# FAITH, ANGELS AND OVERCOMING GBS

## The Jim McKinley Story

JIM MCKINLEY AND PAUL FUNK, JR.

WESTBOW
PRESS
A DIVISION OF THOMAS NELSON

WestBow Press books may be ordered through booksellers or by contacting:

WestBow Press
A Division of Thomas Nelson
1663 Liberty Drive
Bloomington, IN 47403
www.westbowpress.com
1-(866) 928-1240

ISBN: 978-1-4497-7693-0 (e)
ISBN: 978-1-4497-7692-3 (sc)
ISBN: 978-1-4497-7694-7 (hc)

Library of Congress Control Number: 2012922244

Printed in the United States of America

WestBow Press rev. date: 5/6/2013

# *Table of Contents*

Thank you Judy Hefty, Jim Keenan and Sue Porter for submissions. Also Jeff Beard for wise input.

Special Thanks to Ron and Rita Melendy for their editing, title ideas and general encouragement. Their insight and perspective proved invaluable.

Thanks also to Janice Reynolds, Pastor Ray Kerr, Betsy Keenan, my Mother and any others who read the manuscript with a critical eye. I appreciate their help and friendship.

Thanks to Robin Zubler and Jeff McKinley for providing needed information and support, Dale Benner for photos, advice and more. Also, the members of camp Middle Branch who shared with me.

A Special thanks to my wife and family for allowing me the freedom to travel to see Jim. They also endured my absence during the countless hours I spent before the computer, too.

A plaque on Jim's wall;

**I always know God won't give me more than I can handle but there are times I wish He didn't trust me so much.**

**-Mother Teresa**

# *Tid Bits*

During our 5-3-08 visit Jim told me about the Relay for Life held inside Centre Crest home. Patients were walked, pushed or wheeled around the halls to raise money for cancer research/cure. Jim won a plastic cup during the drawing or raffle and the woman beside him won nothing. He told me of giving her the cup because it seemed so important to her. He said she was seen carrying the cup with her for days afterwards. It's been my experience that that's a typical thing for Jim to do.

"If I've learned anything it's that everything is in His time. The Good Lord will have the bottom drop out so we return to Him." Jim's comment is a reoccurring theme.

"Sometimes it's like you're on an island. You need to go to church to keep motivated that it's all good; even if most people don't believe," Jim told me.

# The Clock of Destiny

Mortality is a huge time-piece wound up by the Almighty Maker; and after he has set it a-going nothing can stop it till the Angel swears that time shall be no longer. But here it ever vibrates and ever advances - ticking one child of Adam into existence, and ticking another out. Now it gives the whirr of warning, and the world may look out for some great event; and presently it fulfills its warning, and rings in a noisy revolution. But there! as its index travels on so resolute and tranquil, and what tears and rapture attend it's progress! It was only another wag of the sleepless pendulum: but it was fraught with destiny, and a fortune was made - a heart was broken - an empire fell. We cannot read the writing on the mystic cogs as they are coming on God's errand, and carries in its graven brass a Divine decree. Now, however - now, that the moment is past, we know; and in the fulfillment read the flat. This instant was to say to Solomon, "Be Born!" this other was to say to Solomon, in all his glory, "Die!" That instant was to "plant" Israel in Palestine; that other was "pluck him up." And thus, inevitable, inexorable, the great clock of human destiny moves on, till a mighty hand shall grasp its heart and hush forever its pulse of iron.

Written by Dr. J. Hamilton; as recorded in the <u>The Preacher'sHomiletic Commentary: Ecclesiastes</u>; Funk and Wagnall, New York, page 43-44. Date unknown.

It has been five years, nearly six now, since Jim McKinley became ill. He still awaits the Lord's decision; is he to recover fully? In the mean time he is telling of God's wonder and glory. Will the healing come to him? I think it will. Maybe not in the way we expect it to, but then again, God does not always conduct business the way we think He should. The end of Jim's story is far from the end. Eternity awaits Jim as a servant of God. Thank Jesus for that promise.

# *PREFACE*

As I scrambled to find time for this project I was spurred on because I knew what Jim was doing while I lamented; recovering – physically. Spiritually he is the Atlas of my friends; carrying the world on his shoulders because God is with him. Even as I consider his disability I long for the bond he shares with the Almighty. I'm pleased to participate with Jim in telling you his story.

Jim and I discussed the design of this book and he indicated the format that appealed to him the most was blending scriptural verses and teaching with the words recorded here. So, I interviewed him and allowed him to speak directly to you. The scriptural verses were added many months after the recorded conversations took place. Listen for God's spirit to speak to you as you take in Jim's story.

In this work Jim tells of seeing an angel and being helped by other angels. He speaks of wandering away from his faith and back again. He speaks very directly about his outlook on the world. This view has not changed in the thirty years or so that I've known him. His message is very thought provoking and challenging. The topics are real to life and, as he told me, 'the truth hurts and it should.' We rarely like to hear the truth.

Take in the truth Jim shares with you and mend it with scripture. I think you will find they agree; suffering is part of this world especially when you follow Jesus. He promised us that.

Matthew 10:34 says it clearly;

*"Do not suppose that I have come to bring peace to the earth. I did not come to bring peace, but a sword."*

He continues that there will be difficulty in our families and that we must not love others more than Him. That is a painful truth. Jim knows well the truth of the Gospel's joy, too.

In the pages ahead he will tell you of how close he has felt to the Lord. Healing him slowly, teaching him constantly and an endless source of comfort for Jim is the Lord. Jim told me he feels His presence, like a good friend - always there for him. The Holy Spirit is also available for you and for me despite our tough times. It is important to note how these things are related; God allows us to be challenged but provides the Comforter to help those who believe in Him, a taste of the heavenly salvation to come. Thank God for this knowledge that it is not in vain that we deal with our trials, but we are drawn closer to Him by them!

Jesus also requires that we deny ourselves, take up our cross and follow Him (Mark 8:34). By denying ourselves we stop living for our desires but instead for His. We lose our life to Him that we may gain eternal life.

Jim has been given a cross to bear that many could not carry. He does not complain but instead seeks to uplift others and devotes time to prayer...for others. His life bears much fruit and the Lord does recognize him as His own. Jim has invited Jesus into his life in a very powerful way. Jesus is calling to you as well.

*"Here I am! I stand at the door and knock. If anyone hears my voice and opens the door, I will come in and eat with him, and he with me." - Revelations 3:20.*

The King wants to dine with you. Listen for His voice and let Him in. I pray you will.

# *Introduction: McKinley*

When I first heard Jim had come out of his predicament and was functioning without a ventilator or a feeding tube, I was astounded. The last vision I had of him was a motionless body tethered to multiple machines. When spoken to he did nothing. Once or twice he twitched a toe, something I believed to be an involuntary response. The starkness of the room added to my dismal feeling. I held Jim's hand and asked if he wanted to pray and he jerked his toe/foot ever so slightly. I prayed for God's blessing and he didn't move anymore. It was a very uncomfortable feeling.

The thought of his recovery brought to mind the word "miracle." I know that is an over used word and improperly in many cases. In this case I had prayed for God's mercy upon Jim but must admit a sense of acceptance in my heart even as I hoped for a miracle. I considered the loss of my friend a closed deal.

In studying the Bible we find much evidence that God does not work according to what is obvious in this realm. He is, rather, concerned with the business of administering the plan He has preordained. We, however, enter into the picture, take a look around, make assumptions and then accept what we believe to be inevitable. I say 'we' because the family of God is one large group covering the past several thousand years. We have all made the mistake I admit to: failing to trust God completely.

Faith and trust in God is a very scary business. It involves letting go of what we sense and allowing His Supreme Spirit to move in and overtake us. This is akin to driving blindfolded and listening to directions to move the car safely. It requires a great deal of patience and obedience. We must change our way of thinking and look for better ways to come into fellowship with God. Crashes are frequent and the driver seeking heavenly guidance will accept the dents and humiliation in exchange for God's promise; eternal life later and a closer walk with Him now.

When I saw Jim incapacitated I was filled with worldly dread. If I had been studying the Bible then as I do now, I can tell you that I may well have seen opportunity: opportunity for God to demonstrate His love for Jim and His power over everything that appears so insurmountable in this life. Matthew 19: 26 reminds us; "with God all things are possible." The Bible also points out the dozens of instances where God moved into a situation where the conclusion appeared evident before the scene was fully established. David and Goliath, in the book of 1 Samuel, chapter 17, is a good example.

I am certain David was the only person on that battlefield who believed himself capable of slaying Goliath. He had undergone life-altering trials in the wilderness while tending his sheep. He had faith that God was his caregiver and the source of all strength. He believed this with what Jesus would later identify as the faith of a child. As a result he knew God would not allow any enemy to stand. Goliath showed disrespect for God and David was outraged on God's behalf. The victory was David's before the fight even began. This process is further explained in 1 Peter 1: 3-9. The text reads:

*"Blessed be the God and Father of our Lord Jesus Christ! By His great mercy He has given us a new birth into a living hope through the resurrection of Jesus Christ from the dead, and into an inheritance that is imperishable, undefiled, and unfading, kept in heaven for you, who are being protected by the power of God through faith for a salvation ready to be revealed in the last time. In this you rejoice, even if now for a little while you have had to suffer various trials, so that the genuineness of your faith – being more precious than gold that, though perishable, is tested by fire – may be found to result in praise and glory and honor when Jesus Christ is revealed. Although you have not seen Him, you love Him; and even though you do not see Him now, you believe in Him and rejoice with an indescribable and glorious joy, for you are receiving the outcome of your faith, the salvation of your souls."* NRSV The Faith Sharing New Testament with The Psalms.

David and so many other faithful have experienced that trial by fire. The gold of their faith could only be proven to be gold when it was heated and all the impurities removed. Their inheritance was gained only through perseverance. This is a painful process but without it the faith of the person is tainted. David knew God was the redeemer and source of all things. He knew it. He held to it and, without seeing Jesus redeem his soul, knew He would do it. Jim knows this too, and did not give into the challenges presented to him. He endured the smelting of his faith and continues to bear the fruit of the spirit.

Jim talks openly about having doubts and fears during his ordeal, but he clung to his faith knowing Jesus would not fail him. There would have been no word spoken of Jim being weak if he had given in to the fear and doubt and allowed his life to slip away. I was actually expecting it. Instead he found the Jesus he loves sitting with him and comforting him. He told me it is like "having a personal friend sit right beside you, just for you, and visit just you." He admits knowing God doesn't operate this way but that it sure feels that way. Having felt the comfort of God, Jim did a peculiar thing: he began to pray for **other** people. People he knew at home and those in great suffering right around him in the care home. He said he gave little thought to his own well-being because God had already loosened that burden. After all he had endured there wasn't much left undone. Yet, through it all, God filled him with comfort and joy. Jim told me of this joy in a giddy tone, almost like a child revealing a secret; he was that excited about it.

Look back to the quote from 1 Peter. Notice that even though we don't see Jesus now, we are filled with joy because our trials have alerted us to the fact that He has tested us and we are nearer to Him. He knows of our faith and we rejoice knowing that our faith has provided the salvation we long for; the salvation that leads us to Him - eternally. To Heaven where there is peace and joy and love and where we will never be hungry, sick, or sorrowful and God will dry every eye. That is what our faith rests upon and that is why I desire to tell you Jim's story.

It is my hope that reading Jim's story will allow you to have the same heartfelt, Spirit filled experience many of us have had.

# Chapter 1
## *A Brief Autobiography*

**The Crew; Back row (L-R)Jeff McKinley, Steve McKinley, Dale Benner, Stephen Miller, Mike Nevling**

**Front row kneeling(L-R) Irv Watson, Jim McKinley, Jack Miller, Darren Miller**

There was a picture of him with eight other men. Some of them were older men, some of them were younger men. Before these men was the cause of the photo session; two large antlered white-tailed deer. He is just off center of the picture with a pleased look on his face. There are many causes for the look. For one, he is with his sons, secondly he is at camp, third he has just participated with friends in a hunt that culminated in two big bucks.

The hunting camp pictured above will be identified in much detail later. For the current concern, I will provide a brief outline. Our camp is located in the big woods of central Pennsylvania. It is an old camp going back to my great great grandfather, just after the twentieth century began. In those days there were no roads and the crew arrived by walking in pack mules. The mules carried supplies for the weeks of hunting to follow. Today, we drive right to the front door. Marcellus drilling rigs are attracting traffic of all sorts and a quick trip to camp for lunch is not unheard of. It remains an isolated place with great beauty, where stars can be viewed in numbers unknown to anyone living near a town. It is a destination people seek out with purpose.

**Old camp picture with Irv Watson holding a towel in front of Granddad Watson.**

Move ahead 30 years after Jim and company bagged those two bucks. Jim has been on a most wondrous journey. However, it has been a very scary journey. In fact, I had basically written him off as dead with all but a string of hope for his survival. Jim has survived and this is a tale that demands our attention because the implications extend to us all.

Jim was trapped inside himself and had no control over his physical being. A machine controlled his breathing, a machine fed him, people made decisions about what to do for and/or about him and he was just there. Stuck. Or so it would appear. Unbeknownst to us, he still had his mental faculties and most importantly his spirit.

In meeting with him months after he began to talk and eat again, I found that he had been aware of much that was going on around him. What he describes is the battle raging around us today as it is reported from the beginning of time: good vs. evil.

The cause of his ability to see this battle is that he contracted a grave disease that stripped him of any bodily control. Jim described the disease to me as 'something that takes the coating off your nerves kind of like taking the plastic insulation off of the electrical wiring in your house. Everything gets shorted out.' He is good with words.

The ailment is called Guillain - Barre Syndrome, here after referred to as GBS. Wikipedia describes it as an acute, autoimmune, polyradiculoneuropathy affecting the peripheral nervous system, usually triggered by an acute infectious process. I've heard it said that GBS tricks the body into attacking itself, especially the nervous system. Without a properly functioning central nervous system he was very close to death. Jim fell to GBS on February 17, 2004.

Because Jim acquired the disease he was able to enter into a world you and I will not likely ever experience. Perhaps we will know of it in the next life. That experience permitted him to sense the strife between the heavenly realm and the evil one. He met angels and dealt with pain inflicted by bad people and events. The insidious part of all this is that he was permitted to leave that world and rejoin ours. His story is very compelling as to the nature of things.

Jim and I met several times to discuss the outline of our work here and he agreed to provide me an interview. I recorded his responses and they seemed to move at a pace of their own. It was exactly what I wanted; for you to hear from Jim what his journey has been like and where he's at and where he hopes to go. This began in spring 2008.

Allow me to introduce you to Jim. He is a man of modest origins and recalls being "pretty poor" as a child. His parents raised his mother's brothers and sisters and their own nine children. His father had a job and the farm. They survived by canning their own produce, from their own garden. They also hunted and fished so they would have food. He recalls some government food, like block cheese, but no food stamps. They always went to church and he had pretty good Sunday school teachers. He told me that he and his sister and daughter made a recent trip to the church they attended years ago. All agreed it still had that same warm feeling they remember it having.

When his family sold the farm they moved to Milesburg, PA. In Milesburg he had a paper route. That's when he went to work on my Uncle Irv's farm. He was about 13 or 14 and it was roughly 1953, 54, 55 "something like that." He met Irv's mother and father, (my great-grandmother and great-grandfather) and my grandfather and great uncles. He indicated that Merril, my grandfather, was a "big, big influence on everybody's life."

Irv and Merril Watson were big influences on him and one of the reasons for that was the camp. They belonged to a hunting camp in the mountains and Jim was able to visit and later join, as I have since done. Coincidentally, that's where Jim and I met and have become close friends because of our love for the place and these great men and the memories.

Camp was a place for Jim to get away and find solitude to enjoy God's creation. "I go there," he told me, "to reflect on life and get away from things." He really enjoyed camp and still does.

Jim worked for Irv milking and working around the farm. When Irv passed away Jim moved to the Watson farmhouse because Irv Watson's widow, Jeannie, moved to town. When Jeannie eventually sold the farmhouse Jim had to move out. The farm and surrounding area still holds special meaning for him.

**Irv Watson and his dog, Jigsey, with the old Army truck.**

Jim considered the Watson's his second family. Irv gave his children and grandchildren sections of property and he sold Jim one, too. Jim said he was going to buy one part and ended up buying this lot. "Best thing that ever happened to me," he announced. All the Watson children gave up theirs but Jim kept his. Irv sold him the property in 1972 and he put a trailer on it in 1973. In 1991 Jim and his wife built a large house atop the hill of his property. This place still holds a special place in his heart even though GBS has taken it from him.

He explained to me the joy he found in watching the squirrels and deer, with his first cup of coffee from the deck. The wood edge was not more than fifty feet away from the house so the animals were close. In the evening he enjoyed sitting on the front porch of the home with Muttley, his dog, while eating a bowl of ice cream.

Their story ends in divorce. "She had a hysterectomy and her personality changed 180 degrees," he said.

I asked Jim about the marital issue and he said he was too good to his wives – or at least that's what he was told. "I never thought I could be too good to them," he said somewhat perplexed. We allowed the subject to vaporize and moved on.

As a result of his first marriage, Jim has three children. He pointed out that they always took the children to church and that early church training is important. He is proud of his children and how well they've done. Jim has a daughter and two sons. Robin is in public education, Jeff works for Pennsylvania DOT and Steve is employed by Cintas, a uniform company. Steve lives in Strawberry fields, a home for handicapped people. All three of them contribute to the greater good of their communities.

In discussing spiritual things, Jim noted that he is like most people; they drift away from the Lord once in a while. "They seem to, anyway," he told me, "even if they have deep rooted faith." He notes that this was his experience. He would stop going to church for a while and then start again and back and forth.

This is the point at which he brings in the topic of his illness and ties it firmly to his faith. "When this (GBS) happened, He (God) was getting my attention. I wish He would have done it some other way, but He didn't." He laughs uncomfortably at the thought.

It's a different laugh than I'm accustomed to. It doesn't sound like the Jim McKinley I grew up with, but that Jim never had a tracheotomy let alone a tracheotomy for months on end. The damage to his vocal cords is obvious. He concludes this little segment of our talk by reminding me "there are worse things, you know?" I'm sure there are but I can't seem to think of any.

His true perspective is; it can't be all that bad because the Lord was just trying to get his attention. When God wants somebody's attention He has very powerful ways of doing that. He wanted Pharaoh to let His people go and when Pharaoh refused he was given multiple discomforts to express God's displeasure. Pharaoh let them go. God wanted Jonah to go to Nineveh and when Jonah avoided the issue, God had a big fish swallow him for three days. When Paul persisted in killing Christians, God blinded him for three days to get his attention. There are other examples, but the point is obvious: if God wants your attention He will increase the stakes. Jim feels certain this is what God was after – his undivided attention. "He got it" Jim said with a chuckle.

I don't know if God was after Jim's attention or if He was/is working so as to reveal himself through Jim. In John 9:2-3 it is written; "His disciples asked Him,

*'Rabbi, who sinned, this man or his parents, that he was born blind?'*

*"Jesus answered, 'neither this man nor his parents sinned: he was born blind so that God's works might be revealed in him'."*

Could Jim's experience be God's way of teaching us something?

In Matthew 10:30 Jesus says

*"And even the very hairs of your head are all numbered."*

If this is the case, and I believe it to be so, would God leave any part of any of our lives to chance? Clearly not. Even parents do not love deeply enough to number the hairs of their child's head!

No, God has a purpose for Jim. His purpose is speaking to us all - if we listen.

# Chapter 2
## *How it started*

I asked Jim how it all got started.

"The morning this all happened, I came out of the house and my hands got numb, so I went back in the house and called Larry. (Larry is Jim's brother.) I don't remember any of that. I remember going back into the house, telling Larry this and that. He said my voice was all garbled, he figured I was having a stoke."

"So, he called the ambulance and they got there. Like I said, I don't remember anything in between. Next thing I knew, we were on our way down the driveway and my legs felt like they were on fire. That's the last I remember until we got to Hershey, but only for a little while and then it's gone.

"When they took me up to the hospital they were treating me for a stroke. The one thing about my GBS was that is was the only documented case in the world, at that time, where is started up and went down. Normally GBS starts at your feet and comes up. So, I'm the odd ball. Maybe that's why it's taken so long for me to recover.

"They found out they treated me for a stroke and the next morning they had me on a ventilator. Trache, too. I don't know anything about that. I don't remember.

"Next morning, they had all this on and a nurse came in and said, back in 1968 a friend of hers had the same symptoms and it was Guillain Barre.

"Right away they life flighted me to Hershey, but it was too late. They tried to give me that stuff to stop it, but it was too late." Jim said blandly. The fact that he used the words 'too late' in two consecutive sentences was tell tale of his feelings regarding the way his case was handled. Yet, he remained neutral, not bitter.

"Where were you the first time, before they life flighted you?" I asked trying to nail down a chronological progression of events.

"Centre Community at State College." He said.

"The nurse said her friend had gotten it from the swine flu shot. Later, we concluded that that's where I got mine from, the flu shot. Flew me to Hershey and let my eyes dry out so they got ruined. Then they sent me to Camp Hill and closed my eyes and put bandages over them, but by then they'd already ruined my eyes. Then I went to Sugar Creek, out near Kittaning. That was a bad place. From there I went to Laurel Crest at Ebensburg, PA.

"I was there for a year and a half. Meantime, I didn't get up and I didn't get any therapy and my joints all froze up. I was on the ventilator when a new doctor came in to see me. He said 'get this man out of here and get him off this ventilator,' which took about five weeks. They didn't take it off at once. I still used oxygen for a while. Not much.

"Then they sent me to Health South for rehabilitation. I couldn't do much because, from laying up there (in Ebensburg) I had developed a bone growth on one of my hips. Only had about a 20% improvement in my one hip. I could only move it about twenty degrees...so, I went out to Clearfield for eight months. Meanwhile, I'd come back to Health South for a check up on my trache.

"I got to talk to the doctors out there and they scheduled an operation on my hip. It was a toss up between my eye and my hip. We decided on the hip," Jim paused for a breath and developed a reflective look. "That was a good choice, cause while I was still under they bent my leg to 70 degrees." His countenance brightened. Clearly he liked the results.

Before this procedure, Jim was moved about like a board. He was pushed up, rigid, with his feet placed upon a lazy susan like contraption that allowed the nurses to spin him the direction necessary and then back again. Having witnessed this on several occasions, I was really pleased at the results, too.

"I was up in the hospital and before I left they took my feeding tube out and they took my trache out, so, I was left with a hole in my throat. The trache had been in there so long it didn't close shut naturally. So, I had to have an operation to close that, which I think was in January. Check the books," he offered referring to the collection of log books that had been gathered during his illness.

"After that I was over Health South for rehab until a place opened up here at Centre Crest. Again the Lord stepped in. I was supposed to come in a week before I did and I was supposed to be in another room. But because the roof was leaking they couldn't bring me in. I ended up in the room with Guy," he spoke of his initial Centre Crest roommate.

*We wait in hope for the Lord; he is our help and our shield. Psalm 33:20.*

Indeed, God has revealed His might as Jim's help and shield, leading him through difficulty to some relief. Jim recognizes this in so many events. I believe his eyes have been opened and he sees clearly God's work. Every step of the journey has a purpose. Jim's case serves as an example for us all. God is our help, too.

"Guy was like I was up at Health South; feeding tube and pretty much out of it. Didn't move or anything. The good Lord put me in there for him because I could ring for him when I thought he was in trouble and a couple of other things. So, I could tell them what he was experiencing because I had been there (Knew the interpretation of the outward signs). The Lord wanted me to be in his room for that reason and the other reason was to encourage me. 'Look what you have learned and look where you are now (compared to a year earlier). We just lost him here two weeks ago." Jim's mood grew uncharacteristically sullen.

"How old was he," I quizzed.

"Thirty nine years old," was the response.

"He was here since you came?" I ask continuing to make sense of the big picture.

"Yeah. He was here long before I was. I felt bad that week because I knew they had taken the feeding tube out. You knew it was just a matter of time before he died."

As I reread these words I am reminded of how emotionally charged this must have been for Jim. He was trying to help Guy and be there for him and ultimately sat alone in the room and watched him wither and die.

"The night he died, the Good Lord sent my sister and she was here when he died. The thing of it was that when he passed I felt a calmness. The Good Lord was letting me know he was going to be with Him. There is no doubt in my mind he went to be with Him."

"The other irony in that was that the maintenance man, Mike, he comes around and plays the guitar for a few of us every now and then. He was going to come in that afternoon and something came up that he couldn't. So, amazingly, that evening he came in when I needed it more, I guess. And, of course, his songs fit the occasion.

"And that's not the first time He's sent me people just when I needed them, ya know? When I'm at my lowest or something isn't going right – He always sends me somebody. People may think I'm being silly and that it just seems that way, but I don't feel that it really is. He sends me people when I need them," Jim says with conviction.

The Psalmist writes of the Lord that,

*"You are my hiding place; you will protect me from trouble and surround me with songs of deliverance." - Psalm 32: 7.*

In this instance God was with both men: Jim for Guy and Jim's sister and Mike for Jim. They were singing God's song of deliverance simply by being there. God provided Jim a safe place and protected him from trouble, too.

"One of the time periods that really intrigues me is when you were trapped inside yourself. You were aware and thinking but because your muscles hadn't come back yet, you weren't able to communicate," I say indirectly admitting my reason for wanting to write his book.

"Well, they used to get me out of bed with what they called a Hoyer lift. I don't know if I was dreaming or if this actually happened. I think this actually happened.

"They put me in this chair, like a homemade chair, and oh my, the pain I'd have when they'd do that. I dreaded them coming to do that," he said. His face and body language changed so much that I knew he was reliving the pain.

"Because of the way the seat was designed, or...?" I am stopped when Jim jumps in knowing where I am headed.

"Well, both. It had been a long time since my legs or anything had moved and if you moved them it was

13

excruciating. Boy, I dreaded them coming to get me out of bed. Oh, no you don't," he said alluding to his thoughts as they pulled him out of bed.

"But you know I couldn't say anything. That's one thing I remember," he confided.

"What did you think while you were sort of encased inside yourself? Did you think about things that had gone on or wonder about things that were going on now? Or, none of that seemed to matter to you?" I was being very open about my curiosity now.

"No, one of the things was dreading them getting me up and dreading them doing this and lay me down to change me. What's the muscle they always pull? Hamstring!" he says after a brief pause.

"Oh, when they laid me back down and things stretched back out, oh, it pained me! I'd think about that and think, 'no, don't come and get me, yet!" He showed deep emotional scarring at the recollection of the horrid event.

"That would be every two hours. That's where I spent most of my time then. I wasn't thinking about...I didn't do a lot of praying then. I concentrated on 'how am I gonna get through that excruciating pain!

"I spent a lot of time thinking about when are they going to do it again. We made it through that. It's like He said, 'I won't give you more than you can handle.' I wish it could have been a little bit less." He gives me the silent stare for emphasis.

I chuckle.

"But, then as I started getting more and more alert I started thinking about my roommate and his problems. I don't think he could ever get well. I think he had Lou Gehrig's disease. I don't know if he's still in there or not.

We'll send him a Christmas card, always do. His Birthday is in December."

The roommate being referred to is not named in our talk and his location or current condition is unknown.

"We've never heard anything" about him or from him, "they (cards) didn't come back, but that doesn't mean they weren't delivered. They might get them up there and throw them out. No news is good news, I figure.

"I did pray for him and people I heard the nurses talk about. I prayed for them. That's when I started to graduate into more prayer life, for my friends and family."

"The more alert you became...?" I interjected.

"Yeah. The more alert I became the more aware I was of people being worse than me. I still hear people say, 'how can you say you're lucky?' That's easy. Look at him." He said gesturing to an imaginary person.

"Right," I agreed.

"I'm glad to see the Good Lord gave me the blessing to focus not on my problems but on other peoples and I think that's why He puts me with the people He does. He has to keep me encouraged," Jim is catching me off guard using the word blessing with his ailment.

"In turn, you encourage them, at least the ones you can," I offer.

"Well, I hope so. It seems that's the way it is. I'm amazed. It's like I'm a magnet I guess, because, it's like those Penn State girls, you know? There are only two helping with me and the next thing you knew each one was coming in to say 'hi', stay awhile, and talk.

"Well, you can read some of their comments in the book," he refers to the journal on his night table.

"It always amazes me when people come to me and say I'm an inspiration to them and they're...It's like you," he said suggesting my interest in writing this book is foreign to him.

"What's the matter with them? You know? I don't know how I can be an inspiration to them, but I am. But you know I don't think about that.

"Like you said, I am a humble person. I'd like to think so. Once in a while I'll blow my own horn, but not too often. I feel good that I can be an inspiration to people, because it's what God wants me to be," he pauses for a breath.

*"I have great confidence in you; I take great pride in you. I am greatly encouraged; in all our troubles my joy knows no bounds." - 2 Corinthians 7: 4.*

I see the encouragement Jim is bringing to others through the pain of his troubles. God's love and grace are being shared because Jim is witnessing to anyone who will listen to him. Faith thrives when we place all our trust in the Lord.

"A beacon in the darkness and there is a lot of darkness in here." I offer a scriptural comparison, but he's having none of it.

"It doesn't mean I don't have my sins," he continues on course. "I get upset now and then and I might say something to the nurses that I shouldn't say. Then I have to apologize." He is very melancholy just now.

"After I say it I lay there and I ponder on it. I tell myself, 'you did wrong', so I always apologize. I said that's no excuse, but I apologize to them. If I don't then I'll lay there wondering what am I going to say to that person that they'll understand?"

FAITH, ANGELS AND OVERCOMING GBS

"You told me one time that they put the wrong drops in your eyes and that burned like crazy. It really struck a cord with me that you could feel that and couldn't move to push them away or anything." I wanted to talk about the unimaginable event of being trapped inside himself and knowing what was going on around him but unable to do anything about it.

"Up at Laurel Crest she put the wrong drops in my eyes and never said sorry or anything. Now my eyes burn because of sweat and it runs down in my eyes. I can't do anything about it so I try to hang on until somebody gets there."

# Chapter 3
## *Four Truths*

Suddenly the topic of God's plan for him morphs into another, closely related, topic of theological leanings. It happens quickly, as if he is struck by the awesome nature of what he has to share with me.

He begins without introduction.

"The Bible is all truth. Four truths that stand out to me;

1.)　**"No matter what happens, trials and tribulations, good will come from it and your faith will be increased.** Your relationship with God will become stronger."

The Disciple Peter knew well this truth. In his first book, 1Peter 4:12-13, he writes to us:

*"Dear friends, do not be surprised at the painful trial you are suffering, as though something strange were happening to you. But rejoice that you participate in the sufferings of Christ, so that you may be overjoyed when His glory is revealed."*

Jim was left all but dead. I know it and joined so many of you in going to see what had become of our friend. But for the purpose of God's Divine Plan he was allowed, like Lazarus, to rise up and serve the Lord. Good has come from his suffering in GBS. I expect more good to be revealed as Jim continues along his life's journey. God's plan is perfect.

2.)　**"The power of prayer.** Oh, my, the power of prayer. I was on so many prayer lists. People who weren't known for praying prayed for me. I was on more prayer list's than

Methuselah has years. The power of prayer kept me. I could have died four times real easy. I know people who have come back from cancer because of the power of prayer and lots of other little things."

The Bible dictates the power of prayer over and over. A couple of examples that spoke to me follow: Ephesians 6:18 - "And pray in the Spirit on all occasions with all kinds of prayers and requests. With this in mind, be alert and keep on praying for all the saints." The author of Ephesians has just finished describing the armor of God when he directs us to use prayer on all occasions. Prayer is that intricate to the battle of our salvation. Further evidence is found in the writing of James.

*"Therefore confess your sins to each other and pray for each other so that you may be healed. The prayer of a righteous man is powerful and effective." James 5:16.*

Jesus, God in a human form, prayed throughout the gospels. Most memorable for me is the prayer at Gethsemane. Our little country church has a painting of Jesus kneeling at the moonlit rock in the garden. Mark 14: 34 adds the words to the picture;

*"My soul is overwhelmed with sorrow to the point of death."*

Feeling that upset Jesus walked off to do the only thing that would help: He prayed.

The healing quality of prayer is clear and present.

Jim shared this anecdotal account with me as to the power of prayer: "An agnostic woman (one who has no faith in God, little belief) that worked at Center Crest (county home where Jim lives) said to me that her husband never took her out to eat. So I said to her, 'I'll pray about that for you.' You don't always have to ask for the big things, you know? Guess what? He surprised her and asked her out to supper that next night. She came in the next day and told me about it and I said, 'I keep telling you what prayer does.'" Jim paused his speech and stared at me with his trademark glare. This unique glare is used to emphasize a point with a dramatic flair.

3.)     "**Miracles**. I believe in miracles. When I was out in Ebensburg and they had me lying on my side, I found myself unable to breathe. I couldn't talk and I couldn't move, then, but I was aware. There was nobody around. There was a pillow stuck behind me preventing me from getting a breath. There must have been an angel there that pulled that pillow out from behind me and allowed me to breathe.

"It was the day before or so that I had seen an angel. It had to have been that angel to do that. There was a couple of other times where I almost quit breathing, but we survived that, too. I told the minister here that I not only believe in miracles, but I've almost come to expect them. God's been so good." This time he pauses to shake his head slightly. It's obvious he is still in disbelief that this sort of thing is happening to him.

Another miracle is that Jim walked 150 feet in 2009, with a walker. He had braces on his feet shortly after this happened and told me now that he had stress fractures in both feet. He would need surgery to correct it. This would help correct the dropsie. He needs to walk on his feet in order to avoid having dropsie return. He shrugged at the thought and seemed pleased with the improvement. I was surprised and filled with hope. Small, incremental improvements seem to be the pattern of Jim's healing. God is healing him.

This is something I have come to understand first hand as I have watched Jim rise up from a death bed. He now talks with me, joking like we did years ago. Jim's situation is not as profound as many found in the Bible, yet the basic premise is sound; God initiates contact through miracles. Lazarus' ressurection is a good example.

In John 11 Jesus has just learned that Lazarus is dead. As He is preparing to go there He says plainly: *"Lazarus is dead, and for your sake I am glad I was not there, so that you may believe. But let us go to him." John 11: 14-15.*

The power of the miracle is one tool God uses to gain the attention of men/women. As with Jim, Jesus got their attention by defying the obvious. His power is revealed. This Godly approach to building faith has been going on since the days of old. God is the Creator of everything, so we should not be surprised when he reveals miracles to us. Job's friend, Eliphaz, explained what he knew of God's miracles: *"He performs wonders that cannot be fathomed, miracles that cannot be counted." -Job 5:9*

The Psalmist knew it, too. *"You are the God who performs miracles; you display your power among the peoples."-Psalm 77:14*

A most powerful miracle is the one mentioned earlier; Lazarus raised from the dead, in John 11 - starting at verse 38 -44; *"Jesus, once more deeply moved, came to the tomb. It was a cave with a stone laid across the entrance. 'Take away the stone,' he said.*

*"'But, Lord', said Martha, the sister of the dead man, 'by this time there is a bad odor, for he has been there four days.'*

*"Then Jesus said, 'Did I not tell you that if you believed, you would see the glory of God?'*

*"So they took away the stone. Then Jesus looked up and said, 'Father, I thank you that you have heard me. I know that you always hear me, but I said this for the benefit of the people standing here, that they may believe that you have sent me.'*

*"When he had said this, Jesus called in a loud voice, 'Lazarus, come out!'*

*The dead man came out, his hands and feet wrapped with strips of linen, and a cloth around his face.*

*Jesus said to them, 'Take off the grave clothes and let him go.' "*

4.)      **"He will never leave you.** You may drift away from Him, but He will never leave you. He never left me. Through this illness I've come to know the Lord personally, like you and I sitting here. He's with me all the time, like a personal friend."

Genesis 3 is devoted to the fall of man. It explains the fall of Adam and Eve after they ate of the forbidden fruit and the curses issued as punishment. In spite of the displeasure God felt at their disobedience, He ends the chapter by making them clothes and sending them away from the Garden of Eden. At the dark moment of mankind's fall, God still found loving compassion for His people. He spared their lives, served them in making clothes and continued to watch over them. Likewise, Jesus spoke reassuring words to His disciples.

*"I will not leave you as orphans; I will come to you."-John 14:18.*

Jesus was preparing to leave His disciples behind and return to the Father. He wanted them to know, in a most intimate way, that He had no desire to leave them and would not. Indeed, to the present day He has not left mankind.

This is the presence Jim speaks of - like having the Lord sit right beside him.

The Lord comes to people in dire circumstances, such as GBS, because they have lost most, if not all, of their worldly concerns. Jim prays a great deal and the Lord is with him in an incredible way. The price for such intimacy is very high. Faith thrives where there is no hope but God.

Jim did not speak of these truths in a numbered sequence, but rather explained them to me as a professor would dictate notes to students; with authority and overwhelming confidence.

"Those four truths are in that quilt Gail made for me. The Quilt is actually the story of my life. It was the first quilt she ever made and she had to pull it apart once in a while and pull parts out because her sister-in-law said that it wasn't just right. So she put a lot of sweat, tears and love into that quilt."

Jim paused as he grew melancholy.

Gail Benner is Dale Benner's wife, Jim's best friend, and Jim's ex-sister-in-law. She made the quilt for Jim.

"You'll see it one of these days. I'm going to ask the Axemann United Methodist Church to display it for me, if they will, for two reasons. First, to honor Gail's work and second, to remind people of those four truths. The four truths are important to me..." he lets his conversational tone drift to nothing as he stares off, deep in thought.

# Chapter 4
## Family and Friends

"We've always been a close family and they've been so faithful in visiting me, no matter where I am. There have also been so many friends. People I worked with came to visit and still do, too. You know most people when they leave a job are quickly forgotten, but these people keep coming to see me like that man coming up to visit from visiting someone downstairs. He peeked in to take a few minutes and visit with me." Jim said in humble astonishment.

As we were in the early part of this interview, a man just appeared at the doorway and Jim recognized him, somehow, through injured eyes. They spoke for a few minutes and the man was gone, back to his Saturday routine. I wonder if people realize how powerful a few minutes can be to someone restricted to a home or institution?

*"A kind man benefits himself, but a cruel man brings trouble on himself." - Proverbs 11:17*

"Friends, my golly, miss molly. I always used to say I was never lucky at winning anything. Never was lucky that way, but I have always had lots of friends and good health. I'm down to good friends." Jim paused for a solemn moment. The impact of that statement is huge. Silently we sit for another brief period.

"We had a close family growing up and they've been faithful in supporting me during the illness and my children, too. Big part if you know how much love has done. Big part.

Robin has a family and work and does my paperwork, makes my appointments and insurance...she has always been faithful in coming to see me. She does all those things for me and still leads a life of her own. I don't know how the woman does it! She does have her faith in the Lord." He nods his head in recognition.

Jesus told them, *"A new command I give to you: love one another. As I have loved you, so you must love one another. By this all men will know that you are my disciples, if you love one another." John 13: 34-35*

At this point, Jim has been talking for a long period, perhaps an hour. I wasn't keeping track of the time and I didn't start recording our talk until I began using the topic map I had created. He asks me to give him a drink, which I do. He drinks long, hard pulls of water through the straw. I hold the cup for him because his hands have no ability to grasp. His fingers do not bend at the joints and he is just beginning to use his shoulder muscles to lift his arms. His hands hang limp. That's in sharp contrast to the vise of a handshake he had before GBS. Yet it is a great improvement over the first time I came to see him after the illness.

It was a cold, dreary day when we drove to Kittanning, PA for that first visit. Jim had recently been placed there and my uncle and I opted for a visit. We found Jim McKinley on his back with a new pair of tennis shoes on. They still had the tags on them. He was dressed in the normal hospital garb, otherwise. We inquired as to the purpose of the tennis shoes and the nurse told us it was to prevent dropsy (his foot losing it's form). Jim was completely stationary with his eyes taped shut because his eyes would not blink naturally as a result of the GBS.

It had not been diagnosed early on, so his eyes had remained open. He lay staring at the lights and this, along with them drying out, had ruined them. Sort of like closing the barn door **after** the horse has run off. The damage was irreparable. Recall the four truths? Focus on #3, miracles.

My uncle and I spoke to Jim about things that had been going on at home and work and so on. We were trying to sound casual and comfortable. We went on and on. Once in a while, Jim's foot would twitch. I believed this twitch to be an irritated response to our making so much noise and disturbing him. Later, he would tell us that this was the only sign he could provide to acknowledge our presence.

His toe had moved, that was about the extent of it, but it was a sort of violent movement. I wasn't prepared for what we were seeing and we began to run out of things to talk about. He was just lying there silent. That was not like him at all. Somehow I sensed we were conversing with him, although in a very non-traditional way. I asked Jim if he would like to pray. I had been holding his hand during much of the visit and expected that he would grip my hand to signal me, somehow. He didn't. We said a prayer over him and left. Much later I went to see him again.

He was staying at a care home in Ebensburg, PA. During this visit I seem to recall him moving his leg in response to our visit. I repeated the process of the first visit with much one-sided conversation and followed it with the same mistake – assuming he was irritated by our presence due to his twitching. I don't know what made me feel this, but it made me uncomfortable, so I prayed over Jim and left.

In between our two visits I expected some change, some growth on Jim's part. I didn't see any and was really dejected after the second visit. It appeared I was losing yet another of my beloved friends from camp. Initially, I had accepted the fact that he was sick, but to see no growth, to my unknowing eye, was very difficult to accept. I found myself thinking of him often and included him in my daily prayers. Review the four truths; focus on # 2. Prayer.

"I wanted to talk with you, too, about what's been happening to me. I talked a little bit about it with Dale because his interest in the ministry has sort of been spawned out of your experience. And I think I've had the same call to move into a different kind of vocation. So, it's not just what we see outwardly or think is going on, but maybe a whole lot more to that. 'Well, ok, he was sick but now he's getting better.' I think there was a lot more to it than that." I was gingerly outlining the impact our time together has had on me.

"Oooooh, I know that for a fact," he said. "Because I have got this (GBS) how some people's thinking has changed. Dale's a fine example. He's now a lay minister. He use to say about coming to church that if two or three are gathered together it was the same thing; fellowship. I'd say, yeah, but if you go to church your in fellowship with other Christians. But when I got this he started going to church, he got involved and now he's a lay speaker," that last sentence sounds as if it pleases Jim.

I suspect the total impact of Jim's experience will not be known to anyone in tangible terms. The ripple effect of tossing a pebble into a pool is a fine analogy. We do not know how far those rings will travel or who may be exposed and/or impacted by them. God's glory knows no bounds.

"He and I always said we hoped that we didn't live long enough to have a computer. Well, guess what? Dale's got a computer. Because he's on the civil war roundtable and the church and they don't do paper trails anymore. Everything is e-mail. So, he had to get a computer to get these e-mails."

Jim paused before moving onto other topics.

"It is amazing," I offer "To see how Dale deepened his involvement in the church since you've become ill."

"Ya know they say good comes from bad. Well those are just a couple examples of good that have happened."

"I don't know if Jeff told you, but I developed Lyme disease this spring." I said changing the subject.

"Oh, how do you figure you got that?" he quizzed.

"Tick bite. We were hunting and fishing this spring and I must have picked one up. I did a tick check every night. I never found one but the doctor told me those ticks are so small and they get in your hair and are very difficult to find. That put me down for a while. But I think prayers and healing requests have done the trick. I did the antibiotics, too, but I have to give a lot of the credit to the power of prayer." My thinking was that Jim prayed for healing and it worked, so I used the same route. After all, God's promises extend to us all.

"Oh, yeah, my golly, yeah. That's what's sustained me. There are a lot of prayer lists I'm still on. My golly, yeah!

"How long did it take you to figure out?" he asks of my Lyme's disease.

"Oh, about a week. I was real tired for about a week. I started to develop red splotches all over my torso. I felt sick, like the flu, and over the course of a day it went from flu like to malaria like; soaked with sweat and shivering. I couldn't get warm. I was in bed for two days and didn't get up. I had no energy, just laid there. Bundled up like I was freezing. It was June, so you know it wasn't cold," I explained.

"Did they find the tick or did they do a blood test?" he asked, his curious nature showing.

"A blood test." I respond.

"Never found the tick?" Jim inquired.

"My doctor said 'you probably washed it off when you took a shower'."

"Don't they burrow under your skin?" he continued his questioning.

"That's what I thought. He said you could still break them off. Then when my blood test came back positive I received a questionnaire from the health department to fill out. After that, my doctor told me I had to go to see an Infectious Disease Specialist. He went all over me and gave more tests and exams looking for whatever. He said the initial antibiotic attacked the first chemical that comes from the tick and there is a second chemical. So, he gave me an antibiotic for the second round. He said the first chemical makes you sick real quickly and then drops off quickly. That's when I was in bed sick. The one we worry about is the one that comes on very gradually after that and that's the one that causes joint replacements and organ troubles cause it settles in around the organs. So he gave me a second round of antibiotics and if I had any other symptoms I was to go back and see him. I had a tingling of my hands and feet." I left out the part that it continued afterwards and prayer had resulted in the final touches.

We moved on to another event.

"Did you hear the story about Doug?" He asked suddenly. "You know he was going to go out the weekend they cut the tree down. He went out Thursday and stayed till Friday before he went home. He was out there and he got himself a compound bow and he was practicing. He lost one of his arrows. So, he wrote this note and laid it there by the book, if anybody finds an arrow in the yard, it's mine. I lost one. Signed Doug McDonald, a.k.a. Robin Hood." Jim is really enjoying this tale.

He was looking at me with his silent stare of sarcasm. It had the desired effect - I laughed out loud.

"So, anyway, Dougie comes in and Dean came in and said about the note. Doug left and Dean said, 'now when he comes in you tell him somebody's looking for him; the Sheriff of Nottingham!'" Jim hit the punch line on cue.

That resulted in our sharing a few more minutes of laughter. My side was beginning to ache.

"So when he came in I said to him 'heard you lost an arrow and left a note signed a.k.a. Robin Hood?' Jim laughed. Then he said, 'somebody's looking for you.'

"Oh, yeah? He said. Who's that?" Doug asked.

" It's the sheriff of Nottingham!" Jim delivered the final jab. Then we really laughed!

My laughter had continued throughout the tale.

"Speaking of a colored person, we had a women come in here, she was a volunteer sent by her professor. I told her about Doug and taking him to camp. And she said 'and they accepted him?'

"I said, 'what do you mean did they accepted him?'" Jim's displeasure was obvious.

"She said, 'you know he's a midget and black.'"

"I said, 'what's that got to do with it?'"

"So she and I got into this discussion. I said, 'you know the stigma people have about things. You know not all whites are bad just like all black ones aren't'. I said, 'Doug, to us, was just another person.' I said, 'sure he's black and he's little, but to us he's just another person!' She couldn't get over it. I said, 'sure, look there, I got a picture of he and I right there on the wall. We're sitting on the swing (at camp). She couldn't believe it.'"

**Jim McKinley and Doug McDonald on the camp swing.**

"One day she came up here and said she had trouble believing me. I said to a nurse standing there, 'tell this lady, if I say something you can believe it.' So, maybe we got a convert there. Yeah, I just about dropped over when she said; 'and they accepted him?' Jim was shaking his head with disgust.

"It's a shame that people think that way," I said.

"My golly, miss molly!" Jim exclaimed.

"That sort of thing crosses all boundaries, though. It's terrible." I said.

"Well, it's like when he came to work up there. Everybody was afraid to say anything, afraid of saying the wrong thing. I told him one day after we came in from playing volleyball and he'd been watching us. We had to go through a garage door. He lifted up the garage door and went in and I said, 'sure, you lift it high enough for you to get in, the heck with the rest of us!'" Jim enjoyed the recollection.

"After that I sort of took him under my wing. You know how guys in work can be, teasing and all that kind of stuff. So, I said, 'I'm gonna teach you how to get back at them.' Then one day, I don't remember what I said, but he laid it back on me. I stopped and said, 'now wait a minute!' Pretty good, he was coming up with them after me!" Jim said of Doug's jab back at him.

We laughed.

Another friend of Jim's is a woman who developed Muscular Dystrophy. Her name is Beth and she came to Centre Crest between our 2009 and 2010 visit. Jim alerts me to the fact that he really enjoys her smile. He takes her to church and outside for fresh air and sunshine. He watches her to see when she's ready to come inside. They attend activities together as they come up.

Jim told me, "she just likes my company and my jokes, too."

He told me of the joke he shares with her about a trip across the continental U.S. They would take route 66 in a big convertible with a trunk full of briefs! He laughed at the thought. Beth smiled. It was obvious they enjoyed one another's company.

Jim shared with me that his brother Larry had come and thanked Beth for making Jim happy. He had given her a big hug!

Beth is entering into the depths of her ailment while Jim is on the mend. She cannot talk or sit straight anymore, twisted as she is. Jim is able to interpret her signs, however, like he did for Guy. He had me get her a peanut butter cup from the cupboard. I had no idea of her desire for candy. She sipped her milk and ate the candy, with twisted hands, as we visited. It was very inspiring to watch them interact, because they are both broken but it doesn't matter; the human spirit is too strong.

"Big miracle I want before I kick the bucket is for the healing of Beth... a full healing." Jim nodded emphatically as he told me of his wish for her. I recognize his sincerity and know that he will work for that healing. Recall his four truths, # 3 miracles.

In considering Doug and Beth further, I was struck by a revelation of sorts. Doug and Beth were sent to Jim and he to them for a purpose. Doug was sent to Jim as the new hire at work and Jim took him "under his wing." They enjoyed spending time together. Now, guess who visits Jim often? Doug.

Doug is small and has had many health problems. Very few of us can understand the suffering he has endured. I see the scars left by many operations and watch him struggle to get around. Regardless, I have never heard him complain and he is always pleasant and laughing. The physical impediments the two share have created a bond that, without suffering a similar fate, we cannot comprehend. The friendship the Lord blessed them with is a unique club. Members must suffer and endure to belong.

Likewise, the friendship Jim shares with Beth is special and unique, too. She came after he began to recover from GBS, so he understands many of her needs. You and I will look at her and see a woman in a wheelchair, but Jim sees a dear friend, a kindred spirit.

I know Jim has another good friend in Dale Benner. These two have been in on more hunts, gags, work efforts and the like than I will ever know. I have witnessed many during my lifetime, heard many more stories, and viewed pictures of events I was not privy to. How did God connect these two? This has eluded me for some time, but I think I found the answer.

They have shared in suffering, too.

Dale observed much of Jim's life; raising three children as a single parent, sinning on many levels, preaching the gospel, and sinning some more. He watched up close as Jim went right to the edge of death and then the Lord pulled him back. Dale knows of answered prayers and God's miraculous healing. Now Dale serves God.

I think this was God's plan all along.

Dale is a tough man with a very hard exterior. He worked many, many years in a very demanding line of work. Sometimes he worked two jobs. He didn't have time for church, really. He was working all the time. During this trying time Dale may have drifted from God and the church. Jim's experience pulled him up close to the Lord. None of this was accidental. God established His plan and it worked perfectly.

All three friends fit this pattern because Jim fell to GBS and was raised up. These are not coincidences. *And those he predestined, he also called; those he called, he also justified; those he justified, he also glorified. - Romans 8:30.* God is calling you, too. Are you listening?

# Chapter 5
*Dreams and Visions*

"I have these dreams," he tells me suddenly with a less than enthusiastic face. "Always holding me down. It didn't matter where I hid, they'd find me. Like I had a chip in my skin to find me. I hid in some of the dumbest places. One of the things that was really strange was that everybody, Jeff and Troy and a couple friends, were allowed to hunt and fish at night for anything. Deer," he waved a hand, "it didn't matter. Sometimes I could fish with them and sometimes I was just watching.

"Everything being paralyzed, it was interesting that my mind comprehended everything. In fact, I think my memory got better. I can't understand it other than it's another blessing the Good Lord gave me that I can communicate with people and be a servant to them that way." He was melancholy now.

The dreams occurred primarily while he was immobile and residing at the Ebensburg care home.

My interest of such curious dreams overcame me.

"Was there a theme to your dreams?" I ask as he pauses for a breather and another drink. This prolonged speech is causing him fatigue and a dry mouth.

"Yeah, there were people trying to kill me. I figure it might have been the medicine." He spoke with some agitation. We paused the conversation.

I opted to change the subject, because I didn't know what to say.

"You said you saw an angel." I reminded him of his reference to that fact.

"Oh, yeah. When I was at Laurel Crest, when I was first up there. My body was completely paralyzed but my brain had come back, evidently. I knew what was going on. They'd put you on your side, but they'd only check you every two hours.

"I couldn't breathe. There was a little space of air there that I had to get to. I couldn't breathe. I was on a ventilator and there wasn't anybody around and yet the pillow was removed from behind my back, so I could roll over on my back, to breathe. I can't remember if it was before or after that incident, but I could see an angel. It was only days later, if later at all, there was one there," he said very matter of fact. He told me she was above him along the wall, wings spread. He added that he didn't think you were supposed to be able to see an angels face, but he could see her face. "She was there for me" he concluded.

"Maybe in light of your dreams, it was somebody... you know how we are always told this is a battle. This is a spiritual battlefield; just letting you know the other half was here," As I spoke my mind raced with the possibilities.

"It could have been she was there. I know she was there for me. Angels are...You ever listen to Alabama? I believe there are angels among us? Ooooh, I always did believe that. It's like the song says; they may not be angels as we imagine them. They could be that old man or one of the women. You never know. Could have been any...like Touched By an Angel (the TV show), the shapes they took. Just like Jesus and that Christmas story, that man knocking on the door; Jesus in many forms. He says, 'I was there to see you. I was this and I was that.' I always liked that story," he said.

After considering Jim's experience further and reading of such things I found some suggestive language regarding guardian angels and angels watching over us.

And Jesus said; *"See to it that you do not look down on one of these little ones. For I tell you that their angels in heaven always see the face of my Father in heaven." - Matthew 18: 10-11.* The little ones He refers to have angels that belong to or are assigned to them, individually. Perhaps the same is true of us all. Certainly Jesus teaches more of the same subject; *"Do you think I cannot call on my Father, and He will at once put at my disposal more than twelve legions of angels?" - Matthew 26: 53.* He said this concerning His arrest after Peter's wielding of the sword. A legion in the Roman army was six thousand soldiers. That's a large group of angels!

Yet more evidence exists in the encounter between Zechariah and Gabriel. Gabriel is telling of the coming birth of John the Baptist and Zachariah is having doubts. Gabriel explains to him; *"I am Gabriel. I stand in the presence of God, and I have been sent to speak to you and tell you this good news." - Luke 1: 19.* On and on the evidence continues as we are told of the reality of angels. We should not be surprised when such sightings are reported to us today.

The dreams, terrors really, and the breathing difficulties sought to discourage Jim and take his life, but the angel of the Lord stopped them. This lesson is advanced by the writing in Hebrews 1: 14; *"Are not all angels ministering spirits sent to serve those who will inherit salvation?"* Jim needed help and was sent an angel to do God's bidding. I think that is true of us all. The difference is that Jim was stripped of most everything worldly, therefore he could perceive things of the spiritual world clearly. Whereas you and I are too caught up in the day to day trappings of life and don't find time to pray or study as we should. This could be yet another lesson for us from Jim's experience.

The angel appeared at the first place I had gone to see Jim with my uncle. It blew me away to contemplate his being aware of our presence but not having the ability to do anything but wiggle that big toe. More powerful yet is the thought that there were angels about us and we didn't know it!

"One of the dreams I had was... you know how hot I get?" we moved back to the topic of dreams.

I nod, because Jim would often be without a shirt on a day when I was wearing long sleeves.

"Well, I was hot and took off my clothes and they reproduced themselves. Take off and the other ones there. Take it off and another one is there. Taking layers and layers and layers off and give it to them, people from the company I worked for, another one was on me and I'd take it off and so on. Those people just kept taking the uniforms from me. Doug McDonald was in that one.

"Another dream I had was with a big coat I had and I could fly with the updraft." He said matter of fact.

"With the big coat?" I asked quickly in disbelief.

"Yeah," was his reply.

"Wow" was all I could muster.

"I could stay up there and look down on people and they'd try to get me; grab onto me." He was in a zone now.

"They were after you?" I asked incredulously. I couldn't imagine anyone wanting to harm Jim.

"Oh, yeah. Always after me." He said.

"That would be pretty disturbing if it happened over and over and over again," I said verbalizing the obvious.

"Well, it's not just the way they were or the kids were or others. I even had a dream that an ambulance driver was cutting my throat," he explained.

"Wow!" I said again. So much of this was hard to follow.

"Yeah, really scary," Jim admitted.

"Really scary," I agreed.

"Another thing was I'd be out in these places (dream land) and drift back to my bed and then it would be gone. Everything would be gone," he said with a look as if it were hard for him to believe.

"You'd be back here in bed and that world would go away?" I again sought clarity.

"Yeah," he said with a nod.

"Wow," I again made my disbelief known. "That's mind boggling," I said.

"Maybe it was the devil," he suggested to me.

"Trying to make you feel some kind of way. What are you thinking? What made you say it was him?" Jim's deep philosophy was catching me off guard.

"Well, cause that's the way he is. He works on our weaknesses. At that time my mind was kind of weak!" he spoke sound theory.

"Yeah, those certainly weren't uplifting dreams," I observed.

"No. That's why I say maybe it was the devil causing those dreams." He took a breather and we sat for a quiet moment. He was distant and reflective.

# Chapter 6
## *Jim's Sermon*

I reminded him of my uncle and I visiting him.

"I remember that," he tells me coolly. "You know how people have a near death experience? I don't remember seeing any bright lights or black holes. It was sort of gray. Maybe I'm on the fence," he managed before taking a deep raspy breath that crackled as he inhaled. He struggled to swallow.

"Middle area is not there, do you think?" I asked reminding Jim of the Bible verse about being either hot or cold, but he has something to teach me.

"Yeah, I think if you're in the middle that's when he (satan) works the hardest to get you to come to his side." Jim held a very serious expression as he spoke.

"A couple of times when the ventilator got plugged up and I couldn't breathe, just in the nick of time the people who needed to just showed up did. I couldn't ring a bell. Then one time, later, when I did ring a bell it didn't mean that anyone was going to answer it." He paused for effect to look hard at me.

"Showed up just in the nick of time, twice. The one time they took me to the hospital because of my breathing. But we survived all that. And now look what you got!" He gave me another patented Jim look; a blank, silent stare.

I grinned.

Through my smile, I said, "You have to believe it's all good."

"Oh yeah. It's like I told that guy the other day. He had lost his wife and I talked to him about it. He had turned against God. There was a Christian woman at Clearfield. She lost her son in a bad accident. She turned against God. She said after she talked to me she felt better about the whole thing. I never saw her again." This is the serious Jim talking, again. It's difficult to calculate the power of his witness to those two people. He may have rescued their faith.

"You don't know the power or influence you had there," I said.

"I hope enough," he replied simply.

As I have had opportunity to review these trans-scripted conversations, and reflect upon our years of friendship, I must admit this is a typical comment for Jim to make. He is so loud and talkative that you would never consider him humble. Yet, as I think of him further I must use that term, because despite all the outward appearances to the contrary, Jim is a humble man. And he is a proud man, in the best sense of the word. In this case, he wants to do the right thing and serve the Lord.

"The man that's in my room here, now and the guy that does the Bible study both go to the Baptist church with Dick and Judy (my cousin and her husband). I got to meet a lot of new people like that (due to GBS)."

"Open new doors for you?" I asked without thinking.

"Oh my, yeah! I hope I opened new doors for everybody else, too.

"I told you about my son and his first wife...? She had a daughter when they got married and I always considered her my granddaughter. But when they got divorced, she wasn't allowed to come and see us. Now she's 18 and came in to see me and wrote (in the book) about how she missed her Pap. Of course there's no blood relation at all, but to me there is and to her there is.

"Ashley is her name. When she came the other day she brought my great granddaughter with her. We talked about the times we had at camp and I invited her out to the picnic. Jeff said about inviting her and I said, 'already did'. So, you'll probably see her out there. Her little one is about six months old," he said with a look of disbelief at his being a great grandfather.

"She wasn't allowed to visit and she did say to me, after I told her that I always got along with her mother, even through all of that," i.e. divorce, estrangement, etc. "that her mother said, uh, I was one of the few people she liked." He laughed with a slight shrug.

"There's not anybody I don't like. There's people I don't like how they do. The good Lord tells you... what do you pray? Forgive those who trespass against you, as you would have them forgive your trespasses against them. Everybody, me included, have some trespasses that need people to forgive. I still do. Like that one LPN I told you about."

The LPN he is referring to was hurt by an indiscriminate comment Jim made. So, he explained how he worried over hurting her feelings and soon made a point of apologizing. His conscience bothered him too much.

"It's part of this world," I offer sadly.

He nods.

"There's only one perfect man and we ain't him," he laughs a short burst. "We can only try to be like him. There is no perfect person. We all have our trespasses," Jim pauses to collect a breath.

"But after realizing we are not perfect..." he shakes his head lightly in a reflective, astonished way. "How does He tell us to pray?" Jim asks; "forgive us as we forgive those who trespass against us."

"God is not just such a loving God, man, he's got to be something to forgive us of our sins. Jesus took that away." He spoke while shaking his head in disbelief.

Discomforted by the overly serious route we took, I said mildly, "sometimes that's tough to comprehend, why or how."

"Well, I keep reiterating that things that happen are always for good. And your faith is increased. Boy, nobody knows that more than I do. Certainly your faith is increased to the point I feel, now, where you will be in fellowship with Him and He'll be right beside you. I feel like He's right beside me, just for me and you know that's not true, but you feel that close. You feel like He's there just for you." Jim's voice is filled with emotion.

"It's a good feeling," I say imagining what it is like to be that close to God, given the limited exposure I have had with avoiding sin and gaining closeness with God; a limited but nevertheless very powerful exposure to His Spirit.

Jim is quick to reply.

"Oh, when you accept Christ, that's what He says will come. I always knew God and tried to do what He said, but you know in my life I did a few things He's not too fond of. But then I thought - you haven't accepted Christ. But I guess it's ...you have to grow in the way you feel so that you only get better and sin less. All sins are bad. Doesn't matter how bad they are, but the closer to Him you are the less you sin. Does that make sense?" he asked me.

I nodded.

This was one of those moments when it was so apparent that he was mentoring me just as my forefathers had mentored him.

"It makes sense. I think that's the way it's supposed to be, too. That's the idea." I said nodding.

"Oh," he starts off with an excited tone at the topic we are discussing. "The Bible will tell you never stop growing in Christ."

"Sometimes I think we have the misconception that once you accept Him, then that's it. You're at the end of the road." I was vocalizing some of the thoughts I've had while on my life's journey.

"I don't know if you feel that way because there's always that longing for something more, I think. We all regress. I think maybe that's what's happened to me, but maybe I regressed a little further than He thought I ought to, so He had to bring me back. Like I told you before, I wish there was another way of doing it, but maybe I had regressed that far." He said softly, deep in reflective thought.

"I don't understand it either," I offered weakly.

"Oh, who does? I've often thought the first thing I'm gonna ask Him when I get there (Heaven) is, why? But you know I really think that once we get there we won't have to ask. We'll know why."

"It will be plain," I add.

"It will be right there, why..." he nods gently.

This topic greatly constrains my desire to talk openly with Jim. I feel so helpless. He is open and vulnerable so I want to choose my words carefully. Yet, it is apparent that he is much stronger than I am, walking with the Lord as I wish I could. The fear of God drives me deeper into my own thoughts. What if I did things that angered God that badly? Maybe his relationship was designed to teach me of such things vicariously. Regardless, I didn't want to have Jim disturbed by a blunder in my word selection.

At some point I asked Jim to talk about 'coming out of it' and how his prayer life took shape and his faith was increased.

"Gradually. I listened to Pat Boone and his gospels and Elvis – Elvis was a gospel singer before he got into rock. Those were my two favorites until I got one the other day. Johnny Cash is in there (CD player) now.

"I got good enough so that I wasn't worried about myself or what was the matter with me. I got so that I would pray. Of course, I was asking Him, every time I prayed, for the ... each person I knew. He knew what they needed. Sometimes I would just say a prayer for - not actually what they needed. I would just say a prayer for them and other people; 'God, you know what they need.' Healing and stuff – you know? Sometimes I pray for a lot of people at once. Likewise, at the nursing home and the other ones. Just plain people around the world that need to be comforted and healed. Then I pray for individual people that I think especially need prayed for. In other places – I'll bring up people from other facilities. Some of them I know what happened to them, so I still pray for the people who came to see them, even though they've passed," Jim explained.

"I very rarely ask for myself because I've accepted it; 'God you know what I need.' And as it is said – it's His time, not our time, when anything gets done. He has all the power." Jim said and then drew silent.

"God has a sense of humor!" he says suddenly. With this opening line I begin to wonder if we're headed into some sort of comedic bit, but Jim is not.

"For example; I was looking for these marshmallow cookies that have a cookie bottom, chocolate covering, and coconut on top. I've been wanting them and wanting them. Looking, but I couldn't find them. My sister found them at a meat market on the rack. Funny thing about them is the people that made them is Mrs. Allison's cookies. Funny part about that is my sister, her mother-in-law was Mrs. Allison." Jim shows his dramatic silent stare.

"I said to pastor; God, as powerful as He is, has a sense of humor. And there's been other things like that happen, you know?

"Then again, it's like I've always said about God – everybody says He's dead, because they can't see Him. But they're not looking. I don't know how many times in my life, before I got sick, things were going wrong and you're thinking you need an answer, and drive by the church and on the sign out front, boy, right there's your answer.

"Now we may not be able to see God, but if you're looking for Him, He's there. So many times I drove past the church and there's my answer. If you're looking, you see Him everywhere; in what people do, nature and everyplace you look...if you know what you're looking for," Jim was speaking his conviction of truth.

1 Peter 1: 8 supports this saying; *Though you have not seen Him you love Him; and even though you do not see Him now, you believe in Him and are filled with an inexpressible and glorious joy.* The same joy Jim radiated while telling me of having the Lord with him, like a close personal friend. This is the close relationship we all desire.

"And if you believe it," I added.

"Well, I don't know. I guess most people might not believe it, but who do they call the first time something goes bad? "God, I need you!" he mimics someone in trouble.

"That isn't when He wants you to call for Him, but even then he's there." Jim takes a moment to pause.

I pick an obvious question, especially given Jim's last comment. I compare him to the biblical character Job. It is a rather uncomfortable topic in and of itself, but we are in the heat of conversation, so I proceed.

"I often think of Job in the book of Job and wonder about your circumstances. It's as if God allows these things to happen to put a little pressure on you and then sits back to see whom you will go to then. Don't you think?" I ask.

"I agree. Right. My daughter had said that; comparing me not completely to Job, but sort of like him. Some of the things that happened to Job I can't even imagine. What happened to me ain't nothing, you know?

"God does not do bad things, the devil does the bad things. God allows him to do the bad things only if He thinks you can handle it. There's something else I remember; God will never give you more than you can handle. I don't remember ever blaming God for this or that. I've always said it's the devil that causes this stuff and God will allow it. As I said, if He thinks you can handle it."

Once again we pause and the subject changes.

"There's so much stuff going on now a days that, my, it seems like the end times with the weather the way it is and all these catastrophes. It (the Bible) says about the devil being released. I'm not sure that tsunami wasn't him being released. That was about where he was supposed to be released, isn't it?

"So many tragedies, in New Orleans, too. But strange thing about that was hardest hit was down there where gays were and all that. Is God telling us something?" Jim paused for a breath.

"I've wondered that many times about that incident, because it was an area of great sin. One big party, so if it's a den of sin then it has to go," I say adding my two cents.

"Housed people in that stadium and what do they do? They're in there raping and killing one another. I thought all these things and today right is wrong and wrong is right." He says confirming the truth of scripture.

"I think we were told that was coming, too" I say agreeing with him.

"That was told," Jim nods in agreement.

Jesus spoke of the age coming to a close. Regarding the interpretation of the times, *He said, "When you see a cloud rising in the west, immediately you say, 'it's going to rain,' and it does. And when the south wind blows, you say, 'it's going to be hot,' and it is. Hypocrites! You know how to interpret the appearance of the earth and the sky. How is it that you don't know how to interpret this present time?- Luke 12: 54-56.* Later in that book He adds detail to what signs we will see: *Then He said to them: "Nation will rise against nation, and kingdom against kingdom. There will be great earthquakes, famines and pestilence in various places, and fearful events and great signs from heaven."- Luke 21: 10-11.*

We have seen all these things, in great quantity, over the last one hundred years or so. Yet, so many continue to deny the existence of God. People continue to sin in ever widening spheres, leading others into the mix. Share the word of God's love with people you meet so they will believe and be ready.

"I try not to read newspapers, but every time I do, there's more and more that indicates what you're saying. Just crazy things going on," I say.

He continues to nod.

"We may be the last great nation to fall. Ya know they say about Israel being the chosen people. I don't know, I think the U.S. had to be a pretty chosen people, too, for all those years. Because everything was built on God." Jim's tendency now explains much of his patriotism.

"This was a safe place for the Jewish people before the reunification of their nation state. This was one of the few places they could come," I said adding to his observation.

"Yeah, that's what I thought. This was a chosen country like Israel, but you know what destroyed all the great civilizations of history? Immorality and homosexuality.

"They were destroyed a generation after homosexuality became normal. We're pretty close to the people in the U.S. saying that that's pretty normal," he says.

As I listen I wonder how many people in this country have never heard of Sodom and Gomorrah; Genesis, chapters 18 & 19. It is the story of how God dealt with two cities filled with wicked people. He destroyed them.

Jim said he prays daily for some of the sins he's committed. One of the concerns he explains this way: " I catch myself swearing. You know what I mean?"

"Yes. It happens to me all the time" I admit freely. I'm not trying to make him feel better but rather to express the readiness with which we sin.

"Well, then you wonder how He can forgive you. I mean, it's beyond my comprehension. We do what we do and His ability to forgive us," Jim's difficulty in understanding the enormity of our Lord and God is something else I mirror.

I add; "I cannot understand how God can forgive people who commit the same sin over and over. Like me."

"Especially in today's world. You have to wonder how He can put up with that. 'One day you will feel my justice and vengeance will be mine' He says. That's why He's so gloriously powerful. So compassionate and loving. Well beyond our comprehension, I can tell you that. He can put a stop to it." Jim said nodding with confidence.

"All things in time," I offer his physical improvements.

"Well. It's funny about that." He said. "Every time we are in church or Bible study or the pastor comes in, any place scripture is being read and stuff, you'd be surprised how many times "in His time" comes up. You know what I mean? We always get in a hurry. But that's the one thing that is my problem because it's so slow they don't want to do anything. They don't want to do anything because I don't show a marked improvement over a short period of time."

*"There is a time for everything, and a season for every activity under heaven: a time to be born and a time to die, a time to plant and a time to uproot, a time to kill and a time to heal, a time to tear down and a time to build, a time to weep and a time to laugh, a time to mourn and a time to dance, a time to scatter stones and a time to gather them, a time to embrace and a time to refrain, a time to search and a time to give up, a time to keep and a time to throw away, a time to tear and a time to mend, a time to be silent and a time to speak, a time to love and a time to hate, a time for war and a time for peace." - Ecclesiastes 3: 1-8.*

*Ecclesiastes 3: 11 adds; "He has made everything beautiful in it's time. He has also set eternity in the hearts of men; yet they cannot fathom what God has done from beginning to end."*

"In His time" - this is the emphatic part of the sentence. Funk and Wagnall's <u>Homiletic Bible Commentary</u> offers great insight into this topic. The fitting time is "one of the chief elements in the ways of Providence, which raises in us the thought of an Infinite Wisdom".

Providence is what the Westminster Assembly defined as God's work as his "most holy, wise, and powerful preserving and governing of all his creatures and all their actions."

In all the "afflictions of the good, it is an element of consolation that the severe season will have an end, and in the future a brighter one will arise." It is the "highest wisdom" to await in "patience God's time."

"The fact that there is a divine plan to be observed amidst all the seeming disorder of human beings, is the charter of our liberty, the very foundation of our hope. Under the dominion of a wild and reckless chance, we could not walk sure-footedly in this life, nor cherish a deathless hope of better things awaiting us in the life to come. Without the recognition of a superior power controlling all things, the torch of hope cannot burn."

Even Jesus was subject to God's plan. He waited the hour of His baptism and none of His enemies could win over that plan. Neither will Jim, or you or me, circumvent the will of God. We must await His time.

We must also find wonder and beauty in the words of our creator - in his plan. Even when we find the works of our Lord dark and cruel, there is a "plan of His grand design", perfect for each one of us. "Joseph's being sold into slavery was required that, hundreds of years later, Moses would display God's awesome power. Job was plagued and ruined", but shared much wisdom because of his suffering.

"Daniel in the lion's den" displayed the "love of a wondrous and caring God to an unknowing people." "Christ betrayed and nailed to the cross created a passage for God's people" to have access to Him. All these events begin with an "appearance of sheer terror and evil, but God uses them to reveal a beautiful and wonderful purpose." God's work has a "great deal of ravishing beauty."

# Chapter 7
## *Worldly Observations*

"People anymore! It's like the media, they have a big storm warning and people go nuts. Well, whippeee ding! Like they don't have anything at home." He eludes to folks rushing out to buy last minute toilet paper and milk in the hours before the storm. "And every time there's a big wind there's a tornado warning."

"I think people are out of things to talk about and the weather is it," I reply.

"The media scares people and these people haven't been taught to think for themselves. They can't figure out, 'now wait a minute...' They just accept anything they're told anymore. Computer does everything for them. They don't think. My kids made my grand kids do the homework in their head and check it with a computer. I told them, you give em all the education you want and I'll teach em their smarts.

"I did teach my kids common sense. Robin and Jeff are smart, they got smarts, real smarts. They don't just accept anything that comes along. They think about it and then, if it makes sense, okay." Jim is pleased with how his children have grown. If you meet them it's easy to see why.

"Now the weather – who cares! If the weather is doing this then this is what I'll be doing. I always figured if the weather is like that (rainy, cold, etc.) then I'll do something else. I'll go out and check my weather rock first – see what it's doing.

"I'll tell people about my weather rock. 'What's that?' they ask. I have to tell them; well if I go outside and it's wet then I know it's raining, right? If you go out there and there's snow on it, what's it probably doing? Snowing, right?" I listen to him with a grin.

*Blessed is the man who finds wisdom, the man who gains understanding, for she is more profitable than silver and yields better returns than gold. - Proverbs 3:13.*

Interview session 3 begins with a constant theme.

"Like He's standing right beside me like I'm talking to you. Personal friend. I know He's right beside me, but when you really grow close (to Him) it just seems like He's there with just you. Just as you're sitting there – it's God. Do you feel that way?" he asked me.

I looked at the floor, dumbfounded.

"Um, in all honesty it comes and goes. It seems like that whole issue of sin comes into play," I said before pausing further.

"Oh, yeah, well..." Jim tried to interject but I rudely continue my thought.

"My mind starts to focus, I get all worried about bills or work and I lose track of those things (spiritual connections)." I realize my behavior is rude but it's too late. My mouth was already in gear.

"That's what I was gonna say," Jim affirms my rude behavior. "The difference between you and me is you got a whole lot more to think about than I do. I don't have much to think about in everyday life, like you do. You're raising a family and you have your work. Um, you're doing this and you still find time to go hunting." He stops speaking and looks dead into my eyes, a frozen glare to emphasize his note of sarcasm.

"That's the plan. Once it gets warm out, a lot of these guys," I say referring to other hunters, "Will find something else to do. I usually find the last two or three weekends I have the woods to myself. There's nobody around." I say expounding upon my spring turkey hunting plans.

"Yep," he nods. "Well, you might have to shoot a hen!" he laughs his raspy, hoarse laugh.

I join him laughing.

"Boy I remember I was up back of camp in that clear cut. This dang four point came in about here to the window," he motioned the length of the room. I couldn't shoot him because of all the brush. Course, you can't pull like you can with these..." He looks at me searching for the name of the modern bow, but before I can say 'compound bow,' he moves on.

"With a recurve, I waited and waited. My, my he kept looking back. I should have known there was another one back there. When he finally moved out to a place where I could get a shot, sure as heck, there he came. He took a leap over that log and I shot under him. He leaped and I didn't know he was going to. I'd have been alright if he hadn't leaped. Boy, he was legal!" As Jim told the story I knew he'd been reliving the event in his mind, play by play.

"Big buck?" I asked the obvious, enjoying the story.

He nodded.

"But I enjoyed it," he said eluding to the fact that not killing the deer didn't take away from the pleasure he enjoyed while being in the wilds.

"A lot of fun," I say feeling the same way about the time spent afield in the pursuit of game. He and I agree, it has little to do with killing but a lot to do with the thrill of seeing God's creation.

"I guess throughout this whole thing, I've been talking about nature and God's creation. That sort of thing, haven't I?" he asked.

"Well, we've talked about your prayer life and that sort of thing, too. Yeah, anything you see fit to add?" I asked opening it to his free thought.

"Well," he started and then halted.

"I think the most inspirational part of this is your ability to see good from all of it. Most people say, 'Oh my gosh, that's terrible. I can't even imagine that.'" I explain to him as the thought jumped into my head.

"Well, I'm... to begin with, you know my outgoing personality. I've always been outgoing. Say what I mean and mean what I say, which gets me in trouble," he said.

I bet there are a lot of people with outgoing personalities who would have quit the moment things got as ugly and rough as they are for Jim, I thought to myself.

"But, uh, like I keep saying, first of all, God has showed me that I have a lot of friends and family and staff around me, you know? Being up lifts everybody else up and makes it easier for me to be up. You know what I mean?" he asks me.

"Mmmm, sort of a cycle." I observe.

"You know the old saying about contempt breeding contempt? Well, smiles generate smiles. Oh, that's something I wanted to do, too," he said in a tone and cadence I recognized. He showed an ornery grin.

"Ought oh," I said knowing the kinds of events that often follow that look and those words.

"Laughs...the one nurse here, she's always saying she's gonna shave my chest." Jim has an unusually hairy chest. "So, the other day I said to her, 'I have the chance of a lifetime for you.' She said, 'what?'

"I'm gonna let you make a smiley face on my chest. Oh, right away she backed down. But the guy on second shift, he wants to do it," We share a good laugh.

"You know, just for them. Just for the – they open up my shirt and see a smiley face. That'll throw em back, won't it? Besides that, I can stand to lose some." He and I take off again in our laughter, harder this time. My sides begin to ache.

"We're gonna do that. Actually, the more of the crazy stuff ya do it livens the place up. It ain't gonna hurt me," he says.

"No, just a little bit of hair," I agree.

"A lot of hair, actually," Jim corrects me. I laugh out loud.

"But I said, yeah, you have the chance of a lifetime. She said, 'oh, I can't do that.' Ok, you're blowing it, I say. Wait till she sees it," He grins broadly.

"Oh, mercy!" I offer. We enjoy another good laugh.

"I like to mess with their minds a little," Jim admits.

"Sure, keep em guessing," I support him.

"I think that's another reason they like to visit with me. I keep em on their toes." He spoke showing the shadow of a smile.

We both enjoy another good laugh.

It is important for you to consider the situation as it really is. Jim is unable to walk now, but he is learning. He has learned to talk again and eats semi-solid foods someone else spoons into his mouth. Most all of his needs are met by others. He cannot accomplish even the simplest of tasks without help. He cannot operate a telephone, music or movie player. He is a very social man chained by a very limiting situation, yet he rejoices. Why? How?

The Bible explains why; *Consider it pure joy, my brothers, whenever you face trials of many kinds, because you know that the testimony of your faith develops perseverance. Perseverance must finish it's work so that you may be mature and complete, not lacking anything. - James 1: 2-4*

Jim has come to know pure faith many people will never know: he is following the Lord and Master of all creation through this world's pain on to glory with God. Jim's love of the Lord is being woven with suffering into a tight, strong tapestry that is faith. I have learned this lesson with such clarity in watching him struggle and cling to Jesus.

"I want to get you a copy of them books (the journals of his trek through his illness). Like a diary, they're kind of like my diary." He begins shifting back to serious business.

"So you attribute...we started to talk about seeing good come from all of this. You attribute that to just being who you are?" I ask joining his change in direction.

"Oh, well you have to see good come from all of this because I have. My biggest example is Dale (Jim's best friend among many) and people around me. Because of my disease, how they have changed their lives! People are praying. It may only be when there's a prayer at church or something like that, but good people praying who'd maybe never prayed before or not for a while. They got caught up in everyday life and I was one of them.

"After I... there was a while there when prayer wasn't in my life. There was always a thank you if I saw something

God created or if He protected me from something. I always thanked Him for it.

"Now, I always pray at night. I still pray the old fashioned 'Now I lay me down to sleep', I still pray that. But when I got like this I had much more time for prayer. Like I said, the good has come from it.

"People I prayed for had cancer and they'd go into remission. They've become clean. People with operations, too. We had a lady the other day who had a sister that needed a kidney; she got her kidney because of prayer. All these good things because of prayer," he said.

"If God hadn't put me in here like this, I wouldn't be praying like that," he further explained. The bitter hour has allowed Jim to bear fruit.

"Yeah. You don't have the time. Life is too hectic," I said without thinking.

"Yeahhh," Jim begins with a drawn out pronunciation so that I know a lecture is forthcoming.

"But we're supposed to take the time. It's like Sunday's. In the old days there were no Sunday sales. Families went to Church together, they prayed together and visited. Now, all the stores are open and all kids things are on Sunday. Now, you know it's the devil's work doing that." He paused to give me the emphasis of his silent glare.

"Soccer, football, baseball on Sunday," I chime in.

"They don't let the kids be kids, anymore. We played baseball when we wanted to. Now, they have a schedule and play when they're told to. The kids are in the outfield picking flowers. They're not interested in baseball. They're kids! Let them be kids!

"There are a lot of girls' teams, nowadays. The boys are getting lazy with computers and all. Let them play outside.

Women are taking over. I think so, a role reversal." His thoughts were really flowing now.

"Yeah, I think so. Men are taking a real relaxed attitude. There's too much fun to be had, why bother?" I add.

"I didn't think they were so irresponsible anymore. And the women, they're told if they don't do it (work full time) they are not reaching their full potential. Well, raising kids is the biggest job anybody could ever want. But they don't want to do that because it's not what the feminists say they should do. And with gas prices, I'll bet you it costs them money to work, nonprofessional women. Gas, child care – child care is out of sight. Extra car, extra insurance, plus the price of food, it's very expensive.

"They feel degraded if they're not working. It's degrading to be a housewife anymore. Well, according to society," he quickly clarifies.

"The man that's in with me now, his wife never worked. She raised four kids," he pauses for the emphatic, silent glare. I see the opening and take it.

"Well, if she raised four kids she did work," I said.

"What I mean is the only pay she got was satisfaction. It's just like us and living; our precious things in life aren't material things. Our most precious gift is eternal life." He pauses to give me the dramatic look.

"That's a true statement," I said.

"Well, it doesn't matter how many treasures we build up here, it won't help us a bit up there," he says referring to heaven.

Jesus taught us; *Do not store up for yourselves treasures on earth, where moth and rust destroy, and where thieves break in and steal. But store up for yourselves treasures in heaven, where moth and rust do not destroy, and where thieves do not break in and steal. For where your treasure is, there your heart will be also. - Matthew 6: 19-21*

"There's a couple that owned the store in Milesburg and they use to record music. I bought one of their tapes and there is a song on there, 'we must be ready, for when the day of rapture comes...there will be two men in a field and one will there and one will be gone.' That day you could buy a loaf of bread with a bag of gold. That's how much gold will be worth – nothing." Again he concludes with his silent stare for emphasis. The verse he refers to comes from Matthew 24: 40; *Two men will be in the field; one will be taken and the other left.*

"Oh, everything today. Says in the Bible, in the last days what's right will be wrong and what's wrong will be right. Boy, you see it so much. Then the weather, it (Bible) says about the weather. It's such strange weather we've had," he eludes to the multiple hurricanes and tsunamis and earthquakes.

"I saw something like that the other day. It made me think, boy that isn't right, it's backwards," I share.

"Yep, that's entirely right, it's backwards. Like I told you about the side rails on my bed..." Jim referred to an earlier visit when he told me he had asked for bed rails and they told him, "no." He was informed that bed rails are illegal restraints, yet he wanted them because he was fearful of falling out of bed.

"You don't have to wear a motorcycle helmet but you have to wear a seat belt," he shook his head slowly.

"I've never been able to figure that one out, either," I admit.

"It's the motorcycle lobby and the ACLU. Did you know a communist was one of the ones to start that (ACLU)? And when I got sick there was still one of them on the board. Everyone has rights but the people that deserve them.

"That privacy act, which is a joke, was brought on by HIV people," he paused.

"Is that right? Want to keep it hush?" I followed.

"They don't want people knowing they have HIV. Where it hit hardest is where you give blood. All those years they had volunteers filling out the paper work. They're not allowed to do that anymore.

"They have to be an RN to get your license and swear secrecy. And when that happened almost all of the questions (became) about sex. She asked me, 'did you ever pay for sex?' I said anybody that's ever had sex paid for it one way or another.

"You either buy them a couple drinks and have sex, buy them drugs and have sex. Paid for that new car for your wife? You pay for it one way or the other. She got mad at me. Truth hurts," he nodded sincerely.

"The truth is a painful thing," I offered.

"Mom always said the truth hurts and it should," he agreed.

"That lady, one day when I went in to give blood, you know? They prick your finger to do an iron test. She said, 'we don't do that anymore, we prick your earlobe.'

I said, 'you ain't getting it out of my earlobe.'

She said, 'oh, yeah. We have to get it out of the earlobe.'

I said, 'well if you have to get it out of my earlobe then I won't donate.'

"The other lady at the end of the table heard this. She knew me. Boy, she came running down there and said, 'if he wants to give it out of his finger, you let him give it out of his finger!' Cause they know I have O negative. Ah, that was funny."

I chuckled.

"That was something they tried and it didn't work out. They went back to the finger," Jim said.

"I don't know how that would work, anyway. There's no real meat in the earlobe," I suggested.

"Well, there must have been some blood or they wouldn't of tried it," Jim said showing off his logic again.

"I don't know," was all I could say.

"When they pierce your ear, does it bleed?" he asked.

"I don't know," I replied.

"You never had your ear pierced?" he asked with his dramatic glare.

"No," I grinned, enjoying the jab.

"You're kidding?" he said continuing the drama with a touch of sarcasm.

I laughed a good laugh.

"Oh, I don't know. It seems to be coming to an end, Paul," he said softly.

"What's that, Jim?" I inquired.

"This country," he noted changing his countenance.

"Yeah, I'm afraid. Grandma tells me that all the time. She is just so worried about our country. The way people treat one another," I said sharing her concern with him.

We paused for Jim to drink. When he resumed, we were onto another subject.

"Up behind my house, near the Johnson farm, lots of blackberries, really nice raspberries. I was mowing the grass a few days earlier, and this black snake ran across in front of me, a big one. A couple days later, I was picking berries and there that bugger was, curled up down over the hill there. They must travel a long distance. Heck, that's a long way. He was a big sucker. I just went around him and kept picking. Never saw him again after that," Jim said recalling fonder days when he was doing what he wanted.

"That's the kind you like to see," I said as they are non-poisonous and great pest control.

"Sort of like that cat I had. The whole time I lived up there we never had a mouse in the house. I'd let him out in the daytime. He took care of mice, chipmunks, snakes. I did see a crow with a snake in its claws, flew across. It was a pretty big one (snake), I don't know how he ever did it," he swallowed hard, his reflex needing to be coaxed. I offered him some water.

"They're pretty strong," I said matter of fact.

"Must be, especially if you have a wiggling snake under you," he said mildly.

"Right. Did I ever tell you about the one we saw out there last summer, after you left the picnic," I quizzed him regarding the trip to the camp picnic.

He shook his head.

"We got past the next to the last cabin in that long barren stretch and I saw this snake stretched across the road, coming off the bank. I had the girls in the back and pulled over where they could look out the window. I got around the back of the truck and he started coming up the road toward me. His buzzer was down in the grass and his head was out over the crown of the road. He was the biggest one I ever saw out there," I said.

"Killed him, I hope," Jim said giving me a serious look.

"Naw. I didn't have anything to kill him with. I had my pistol but I don't like shooting into the gravel," I explained.

"That snake you're talking about ain't nothing. I was coming in one time and saw this snake and his head was bigger than my hand," he said.

"Wow," I replied.

"He was stretched across the road," he added.

"Oh, my goodness," I said in disbelief.

"He went up there into those ferns and I wasn't going in after him. I didn't have a gun either," he added.

"One other time, near the burn out, there was a couple guys standing there. They was holding this rattler above their heads and it was touching the ground. And they were as tall as I am," he said with the dramatic, silent glare. Jim stands six foot, easy, so the snake would have had to been closer to 8 feet in length.

"Wow," was all I could say.

"Did you know that if you participate in the snake hunt you have to buy a permit for 25 dollars?" he asked with a related topic.

"To participate in the hunt?" I was incredulous.

"Yeah. And then you have to let the snakes go, anyway. I figure if you see them and kill them it doesn't cost you anything," he said showing his common sense again.

"Right," I nodded.

"It's amazing. These animal rights people are so protective of these snakes. They have to keep them a certain temperature and everything. The one kid made a move and the snake struck the side of the cage and he got on the kid." Jim was referring to a boy near a rattlesnake caged at the snake hunt.

"That's when you know things ain't right.

"You remember a couple of years ago when that boy got lost in the wild area? They weren't allowed to take vehicles in there after him. They spotted him with a helicopter and I guess it ended up they had to walk in and get him," he shook his head, disgusted.

"Holy cow," I breathed in disbelief.

"Then there was the time a sort of celebrity got lost in a wild area. They used snowmobiles (for the search) and they fined the devil out of them. Things ain't right here," he gave me the silent, dramatic look.

"It's gonna get worse before it gets better. This gas crunch is causing people to think we need to be more environmentally friendly. They're transferring to 'it's a wild area; you can't hunt there, fish there. You can't even go in there," I said with a bit of ranting at the idea of such radicalism.

"Unless you did something like out in Los Angeles and plant a tree every place you see a bare spot. That would soak up a lot of that smog. I don't know if you remember science class; trees take up carbon dioxide and give off oxygen.

"Now the Good Lord with His knowledge knows how to do things. Some of these people are too stupid to even plant a tree. They won't let you cut one down..." he shook his head.

"Wouldn't that alleviate a lot of that?" he looks at me questioningly.

"A lot of that," I nod. "A tremendous help. It's like you said; it's all flat and there's no trees."

"There's bare spots," Jim suggests areas to plant trees.

"Why wouldn't they line the sidewalks with trees?" I wonder aloud.

"Yeah, they have the planters where they..." he ends to swallow or breathe or both.

"Grass next to the sidewalk," I say.

"Yeah. Any open area, plant a tree there," he says in a disgusted tone. Then adds, "too simple."

"Too simple," I echo.

"Man(kind) can't do that. We think we can do everything else but we can't plant a tree, you know? Do you think a lot of society...they don't believe in God because they think they're gods themselves and tell you what you ought to do. Make sure you wear your seatbelt, but don't put a seatbelt on a wheelchair for an old person," he uses the look again.

The Bible supports his line of thinking regarding wisdom. *I saw that wisdom is better than folly, just as light is better than darkness.* - Ecclesiastes 2: 13. Jim's observations about the world are accurate and contrary to most people's thinking. It is still part of his 'say what I mean, mean what I say' philosophy.

"Oh, yeah, well I just look at history. They don't want you to look to history. They don't want you to know history. We ask these people today about global warming, you know? I asked one the other day. Do you know when most of the hottest temperatures were recorded? Back in the 30's, during the depression. They had what they called the dust bowl. Out west they plowed everything up and it got so hot the dirt turned to dust and the wind blew it like a tornado and sucked all the soil up cause it was so flat and there was no wind break. Their houses were filled with dust. It just cleaned the dirt off the top of the ground.

"If you ever go out west, you'll see all around the houses – you'll know where the house is because there's trees around it. In Iowa, they piled stones around them. Stones they picked. There can't be any stones left in the field. They made wind rows out of them," he explained.

"Wow, just something to break the wind," I echoed.

"But you always knew where a house was," he chimed.

He paused to take a serious turn.

"Going back in history as far as the countries, all the great nations fell a generation after homosexuality became normal. Well, you know we're in that generation now where it's almost normal. It's getting to be that they consider them normal, so, unfortunately, that's what generation it's in: my grandkids.

"Hillary gets in there, we'll have terrorists in this country the next day, probably," he says with a bit of sarcasm.

"Maybe by invitation, it's hard to say," I reply.

"Oh, it will be by invitation," Jim asserts.

"She uh, they use those kinds of tactics," I mutter.

"One thing about liberals, they have patience. They'll take one little victory at a time. It's like the gun laws, they'll take that little victory about having them registered," he pointed out.

"I don't know if you've been following that ammunition debate or not," I inquire.

"Well, there's the other thing. No, but I'll bet I can guess," he said.

"They've mixed it up with the environmentalists now. You're not allowed to have lead anything now. So, they can regulate what kind of ammunition you can use and they're going to regulate it to death," I explained.

"Yep, that's what I mean by little victories. They don't attack it right away with a bill to take away your guns. It don't work, so, they're content to take these little victories just like that," he alludes to the ammo regulation.

"That's one of the tactics they use. They're content to take one victory at a time because they know they can't regulate guns out of existence," he says.

"But if there's no ammunition for them..." I said connecting his thinking pattern.

"That's right!" he said as any good teacher would.

"Now what good did it do you to have them?" I asked from the perspective of any gun control lobby.

"That's right!" he said again. "I figure that business is doing pretty well – reloading. But the problem with that is you can't buy powder," Jim was moving in a logical order.

"I think it's already where you have to sign for it and you're only allowed so much," I added my two cents.

"Uh, huh," Jim said nodding lightly. He knew where I was going.

"It could be part of that Patriot Act or something cause they are afraid of you making a bomb," I concluded.

"Yeah, go on line and it shows you how to make one," he says emphatically.

"Go look at the bombing of that federal building. Those guys used fertilizer. They didn't use gun powder at all." I said using supportive evidence.

"Yeah, you can regulate and regulate all you want, but those guys who do that, they'll find a way," he concluded.

"For sure," I agreed.

"I'll sign for my gun powder, do you think they're going to sign for theirs?" he added to emphasize his point.

"They'll steal mine," I observed.

"They'll steal mine," he agreed nodding.

"That's one more thing you're going to see more of as the economy gets worse; holding up grocery stores, gas stations, liquor stores and bakeries. You're gonna see more of that. We said when I-99 came through the crime rate would go up and it has. We've had more murders in the last year than we've had..." his look indicated that he couldn't recall a time when with a murder rate near what it is now for the State College area.

"And you know, they don't think anything of it. There's no remorse about killing anybody," he said openly upset by these circumstances.

"Not anymore," I added not sure if there ever had been such thing as true remorse for murder.

"Well, you see it on TV. You kill em and whip-pee ding. That's why I think our days are numbered," he said.

"What time is it?" he asked of a sudden.

"Ten till one," I said a bit surprised at how late it was.

"Oh, we missed dinner," he said matter of fact. "We'll go back to my room and have cheese and crackers," he said. I knew he was hungry.

"Oh, that's ok. I'll go out and buy us something," I offered.

"Oh, no! You ain't going out to get me anything. I told Jeff to bring me a couple fried eggs. Real eggs. They actually are almost organic because his chickens run free," Jim said softening the hard reality of our earlier conversation.

"They are organic then," I chimed.

"Well, ok. Let's see. The Amish may have sprayed those fields with something..." he gave me his dramatic stare.

I laughed.

There is a pause and long silence. I think maybe it's time to turn off the recorder and move to his room. Jim seems more interested in conversing than eating.

"You have fellowship with other Christians to renew your spirit, when you're down. So much bad around you and people seem so disinterested. I guess the good thing is you very rarely hear anybody say, 'well, I don't want to talk about that.' Don't do that in front of me, you know, praying. We pray.

"We were down at therapy one day and we were gonna pray before she left. She said to the girl, 'do you mind?'

"This girl said, 'no. I'll join you.' The other ones didn't pay any attention. That's bad when you have to ask to pray. I'd of just gone ahead and prayed," he said.

"I need to stop these discouraging thoughts," he announced.

"Focus on the good," I offered.

"There's a lot more good than bad. You just don't hear about it," Jim observed.

"That's for sure," I agreed.

"Did you give your mom a hug for?" he asked changing the subject.

"No. I haven't seen her, only talked on the phone, but I did give my grandmother one for you," I said hoping that would be a suitable, short term substitute for hugging my mother.

"Oh, give her another one for me," he said. His eyes were ablaze.

"And I told them you asked about all of them.

"My mom had an incident reading in bed. She didn't have to get up early in the morning. She heard a popping sound. She got up and crept around the house. Nothing. Back to bed reading. Room felt warmer. Then she smelled smoke. Jumped up and ran to the basement door. Opened it and smoke billowed out. She covered her face and ran down, turned on the laundry tub, after unplugging the freezer, and hosed the fire down.

"Here, the freezer compressor had burst into flames. It burned up the wall behind the freezer and started to burn the ceiling. Then she was afraid to go back to bed because of the hotspots in the wall. So, she called 911 just to check it out. Next thing she knew, there were four fire companies and firemen everywhere," I said giving an abridged account of what happened.

"That's another thing; over response. That's the reason I quit the fire company. They had a fire at the trailer park so they take the ladder truck," he said accompanied with his silent, dramatic stare.

I laughed out loud.

"But they're required to respond to every 911 call with ambulance, fire, and police – depending upon what it is. They had a guy holding his wife hostage with a gun. They blocked the road, evacuated houses, called in the SWAT team. One man, one gun, too many guys. They over respond. Costs money.

"You get in an accident. Fire trucks, no matter what, got to go. Just in case the car catches fire. They had an EMT up at the hospital, they have to come out if an ambulance is on the way to the hospital and they have to come out to stop them so he can check em. People on the ambulance are trained EMT's," he emphasizes the words trained EMT's.

"But every time they move that vehicle it costs money so, they have to check somebody. They'll pull an ambulance off the road," Jim says.

"It makes you wonder," I offer.

"Well, they're idiots. Everything's a calamity. If you used your common sense it wouldn't be a calamity," Jim said again showing his 'say what I mean, mean what I say' approach to life.

"I see this all feeding in with the Patriot Act, now. I just passed a whole line of military trucks and we have black hawk helicopters flying overhead. People are being desensitized by sirens and things. I don't think it will be anything for people to accept the military is going to roll in and do this or do that," I said sharing a secret concern.

"Well, there's the other thing. There could be military rule," Jim replied.

"Or at least some sort of marshal law where somebody just takes over," I said hoping I was wrong.

"Yeah, everything will be... You won't be allowed to come out of your house at certain times. All that kinda stuff. There's another thing, you know, with these gun laws, your freedoms are slowly being taken away a little bit at a time. Gun locks cause of kids. They always use the kids.

"They'll give you a questionnaire asking if you feel safer for your kids with gun locks on there (gun) would you vote for it?

"Well, women especially, as soon as you say kids, they'll vote for it. Not realizing if you do this, there goes one more of your freedoms. But they always use kids as a crutch."

"Emotional part of it," I offer.

"And most of your questionnaire's are geared to get a certain answer. I use to answer questionnaires but I wouldn't give them a yes or no vote. They wanted a yes or no answer and I said I'm not going to. They want that yes or no vote so they can turn it into whatever they want. I'm not like that.

"This depends on that and that depends on this. You can't say yes or no to that question. Too many variables and they know that!" he exclaimed

"That's why they do it," I said.

"Well, I'm sorry, but you can't be a reliable respondent then," he says mocking the survey people.

"The problem of it is that I'm too reliable a respondent. They hang up," he explains.

"I think there's probably a lot more in this country who feel the way we do and don't bring any attention to themselves," he was becoming melancholy.

We paused for a few moments.

"I don't know. I haven't done a lot of praying about this book. I have prayed some. It would be something that...if it touched them like it did me, have the Lord change my heart like He has. I'd be praying for that, but if it happens it will be a pretty good one. If it happens it's what the Lord wants," he said solemnly.

"True enough," I agree.

"The fact that He put the idea in your head was amazing because I still feel insignificant as far as things happening. But when they make me sit down and think about it; I guess it is kind of amazing. But I do thank the Lord that...( he shakes his head slowly) I really do. I am a humble man.

Jesus said, *"For whoever exalts himself will be humbled, and whoever humbles himself will be exalted."* Matthew 23:12.

"It's like I played pool and darts and stuff, ya know. When they win, almost all of them, there weren't too many like me. A few. When they win they feel good inside, they don't have to bring attention to themselves, ya know? By going nuts like some of them do. I don't know, I've always been that way. If it is good it's better to have someone else recognize it for us instead of us having to tell them, 'hey, I'm this or that. I'm this. I'm that, I, I, I , I , I, I, I.

"Told you about a friend of mine. Right inside the door (of his room) is a picture of his stepdaughter, there. I am this and I am and I am. It's to build up self-esteem. Self esteem you don't build up, you earn it. You don't have any self –esteem unless you earn it. People can't come out and give it to you," he paused with the silent drama stare.

"Wise words, very wise," I nodded.

*Pride goes before destruction, a haughty spirit before a fall. Better to be lowly in spirit and among the oppressed than to share plunder with the proud.* Proverbs 16: 18-19.

"But they try so much to give self esteem. Another thing I don't understand is about these blacks. You can't say anything about them. I told you about the guy that worked with Larry?" he asked.

I shook my head.

"Well, there's two black guys that work with Larry. One of them had been there quite a while. A lot of guys come in there, work a little bit and then they're gone. Larry come into work one night and the one guy, who'd been there quite a while, had the other guy up against the wall, by the throat. He was telling him, 'It's niggers like you that give blacks a bad name.' Larry said I liked the guy a lot before but after that I liked him even more. That's the truth," Jim concluded eluding to the fact that he agreed with the sentiment.

"It's guys like that that give blacks a bad name, just like some white guys give us a bad name. I don't care what color they are as long as I don't have to cater to them. They have their place, just like any other guy does. Even Dougie," Jim says chuckling. Doug is another of Jim's closer friends and he is of African-American descent. Doug is also a regular visitor to our camp. He is very down to earth and admired for it. In fact, he was recently made an honorary member of our camp!

"And the second is like it: *'Love your neighbor as yourself'.*" *Matthew 22: 39.*

We pause for a moment. He starts talking about the problems with the nursing staff.

"It's like the one nurse's position here. Her job is to do the paperwork and make sure it gets done and that's it. She won't do anything beyond her job description. The one lady that was in there before her would help the care nurses. She would give a hand changing people. She'd be out there and hear my bell ring and go get somebody to answer it instead of coming to check on me." Jim adds a sense of practicality to our conversation.

"She had to resign from her last job or get fired, she had a choice, but they hired her (here)," he says with a disgusted tone.

"Wow" is all I can say.

"The people who really care take the brunt of all that and make up for all the slackers." Jim's observations remain on target.

"Right," I agree.

"The amazing part of it is they cater to the slackers." He continues his observation

I chuckle before adding; "I see it at work, too."

"Oh, it's not just here. It's everywhere. They go around and place the extra work the slackers don't do on the ones that do work. They'll complain, but they'll do it. They say, 'oh, they can handle it.' Yeah, but they can only work so long then they get burned out and quit. That's what happened here. They burned these people out and they quit.

"It's just like that nurse. Last night she signed off that she'd given me my eye drops, twice. She didn't give them to me. They sign off on stuff like that all the time. I had to tell her to use gloves when she did my eyes. She wasn't going to. I see them not using gloves when they do other patients."

The scanner Jim's roommate has on the windowsill begins sounding off as to the details of an accident. It was a very loud dispatch. Jim asked me to turn it off, so I did.

"I have to keep speaking up. It gets so frustrating when nothing happens, so I keep it up." He's speaking of the nursing issue.

"Just let them know your watching," I replied.

"Well, they know. One thing I've always been was very observant. I pick up on things real quick. It probably is because I have very good peripheral vision. So I notice things. Dale's the same way. It's like my roommate has a new TV. I came in and it's the first thing I saw."

I chuckle: This from a man who was nearly blind just a short while ago.

He continues; "Or if they get a new hairdo or something; I pick it up right away. Most people don't notice stuff like that."

Brent, Jim's step son, stopped for a visit while I was there.

In talking with Brent I learned that Jim had a big impact raising him. Jim said, ' I don't think he turned out too bad.' Brett, sitting across the table, beamed.

We spoke of the friend Brent had in Iraq and the boxes he had sent him and of the boxes I had sent my cousin, Justin, while he was in Iraq. We talked about the coin rumored to be out with the words "In God We Trust" missing from it. There was a planned boycott.

The issue of age came up and Jim talked about putting it all in perspective. He said, "you take a standard tape measure and pull it out 78 inches, the average age, and look at how much life is behind or in front of you. Keeps it all in line," he said.

Jim began sharing the experience he was having with the therapy people. He was learning to walk! The process was frustrating to him because of the inequity of the system.

"So, they want to hit the high spots and get people in and out of the door quick over a short period of time." I said of the medical insurance folks. "When you're dealing with people that's not the case."

"Well that's what's so frustrating. I'm supposed to get an hour and a half of therapy and I'm lucky if I can get half an hour. And other people sit there and sleep. But they don't care. They're getting paid."

"It boils down to the bottom line, that almighty dollar." I said.

"That's exactly what it is." He nods.

"Too bad" I say.

"Well, that's the way of the world and it ain't gonna get any better. It's like everything else – it's about that almighty dollar. It's like what they did to Christmas. It's about the dollar" he offered.

"Don't even call it Christmas. It's the winter celebration or something," I said.

"Holiday. They call it the holiday tree, not the Christmas tree anymore. People. Ah, I was talking to somebody the other day about the lighting outside and I asked them about a nativity scene or anything like that and they said, ah, we don't do that. I think I told you this one time before, one time I went for a drive to look at the lights and all I saw was two things that had anything to do with Christmas."

"That's a shame" I offered.

"Ya, well, the other day a nurse was in here and said about seeing all the signs in people's yards, 'it's a boy'. She said, 'my golly, must be a lot of boys being born around here!"

I laughed aloud, a good belly laugh! Jim gave me the silent stare.

"You know? Then they found out it was from the church." He shook his head.

"A little slow on the uptake" I said amongst the chuckles.

"Well yeah, but you know, if you're not familiar with the real story of Christmas they don't get it."

"Pastor was in the other day and he read to me from the book of Luke. The part about Gabriel coming to see Elizabeth and telling her she was going to get pregnant with a baby boy. Well, then he said about Mary coming to tell her about her experience and the baby jumped in her (Elizabeth's) womb. I always found that exciting! You know, John the Baptist jumped for joy," he said.

"He knew it from the very beginning." I added.

"Yeah. I always found that pretty exciting.

"The whole story's pretty exciting right down to him not believing it, that he was going to have his own son because of his age and everything. Losing his speech."

A nurse broke our concentration. She tended to Jim's scheduled needs and then left.

"What other kinds of things have been happening for you?" I asked.

"Well, I've been able to go out. I went to my sisters using the county van."

"Oh, wow" I said.

"They pick you up at the door and drop you off at the door. So, I spent a couple hours in the afternoon with my sister."

"Good," I said excitedly.

"I went out to a ball game at State College. Went to the camp picnic. I'll be going to the company Christmas party. I'll be going to the Christmas Eve service. It's in the afternoon this year. Before it was so difficult to get out. When I first went to get in a vehicle I had to bend my knees. The pain was excruciating! Now I can get in there without any pain at all. So, that's an improvement!"

"I'll say," I commented.

Then we took a little break and when we got back to work, Jim told me about his thoughts on Jeep automobiles. He shared several of our favorite stories with me. Then we talked about Jim Wilson's ride UP the mountainside. He said we came to understand that it wasn't the vehicle it was the driver!"

I laughed.

He was referring to the many episodes where various autos drove by the old jeep stuck in the ditch!

We talked then of Dale's Jeep and his old jeep.

"So Dale said to me, 'what are we gonna tell Jim (Keenan), after all those years of picking on him. (much laughter) That's when we figured out, when we rode up the mountain with Wilson, it was the driver not the vehicle." We both laughed aloud.

Jim paused to think. Suddenly he leads me into a deep subject.

"Every place I've been there's been angels. One care nurse that stood out and was more than a care nurse to me; I call these adopted daughters angels. I had an angel up at Laurel Crest and it just seemed whenever I needed her or something wasn't working right, she would show up.

*Are not all angels ministering spirits sent to serve those who will inherit salvation?* Hebrews 1:14

"A couple of them corresponded with me for about a year and a half. I haven't heard from them since Christmas. I heard in the fall that they had a lot of problems up there. I don't know if they even work there, anymore.

"Then there was a woman out in Clearfield, same way. It just seemed like extra special. I got to know her family and she had a little girl. Oh my, she was something else." I knew exactly what Jim was talking about because I had watched him fuss over my daughter and his granddaughter.

"And now, I would guess my adopted granddaughter here is Sara in OT. She looks at me like her grandfather. She has been really close. Her dad is really talented.

"He not only sings em, but he wrote them. Then in the newspaper, last Saturday, he and his two brothers were in an art show down in Millheim. My daughter says he is really talented. His brother did a painting and the price was 1500 dollars, but it was so meticulous." Jim is clearly impressed.

"What's his name?" I ask curiously.

"Carl Lightsell and his brother Greg and I forget the other one. They're all talented," he said.

"I guess we all have our talents of one kind or another," I offered.

"Yeah, (pause) I guess mine's running my mouth." Jim said. I thought he was being too self-critical.

"Conversation is an art. There are an awful lot of people who can sit in a room with 20-30 other people and not speak a word and not want to speak a word. They just like to sit quiet." I explained.

"Well, I get sort of uncomfortable when I'm with somebody and there is silence. I need to break the silence. They're sitting there thinking something and not saying it." Jim said.

I know this to be a very accurate statement because I've been present when Jim broke the silence among a group of men.

"As I sit and think of that, I think that's why so many people find your overall situation so inspirational. You still manage to have an upbeat attitude after having gone through all that. A lot of people would still be very, very bitter that they were stuck in this circumstance after having all those things go on," I say referring to the eye drop incident, the "hoyer lift" and his situation in general.

"Well, the lady that did that, she wasn't a very good nurse," he begins and I sense that he is defending her. He tries to explain her side.

"She's one of those that comes in and once she gets done, she is done and she wants to get done as soon as possible. We have a few of those here, but the good ones look at the care book, which tells you their (patient) history and what problems and kinds of medicines they get and all that kind of stuff. The good ones, they read that every time they see me," he said providing anecdotal evidence of what he's talking about.

"Then they read the instructions on the medicine and make sure it is the right thing before they administer anything. There are others that just don't do it, because they did it last night the same way," he says seemingly in defense of the less competent.

"That particular nurse, she wasn't very good. Put that in there and it burnt and I mean it burnt. She said, 'Oh, that's the wrong medicine.' She went on and got the other medicine and put it in there and that was it. Didn't try to do anything with it or anything," he said sharing the experience.

"Wow, and you weren't able to tell her anything?" I wondered aloud.

"Oh, I was able to tell her. After she put that in there I said, 'that's burning my eye out.' She said, 'Oh, yeah. It's the wrong stuff.' "

"After I left up there a woman gave an overdose of stuff and they fired one of the nurses. That would be the one, too, you know? She's not very careful about things," he said.

"Like you said, It doesn't take too much to be attentive," I affirmed.

"Well, what they want to do is get done so they can go and sit at their nurses station. We have one on second shift who will have her care nurses do her vitals for her. Well, that takes away from the care nurses and it makes the LPN look good. She gets done quicker. She doesn't help the care nurses if they don't get done pulling somebody up. The other nurses, they don't get done sometimes and have to stay late because they were helping the care nurses. They care. It's not required of them but they care about the patients and want to help them," he explains his observation.

"It's too bad people are that way," I said.

"Those people ought not be in the business. I keep telling the other ladies, you all have to be angels; that's the only people who'd do this," he continues.

"12-14 hours and they can still smile about things," I offer.

"We met with the county commissioners and I said to them, 'I challenge any one of you to come in here and spend one day as a care nurse.' Two of them weren't even here and one showed up later.

"One of them said, 'I'll pass that along.'"

"The one I really wanted to talk to, the one who always abstains, he didn't show up. He said he had to abstain from coming because he had the flu. When he said, 'abstain,' it was kind of like...you know?" he paused expectantly.

"Barbing?" I said.

"Yeah, barbing. And I knew who it was directed at. He said the flu and somebody else told us a cold. I wouldn't be surprised if he didn't have nothing." He said referring to the open criticism he had made of this commissioner abstaining from most things.

"They did relay the message," he said finally.

"What he does with it is his problem, his business," I said.

"I was gonna tell him the voters aren't stupid. You saw what happened to the other fellas? But he didn't show up."

I related to Jim some of the symptoms I had from Lyme's disease, especially the tingling sensation in my hands.

"You know that's also a symptom of this here (GBS). The tingling. They can catch it real quick now. There's a lot more people catching this." Jim was warning me now.

"That's what I heard," I said. "I was just reading that somewhere on the internet while looking GBS up."

"They found it's coming from the flu shot. One of the warnings on the flu shot said if you had any numbness of the feet or hands you shouldn't take the flu shot.

"I had a nurse come to me the other day and she asked if I was telling the girls not to take the flu shot. 'No,'" he indicated he had not. "She said the girls weren't taking the flu shot because they were listening to you. I said what do you mean? I didn't tell any of them not to get the flu shot. I just told them if they have those symptoms they should not get it.

"It's like that H1N1. A lot of people won't take that. We had a lady here who had the flu and it escalated into double pneumonia and she died." Clearly Jim sees the serious nature of the charges leveled at him.

"Wow," I offered.

"So if they hear your speech slurred a little bit you better get to see a doctor. They give you stuff now. I think they said it was the anti-rejection drug they use when they give you transplants. I know a friend of mine and she has three daughters. The one is twenty one and she got it (GBS). They caught it and she was up walking with a walker in two months. I met a couple (GBS patients) over at Health South and they were up and walking in six months pretty much normal.

"I heard of other cases. One was a doctor and they should of died but they made it. But they were taken care of.

"You ever get the flu shot?" He is asking me.

"No, I never did. I don't believe in that kind of medical... After seeing what happened to you I just stayed away from them." I speak with some reservation.

"Well, I'll tell you. What happens to these people who get the flu shot? They get sick. They inject you with a live virus that is neutered. That's not the word they use but that's what it amounts to.

"My theory is that they don't let kids be kids anymore. So, they don't develop their own immune systems. Everything is so wash this and wash that that everything is so sterile they don't have a chance to develop an immune system over the years. How many pieces of fruit did you ever eat without washing it or pieces of meat with your dirty hands?" Jim takes us in a new direction.

"Or pick up an apple and just eat it?" I ask thinking of camp.

"Right," Jim nods.

Jesus said, *"Do you not see that whatever goes into the mouth enters the stomach, and goes out into the sewer? But what comes out of the mouth proceeds from the heart, and this is what defiles. For out of the heart come evil intentions, murder, adultery, fornication, theft, false witness, slander. These are what defile a person, but to eat with unwashed hands does not defile,"* Matthew 15: 17- 20.

It is apparent that most folks are more worried about clean hands than their eternal salvation. Our hearts are soiled and nobody cares, just so we don't catch a cold. It is a very mixed up world.

"Hey, I forgot to ask you if Larry got that apple out of the camp yard to you," I quizzed.

"Oh yes. First apple off the tree." He sounds pleased. He was involved in acquiring the trees and planting them.

"Good," I said hoping to hear of his experience.

"Yeah, that thing was sweet!" he exclaimed.

"Good." I smiled.

"It was nice and crisp, you know what I mean?" he said squinting at me.

"Oh, yeah," I nodded.

"Boy that apple was nice and crisp and sweet." He went on as he relived the experience.

"Good" I repeated.

"I told Doug; I told him I had the first pear off of his tree and the first apple off the camp tree." Jim was enjoying this. I chuckled.

Centre County commissioners came to give a check to the physical therapy department. It became a big deal. They stopped on his floor. Jim said, "I knew one of them wouldn't show up to give them an out." He was right, only two showed. Jim waited until last to talk with them.

He spoke about the treatment of nurses and the food they served. Jim has become an advocate for nurses. He told me about one being fired.

She had been engaged in some activity the administration frowned upon even though it was positive to patient's care. She fought back with legal counsel and won her job back with back pay. Jim concluded that they always threaten the nurses for this and that - "you'll be fired."

Jim said, "yeah, right, and I'm the king of Spain."

Our subject morphed into a more specific discussion of Centre Crest. He explained that the nursing home was a county home but was about to be absorbed by a non-profit group. Jim said he knew what was going on. Like the other homes he'd heard of, this home was about to be purchased by a particularly wealthy pharmacy chain. They couldn't buy it outright, so they would use a non-profit group as an initial purchasing body and then run it into bankruptcy and buy it cheap.

Jim explained to me that he's noted the signs: the county was running extra people over the holidays and that was at time and a half or double time. The county also bought new trays and dishes at a cost of 150,000 dollars. They were making a deficit, on paper, so that they could legitimize unloading the home as a financial burden when really it was not.

"Why all the trouble?" He had asked me rhetorically. "Guess who sells the county home all their prescription drugs?" He used the silent stare used for emphasis.

"You guessed it, the same pharmacy chain that's looking to buy the home. This way they would cut out the middleman and sell their own drugs to themselves," He explained.

Jim enlightened me as to some of the other inequality he'd encountered. While on his way to regaining the use of his legs he had to spend a couple weeks at Health South for an evaluation. Tests were done to determine if he had any hope of walking again. Otherwise, the insurance company wouldn't pay for it. Thankfully, they did find some merit in his potential to walk.

Jim was too in tune with the politics of the place not to make note of these things. If the administrators believed they were going to walk around the place and do as they pleased without being caught they were wrong. Jim may look impaired and motivate in an impaired manner and even speak and eat as one who is impaired, but there was nothing wrong with his mental faculties. The administration may have believed he was out of it, but they were wrong. He is very with it.

# Chapter 8
## *Special Places*

During our interview Jim mentioned the Advent Historical Society and wondered aloud if it should be mentioned in this writing. We have noted it here as a point of interest.

The Advent Church sits at the head of the hollow where Jim grew up milking cows on my Uncle Irv's farm, which had been the family farm of my great grandfather, Clyde Watson and his father John Watson a generation before. They had all attended church there. Jim recognized the significance of the church and the work the historical society was doing.

The Advent Church (right) and outbuildings (left).

Merril Watson, my grandfather, and Jane Franco, Merril's cousin, among others, had spearheaded the Advent Historical Society by honoring the church with restoration. I had been privy to their work and knew of the efforts these people had put forth to renew and maintain the local landmark. It was a costly long-term commitment. Jim was married to Barb in the Advent church, too!

I had driven my grandparents to the wedding and was surprised at how late in the evening it was being held. The reason was soon made obvious. By the time the service was underway, the candelabras were needed and lit. That old church, recently restored, illuminated with candle light for the wedding of my good friend. I had been blown away by the beauty of that evening.

Looking out the window, through the old imperfect and wavy glass and seeing the shadows of the tombstones cast by the bright moon was breathtaking. The open heat grate decorated the floor and the soft colors used to paint the walls were lovely. The pews were very straight and narrow. A pump organ provided the ceremony music and the large group in attendance filled the church. It was like going back in time. Jim recently informed me that a half dozen fire extinguishers had been strategically placed and the electrical outlets were all disguised!

That is my recollection of his wedding at the Advent Church. Jim, however, spoke of the Advent church in a different vent. He described the rummage sales Jane Franco had helped organize. The sales had generated large sums of money to support the Advent Historical Society. Jim described these sales as a big deal for the local people. Jane would provide a selection of baked goods that were very good, and as he said these words he rolled his eyes to emphasize how tremendous a baker she had been. He told me, "You could buy everything else there for a whisper, but Jane's stuff was expensive."

He went on to describe the jellies and sweet things, too, again, rolling his eyes indicating that they were awful good. He said they raised a few thousand dollars to keep the church up. Jim explained to me that he had helped out with the church and served on the board for a while.

As was expected, we came to the topic of our camp. Jim and I belong to a hunting and fishing camp in the north central mountains of Pennsylvania. He explained that he personally enjoyed camp for the quietness and as a place to enjoy nature.

"People love that picture in the window," he said directing my gaze to an old wooden four pane window. It was recently removed from our camp and now served as a collection of four picture frames. Each pane of glass secured a separate photo of the camp. It was a beautiful testament to a timeless place.

Jim told me that the picture most people liked the best was the one with the snowflakes falling, big fluffy flakes that blocked some of the view. He adds to why people love that the best by telling me, "especially when they can't get out."

**Jim's picture of the camp in a snow storm.**

"I remember the year all the two wheel drives were snowed in at camp. Merril had said, 'no way I'm leaving my truck down here' at the suggestion. Aahhhhh," Jim sighed with a quick chuckle. "Better start digging!"

"Dale and I always did hope we would get snowed in down there," he summed up with a smile.

"A guy from another camp did get in trouble a week after that story took place. We met him coming down Penrose road," he said. "He was back at that old trailer that use to be back there and he'd been shoveling for three days. 'How much further to the hard road?'" he'd asked them. They had encountered him a couple miles from the hard road and there was plenty of snow-covered road ahead of him.

Jim and Dale explained to him that if he got down the hill he could make it out because they had plowed the lower road. Jim said after they passed him and he made it to the top of the hill, "all you could hear was the roar of his motor as he came hauling down the hill. He was tired of shoveling," Jim concluded. Then he laughed the hoarse laugh he'd been left with.

His laugh was further handicapped by the lack of facial response. If you were out of earshot when Jim laughed, you wouldn't know he was laughing. He showed signs of labored breathing, too. It concerned me.

"Thing about camp was you had those mentors out there. They taught you how to enjoy the things God gave you. So, that was it. Not only to enjoy everything, but also how to enjoy everything. Mentored to appreciate everything, too.

"People who go to our camp say they really enjoy it because of the people in the camp and where it's located and everything. You have people come back, too. One guy who hadn't been there in fifty years came back out to enjoy a visit. Then there's the guy they dumped in the creek. I don't know who he was." Jim was talking about an urn of ashes some folks had poured into the stream beside our camp. It had appeared to be a funeral service of some kind. Neither Jim nor Dale nor any of our members know who the deceased was but it must have been somebody who loved the camp a great deal to leave final instructions of that sort.

Since we were talking of the camp, I mentioned the pictures we have of him with a beard and/or mustache, posing with wildlife harvested, huge chainsaws and so on. The tornado and the blow down...

He stared off, introspectively for a moment. Slowly his head began to nod as if he was recalling the photos as they were being taken. Then he looked in my direction again and said, "there was a time..." He continued to nod.

Since the early onset of Jim's GBS came so late in his years and his eyes dried out, he had very poor visual acuity. So, I didn't think anything of it when he didn't look right at me as we spoke. This time he looked right at me, intently.

Then he paused before speaking and went in a different direction. I expected him to address the topic of the younger Jim McKinley, but he didn't.

**A view of the destruction left by the tornado near our camp.**

"They have trees about this big around (holds his hands at a 14-16 inch gap) just twisted off twenty feet in the air. Stumps are still there. Took the top off (Eluding to the Tornado of the 1980's). Then that fire came pretty close to our camp and then missed it. I think our camp is blessed," he mused.

"When they burned all them other camps down that time, they drove into our camp and backed out. They could see their tracks. Forest Ranger said it was clear they knew which camps they were going to burn before they got out there. I don't know.

"I don't know if there'll be a day when you guys will have to tear it down and build another one or not," he eluded to replacing the camp. "I know that kitchen floor is getting bad. So damp there. You dig down a foot and you got water. I hope it always stays that rustic.

"We were up on the ridge hunting and could look down into the cockpit, they were so low," he is speaking now of the military jets that fly practice maneuvers up and down our valley. "Then there was the other time when the deer were scarce. We were skinning one out and four of them flew overhead in formation. One of them broke off and circled back over camp. We joked that the pilot was so astonished to see a deer taken that he had to fly back around and verify it." He was laughing aloud now.

"So many memories out there. I remember, you know, Tibby and how Mr. Wilson use to wave his hat at the end of a drive?"

A drive is a hunting tactic where one group of hunters push deer toward another group. They select bucks and attempt to harvest them. Some of these drives covered large areas. It's an ancient practice. Mr. Wilson wanted to be sure the approaching hunters spotted him even though he was wearing bright orange clothing and could be readily seen.

"Well, Dale told him if he did that again they were going to shoot. We were over there in the cove of rocks one day and Tibby was there. We had already decided to shoot up in the air if a hat was waved. We got out there to the end of the drive and Tibby, being smart, was standing there waving his hat. Bang, bang, bang, bang, bang. Oh, he threw that hat on the ground." Jim's eyes closed and he looked like he couldn't breathe as he laughed a deep belly laugh. The laugh was raspy and weak.

"Bobby was in on that one." He said matter of fact.

"You know, that's what makes camp so special. Just read the log book." He spoke of the journal everyone contributes to as they visit the camp to share their experiences.

"The one the girls always remember, Penny and them, look it up, is that bat story. About a page and a half on that one. They used a fly swatter and a tennis racket and I don't know what all," he spoke of one of the many instances where a bat entered the camp and flew about frightening the campers. The teenage girls had freaked out.

"I can tell you one thing I learned about that. If they're going this way, you swing the other, because they always change directions. We use to shoot at them a lot out there. Notice how I said shoot AT them. I had the best success out there with that old single barrel 12 gauge with the long barrel. I'd wait until they were going away from me to shoot." He was enjoying the recollection of such events and it was outwardly evident.

"Gail did something for Dale this Christmas...She bought him a bat box. She heard us talking about these bat boxes, so you know what's going up this summer?" he paused for effect. "A bat box," he said nodding.

As Jim is speaking my thoughts begin to wander about the nature of his predicament. He is fully aware of the world around him; past, present and future. Yet he's confined to a shell that restricts his movement and his actually, physically, reliving such events as the bat hunting. Such a tragedy; or is it?

Scripture speaks to such a topic. What we think is so openly obvious and self-evident is often an illusion. In Jim's case God has given him a great strength. He sees things for what they really are. The Lord *"gives great power to the weak, and to those who have no might He increases strength."* – Isaiah 40:29. In this regard Jim is a very powerful force.

As I spent time with him it became apparent that he was stronger than ever. Not in the sense I had been accustomed to, like seeing him lift heavy logs onto the truck or carry buckets of coal in the snow. His strength had changed. Those of us who had known him before GBS didn't like what we were seeing. It made us uncomfortable, because it was change. Change is painful. Jim had changed to become a memory of days past and to illuminate the will of the Lord. He was preaching to me, in this subliminal sermon, as to the real nature of things. His faith was his real strength now.

# Chapter 9
## *Future Predicted in 2008*

"What kind of an outlook do you have for the future and what are the people here telling you?" I began the subject.

"Well, very few people think I'll ever get out of here. I have an appointment with the neurologist in July. We'll know a lot more then. I haven't stopped having them minute changes, for the better. So, I haven't given up hope that I'll get back to caring for myself. If I can even get my hands back, you know, a grip that will be a big step. If I could do that I could feed myself and go to the bathroom myself, if I wasn't able to walk. I can stand myself with help. I would guess I could do that with therapy. I have a problem with foot drop. You know what that is?" he quizzed.

"Mmhmm," I said. Recalling the very first visit when Jim was in bed wearing the tennis shoes and I asked why.

"I don't know. I doubt that I'll ever recover enough to get out of here. If I can only get these stupid hands to work. It doesn't seem like they want to come along.

"Now I am able to press the remote a little. Turn it (TV) off and on and change the channel. It ain't much, but it's something." Jim is showing a little frustration and I don't know how to respond so, I try to approach the topic with an encouraging analysis.

"Like you said, you can't really see your changes cause you're measuring it against yourself. You can't see the growth. It's like raising kids; you can't see them grow but other people can. If they don't see your kids for six months they say, 'wow, did they get tall.' To you it doesn't seem that obvious a change. You may be showing a lot of progress but to you it's everyday and everyday. No change," I hoped to make a helpful point.

"It's like I was laying there one day and the manager came in. I lifted my hand up and put it on the rail. She said, 'well, that's something you couldn't do before.' It had come along until I could do that.

"Everything has come along so slow, but I'm older and the severity of it (GBS) is the second thing. I think the severity of it is the main thing.

"One of the nurses here, her uncle had it (GBS). His did the same thing as mine. He had a tracheotomy and a ventilator and that was three months ago. Now, he doesn't even have a tracheotomy. But he's only 46 now. He wasn't paralyzed as long as I was without knowing anything.

"Evidently he was pretty much able to know what was going on. He moved his head and stuff.

"Robin said the day I was able to move my head it was an achievement. I don't know if I've reached as far as I'll go yet. If I'll ever be able to get up and go here."

"It think that's more than I saw you do this summer at camp," I offer.

"Oh, yeah," Jim acknowledges the improvement with some enthusiasm.

"Yeah, but that's what I was telling them today. Our time and the good Lord's time seem so far apart. (He laughs) I look at it this way; He must have something else for me to do in here."

"Maybe. Even if I don't walk and I can do everything else, I'll be happy. I don't intend to go home. Robin wants me to, until I can care for myself. Even though they have home health, I'm not gonna burden them with that," he said.

"So, you're thinking at least a grip would be necessary to feed yourself and general care; get a drink on your own, that kind of thing," I asked him for clarity.

"I can get a drink of a fashion, now. I can't lift it up but I can move my tray over and get a drink," he said of pulling the wheeled bed tray over to his wheel chair or bed and aligning the cup so that he can reach the straw with his mouth.

"It's one of those little things, like I talked about. I think they can put needles in the skin and see what happens. If there's a reaction, there's still hope and if nothing happens then it's down the drain. If that happens I thought I'd shut it down; quit eating, quit drinking. That thought had been in my head," he said as I tried to cover my shock and surprise.

"If your muscles don't show any sign of coming back?" I wanted to be sure I heard him right.

"If it looks like I can't even take care of myself again, that thought had jumped into my head; that I'll let myself go. But, that only lasts for a little while before the Good Lord tells me, 'If I'm not ready for you I ain't gonna take you, anyway.' I have always had that nagging thought in my head; that I will get well enough to go to the people that have helped me to…Churches and stuff and tell my story of faith, you know? That there's something the Lord wants me to do yet. I've always had that nagging feeling in the back of my head; that there's something He wants me to do and it won't be done until I get well. Maybe I'm crazy, I don't know, but I've always had that nagging feeling.

"I do want to get well enough, it's been a dream, to get well enough to go around to all the people that have helped me and be a witness to what their prayers and everything have done for me and what they can do for everybody else. If it encourages somebody then it was well worth it. You know the story of the one lost sheep? If we encourage just one, God says it was well worth it.

*Then Jesus told them this parable: "Suppose one of you has a hundred sheep and loses one of them. Does he not leave the ninety nine in the open country and go after the lost sheep until he finds it? And when he finds it, he joyfully puts it on his shoulders and goes home." Luke 15: 3-5.*

"I've already encourage one; Dale. He's a good speaker," he says of his best friend at camp.

"There is a significant difference between going to church and saying, 'yeah, I believe and all that and being on fire and knowing that without any doubt at all in your mind that..." I say of true faith. Jim sees me coming and heads me off.

"You're gonna go to heaven. Yep.

"Well, once he got that fire he went to town. We got him involved in the church and he was into their fundraising and everything. He made seventy some apple dumplings for the bazaar. Of course, he didn't charge anything for them or the ingredients. Had trouble-finding pans. He did them individually," Jim paused for his dramatic glare.

"Wow. Holy cow," I said mildly trying to imagine the work in doing that many dumplings individually.

"He didn't use a big pan, he did them individually. Boy, were they good!" Jim said enthusiastically.

"I didn't bring you up any sweets this time," I lament.

"That's all right. One of those Penn State girls made me peanut butter fudge. She brought that in for me the day they left." He licks his lips obviously recalling how good the fudge was.

I fell into a rut with my own life and failed to see Jim for over a year and a half. I did work on his book; transcribing interviews into text, collecting information, learning about GBS and so on, but failed to focus on Jim. It was the visits that were important. We talked like old friends do. It was good fellowship.

The story we have collaborated on is significant, but it is not worth the disconnect we experienced these past few months. Other people are the main element and the purpose of life. That is important. My focus must remain on people, even as I write about Jim or anything else. I regained my sense of this after the December 2009 visit.

It was the twelfth of December when I made another visit after the long time apart. I was quite surprised to find him sitting in his motorized wheel chair with a hand on the controls – that Jim was working! He was talking with some people when I walked in and he never missed a beat. He spoke to me like I had just been there the week before.

It was delightful to hear him tell me about his first steps in six years! He used a walker and only went about 150 feet but what a miracle. From complete entrapment within himself to walking! I was in awe. I noted the brace on his ankle.

"Oh, I hurt my ankle walking," he said.

What a wonderful thing to hear!

I met Annie, his newest nurse. She was wearing an 'employee of the month' badge. Jim pointed it out to me. We talked a little about the perk she gained with it; parking in the special 'employee of the month' parking spot. Jim told me she had been honored, he thought, because she worked at whatever needed done; she didn't wait to be told what to do. She saw something that needed done and just did it. It pleased him that Annie had won.

In his motorized wheelchair Jim is able to lean back or forward: the controls allow him to tilt back or drop forward under his own control. He had been leaning back relaxing when I arrived and was able to lean forward for lunch. There is a joystick beside his right hand. It was seemingly easy for him to operate. I also noticed his right eye was looking clear and bright while the other was stitched partially shut.

When Jim read the writing on the front of my sweatshirt from across his room I was further amazed! He'd been considered legally blind not long ago. He told me the doctors had decided to close the one eye for a while till it healed a bit. Improvement in the other eye was obvious. He told me his vision was now 20/70. I watched the nurse put drops in his eyes. He said some of the nurses told him they had already done his eyes when he said they had not. He explained that he was sure to correct their mistake. He was keeping them straight!

"The Lord is keeping me here to keep their spirits up," he said. Much like the earlier story of the smiley face shaved on his chest. During this trip the nurse asked him how the beans were and he commented, "just like fresh out of the garden...!" he gave me trade mark silent stare with a blank expression. I chuckled. The nurse was amused, too.

*"A cheerful heart is good medicine, but a crushed spirit dries up the bones."* - Proverbs 17: 22.

"That good?" I asked him of the beans he was being fed.

"Not really," he admitted.

Jim had a large, oversized, remote control beside him to work the television. He lamented the fact that he still had to ask for help in getting the remote! He holds very high expectations for himself!

While Annie was feeding him, another nurse came in and asked if Jim was feeding us a line of B.S. We laughed. Jim instructed me to get down a package and hand it's contents to the nurse who'd just walked in. I did as he asked. It was to be a Christmas gift for her daughter. The nurse seemed tickled with the offering. She smiled and thanked Jim before returning to her busy schedule.

Jim then told me of his grandson, Garrett, wrecking Jim's old truck – shortly **after** the collision insurance was taken off of it. "Just so nobody got hurt," Jim said. This was the truck that Jim had wanted and shopped for before he became ill and lost as a result of his illness.

He'd been swinging his legs the entire time we visited. Intermittently he would land his feet on the footrests, like any other man sitting and visiting might do. I mentioned my observation to him.

"Yeah, it's coming along," he said.

I would suggest to you that it is more than coming along. Eighteen months ago Jim couldn't even bend his knees to stand. He had to be stood up like a board. It took two people to get him out of bed. Now he was sitting and swinging his legs!

He related a story of going down a flight of outdoor steps with his wheelchair. It seems he gets around so well with his motorized wheelchair that he often goes outside to sit in the sun. I looked out his window. There appeared to be a garden like layout behind the nursing home. He had been motoring along and went down those steps. Flopped around a bit. He wasn't hurt but said he sure stretched out his hamstrings! Jim always looks for the positive in a situation. Typing this now I wonder if that fall wasn't helpful with his ability to swing his legs and walk those 150 feet?

*"But those who suffer He delivers in their suffering; he speaks to them in their affliction." - Job 36: 15.*

"I can use the walker with wheels to get to the bathroom, on my own. I need help getting around in there, but I'm making progress," he told me. I was in awe. To consider where he started in this process and where he's at now leads to the notion of full recovery. Maybe not to the complete Jim we knew before GBS struck, but full enough to live an independent life.

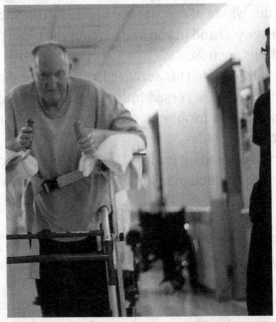

**Jim McKinley showing me how he could stand 2012**

# Chapter 10
## *Scripture interpreted by Jim*

In this section the focus is upon Jim's interpretation of scripture or his reaction to scripture in light of his recent history. The point is to gain knowledge or insight into life through the journey Jim has survived. Not all the scripture verses examined below are useful in looking at Jim's life. Some of the scripture is, frankly, just woven into and among parts that called to me. However, you the reader, in following this story may have something to gain from reading the whole of a scripture verse. Allow God's Spirit to work over you and in you and explain the truth to you as you read this section.

After agreeing to this activity Jim informed me that he wished he was more versed in scripture. He also indicated that it was harder for him to commit scripture to memory now that he was older.

I started by reading Psalm 119: 66-72. I am interested in hearing his perspective in light of the past 5 or six years.

### Psalm 119: 66-72

*"Teach me knowledge and good judgement, for I believe in your commands. Before I was afflicted I went astray, but now I obey your word. You are good, and what you do is good; teach me your decrees. Though the arrogant have smeared me with lies, I keep your precepts with all my heart. Their hearts are callous*

*and unfeeling, but I delight in your law. It was good for*
*me to be afflicted so that I might learn your decrees.*
*The law from your mouth is more precious to me than*
*thousands of pieces of silver and gold.*

At the conclusion of this reading Jim says, "That pretty much sums up my whole situation. That sums it up pretty well, because, yes, I was astray. God put me back where I should be."

I asked about reading another and he said, "sure." He told me "you don't know how many times Pastor Barbara has been in reading me scripture and the reading fits exactly with my circumstances."

**Jim McKinley (seated) and his spiritual leader**
**Pastor Barbara Mosch.**

I replied "His timing is perfect."

"There we go again; His timing!" Jim spoke excitedly.

"I don't know how many times I'd go by that church and they have the sign out front with sayings on it and before I had this I'd drive by and there would be my answer. God is there, we may not see Him but there He is."

## Romans 9:15

*"For He (God) says to Moses, "I will have mercy on whom I have mercy, and I will have compassion on whom I have compassion."*

"Man is going by his knowledge not God's knowledge. God is ever powerful. Nobody can have more power that God!" Jim clarifies.

Jim shifted his focus to the constant clearing of his throat. "I'm sorry about that," he said. "There's stuff in there and I can't get it out."

I have listened to him endure these frequent attempts to remove the material in his throat. It does cause his throat to have a different sound; raspy and hoarse. It is something that bothers me because it bothers him. I hear him struggling with it and there is nothing I can do: a very maddening circumstance. Also interfering with the work we're doing is the constant beeping of the machines and the hissing of air from other machines and the occasional outburst over the intercom.

Jim went on to explain to me that he has never been depressed. "I've been discouraged," he said, "but I've never been depressed." He said people notice right away when he's not himself. 'Why are you so quiet?' they ask. Jim chuckles at the thought of himself being quiet.

I asked Jim about the angel that had appeared to him and how that and the whole GBS experience has made him feel differently about his life. I selected several more verses of scripture and posed them to him seeking a reaction.

Before I got that far I asked him about the angel incident again and how it made him feel. Did he feel like going with the angel? Did he see a need to stay and finish the work he had to do here?

"Well", he said, "I saw the angel a day before or after the pillow was pulled from behind me and allowed me to breathe. I didn't see any light or any darkness so I guess I wasn't very close to death. You know, they say some people see a light above or darkness below. I don't think I was close to dying. There wasn't anybody around, so you know it had to be that angel."

"Did you ever come up with a list of things you've learned from all this. I know we talked about the four truths, especially, but has there been anything else that's jumped out at you?" I inquire.

"Yeah, those four truths are especially important. Another thing that comes up often in the scripture we read is 'in His time.'

"In His Time," he repeats for emphasis. "And the prayers when we're praying for somebody how often those prayers have been answered, the way we want them answered. We were praying for somebody and we knew it was better for her to go and it was His will." He said sullenly.

God's timing is perfect, so we shouldn't worry about things. He has everything under control and will give to us in ways we need when the time is right. Jesus teaches to this in His Sermon on the Mount.

## Matthew 6: 25-34 read to Jim:

*Jesus taught them, "Therefore I tell you, do not worry about your life, what you will eat or drink; or about your body, what you will wear. Is not life more important than food, and the body more important than clothes? Look at the birds of the air; they do not sow or reap or store away in barns, and yet your heavenly Father feeds them. Are you not more valuable than they? Who of you by worrying can add a single hour to his life?*

*And why do you worry about clothes? See the lilies of the field grow. They do not labor or spin. Yet I tell you that not even Solomon in all his splendor was dressed like one of these. If that is how God clothes the grass of the field, which is here today and tomorrow is thrown into the fire, will he not much more clothe you - O you of little faith? So do not worry, saying, 'what shall we eat?' or 'what shall we drink?' or 'what shall we wear?' For the pagans run after all these things, and your heavenly Father knows that you need them. But seek first his kingdom and his righteousness, and all these things will be given to you as well. Therefore do not worry about tomorrow, for tomorrow will worry about itself. Each day has enough trouble of its own."*

Jim's reaction: "God always provides. The Pastor had this needy person and he come up one dollar short and he (the pastor) was going to put that dollar in. They went to give it to the person and guess what? They didn't need that dollar; God had already provided the money. What they needed was already there. It's just a dollar, but it shows you how He has control over everything.

"Another story he (the pastor) told me was that they had coats they had to give out. And this Chinese couple came in and they didn't have much in the way of kids (coats) but they found one for their little girl. Couldn't find one to fit their boy, but while they were in there, a lady came in with a couple coats she had got there the year before and her kids had out grown them. The coats were in great shape, and low and behold one of them fit that little boy. Now talk about when there's a need why should we worry, God will provide. Right there's two stories. Let it up to Him." Jim said impressing me, again.

# Chapter 11
## *Closing items*

While in Centre Crest Jim had a tooth pulled. A bone spur was sticking up through the gum line and chewed his gum all up. He gargled a bit for the nurse to encourage a speedy recovery. He looked at me and rolled his eyes as the nurse tended to him. I sense his full acceptance of staying in Centre Crest. Life is going forward and he's content.

"The chapel is a place I enjoy most in the morning. Light streams through the stained glass and Jesus' eyes are upon you no matter where you are in the room," he said describing how the stained glass mural worked on the worshipper. "It was really beautiful Easter Sunday morning, but nobody wants to hear about it. Very disinterested." Jim offered sadly.

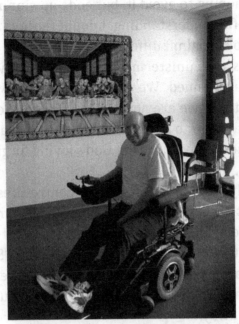

**Jim in the illuminated Chapel and the
Last Supper Tapestry to left.**

Once again Jim tells me of praying for those around him and hanging on to fulfill God's plan for him. The prayer he issued also rid him of the cursing spell he had encountered earlier, during the period of my last visit.

"Well, I'll tell ya. One of my sins; I tell dirty jokes. If I think they're funny I tell somebody." His admission catches me off guard.

I responded by saying, "all men are seeking perfection in Christ, but we're all fighting it from the very beginning. This world is a fallen world and no man is perfect. There was only one perfect man."

Jim agrees.

However, he adds, "people need to try hard to become as righteous as possible." He admitted praying about sin everyday, hoping to avoid it, but ends up sinning anyway. I nod with full understanding. I doubt there is any honest person who can admit different.

He goes on ministering to me of Paul's words that "all men have sinned. We've all fallen short. We have to understand that we are not perfect. I don't know how He finds His way clear to forgive our sins, but I'm glad He does." Jim continues to be amazed at God's loving forgiveness.

"Me too," I echo.

Suddenly he mentions a man in Centre Crest who has Parkinson's Disease and walks about until someone sees him and then calls for a nurse's help. "I wish I could half as much as that guy. I'd get out!" he explained. "So many of these guys are interested in having nurses serve them." It's clear the matter makes Jim angry. "I prayed about it and my anger went away."

"I discovered two more reason's God put me here" he said. Then he explained it was to transform the black women that couldn't believe the men at camp accepted Doug and to uplift Beth. Jim said, "Gillian-Barre really took me to a place where I saw things from a different perspective."

I would add to his list of benefits from GBS the aforementioned item of prayer. When Jim was healthy and strong in himself, he was aggressive and if he saw a wrong he let it be known. He was very boisterous then, but now he relies on God; he prays. There is great power in surrendering to God.

"How do you like my cow?" He asks me out of the blue.

"Nice," I chuckle. "Who got you that?"

"Dale and Gail. Is there a plant in the planter?"

"No," I tell him.

"Is it green at all?" he asks.

"No. I could bring you a plant the next time," I offer.

"What kind?" he asked.

"Spider plant," I reply.

"Oh. I was thinking of a cactus." He had a good idea.

"OK," I accepted his plan.

"How big does it get?" He asked of the spider plant.

"Bought yo high" I say holding my hands an around 8 inches." I did it without even thinking of his limited sight.

"Mmmm."

"Doesn't matter," I say trying to withdraw from the topic without hurting any feelings.

"I think the last one they had in there was watered too much and drowned. Then it wasn't watered at all." He said.

"Hmmm" I nodded.

"Yeah, Dale knows how I like cows. I had em all around the house; on the dinner bell outside the house and everywhere. I wanted to chain one in the front yard." He explained.

I laughed aloud at the thought.

"We had cows in the yard" he explains. I assume he is referring to his childhood but I am having too much fun to clarify such a detail

"By the way, Dick Johnson passed away." He said suddenly.

"Aww." I say. "How old was he?"

"I don't know but he was pretty old." Jim sums it up well.

We reminisce about how long we had been acquainted with Dick. He was old when I was just a boy. Jim admits that farm work will make you old fast. Then he goes on to tell me about the explosion of houses out there on the old family farm. I am saddened, but it is bound to come, State College growing as it is.

I ask about my cousin Russell and Jim explains they moved further down the hollow. Then he quickly interjects that Russell's boy, Billy, works in the kitchen here at Centre Crest. I end up running into Billy as he is coming in to visit Jim. He is a good-looking young man. Reminds me immediately of his father many years ago, when we were kids.

I offer to read to Jim, before I leave. He wants to read from Revelations.

### Revelations 21: 1-8

*"Then I saw a new heaven and a new earth, for the first heaven and the first earth had passed away, and there was no longer any sea. I saw the Holy City, the new Jerusalem, coming down out of heaven from God, prepared as a bride beautifully dressed for her husband. And I heard a loud voice from the throne saying, "Now the dwelling of God is with men, and he will live with them. They will be his people, and God himself will be with them and be their God. He will wipe every tear from their eyes. There will be no more death or mourning or crying or pain, for the old order of things has passed away."*

*He who was seated on the throne said, "I am making everything new!" Then he said, "Write this down, for these words are trustworthy and true."*

*He said to me: "It is done. I am the Alpha and the Omega, the Beginning and the End. To him who is thirsty I will give to drink without cost from the spring of the water of life. He who overcomes will inherit all this, and I will be his God and he will be my son. But the cowardly, the unbelieving, the vile, the murderers, the sexually immoral, those who practice magic arts, the idolaters and all liars - their place will be in the fiery lake of burning sulphur. This will be the second death."*

As I sit and relive that visit it seems only right he should ask for that chapter. The former Jim, the one I knew as a kid, has passed away, but God has given me a new friend of the old. He looks similar with the same personality, yet he is simultaneously a new Jim, completely devoid of so much the old Jim represented. I can't say I like either one more that the other. It is as Solomon wrote; everything in it's season. I have changed, too. We should all be changing. It is our job to change. Jim has shown me that.

Jim's illness came, he suspects, because he wasn't doing the things he was supposed to do, that all things are in His time and that we should accept them. What else are we going to do – fight God?

# Chapter 12
## *Biblical Teachings on Suffering*

In this section I will seek to shed light on the topic of suffering as written in God's Holy word. Our Creator and our Redeemer has much to say of suffering and why it's necessary. I will try to keep my examination of the subject brief, concise and to the point. I have interjected words from the Bible and Biblical scholars to support the observations Jim and I have made. Pray for help in understanding such things so that you might gain the full benefit of the exercise.

A good place to begin our study is with one who suffered much for the Gospel; The Apostle Paul. He wrote a great deal about suffering. In the book of Romans 8:18 he declares; "I consider that our present sufferings are not worth comparing with the glory that will be revealed in us." The glory that will be revealed in us is eternal and free of any evil. Christians suffer now but they are promised something far greater than we can imagine. We must endure our suffering and await the glory to come.

God's will remains a mystery to us. Jim's illness and prolonged recover illustrate that. It is difficult to reason why he became ill to the extreme point that he did let alone the prolonged recovery. We don't understand the good things, let alone the bad. We must trust that God's mercy is enough for us, that he will never try us beyond our limits and that He will never leave us.

William Cowper wrote a hymn to that effect;

> God moves in a mysterious way
> His wonders to perform:
> He plants His footsteps in the sea,
> And rides upon the storm.
> Deep in unfathomable mines
> Of never ending skill,
> He treasures up His bright designs,
> And works His sovereign will.
> You fearful saints, fresh courage take!
> The clouds you so much dread
> Are big with mercy, and shall break
> In blessings on your head.

GBS may very well have been the cloud over Jim's head that he used to dread: horrific illness and disease and disability. Now he sees clearly the mercy from the pain and has shared with us the blessings poured out upon his head. If you are a follower of Jesus then you must suffer. Suffering is the passage into life eternal. Jesus explains the way to Heaven; "If anyone would come after me, he must deny Himself and take up his cross and follow me," Matthew 16: 25.

This means not doing the things you want. Instead, take up your cross (remember the burden He carried up to Cavalry) and follow Him to earthly suffering. Recall how he was tortured, beaten and executed in a most painful and public manner? He is calling you to follow Him through the fiery trial into His loving arms. Be mindful of the triumphant resurrection we celebrate on Easter morning. Your suffering is not in vain.

Peter adds to this a bit; *"And the God of all grace, who called you to his eternal glory in Christ, after you have suffered a little while, will himself restore you and make you strong, firm and steadfast,"* 1Peter 5:10. Did you catch that? You will be put through hardship but He will restore you and build you back up!

It's not all gloom and doom because he has not allowed the evil to rule but has merely allowed it to mingle with the good. As Jim said in an earlier chapter; "He will never give you more than you can handle. Boy, nobody knows that more than I do!" Jim was pushed to the breaking point but was then allowed refreshment of spirit. He now sings God's praises. Again, the Apostle Paul provides supportive evidence.

In 1 Corinthians 10: 13 he writes; *"No temptation has seized you except what is common to man. And God is faithful; he will not let you be tempted beyond what you can bear. But when you are tempted, he will also provide a way out so that you can stand up under it."*

Previously you read about Jim's terror filled dreams. The devil was tempting Jim to give up. He wanted him to lose hope, but Jim didn't lose hope. Instead, he was reassured by the presence of the angel and filled with the Holy Spirit as he resisted the devil. Now Jim proclaims the kingdom of God and the Lord Jesus Christ to all who will listen. No man is exempt from this type of temptation, even Jesus was tempted to give in when He walked the earth.

*"Again, the devil took Him to a very high mountain and showed him all the kingdoms of the world and their splendor.*

*"All this I will give you," he said, "if you will bow down and worship me."*

*Jesus said to him, "Away from me, satan! For it is written: 'Worship the Lord your God, and serve Him only.'"*

*"Then the devil left him, and angels came and attended him." - Matthew 4: 8-11.*

Consider further the advice given in James 4: 7;

*"Submit yourselves, then, to God. Resist the devil, and he will flee from you."*

Jim resisted the devil and his terror filled dreams. He stood with good and evil fled. Consequently, an angel came and comforted him. Now Jim speaks of God's goodness and grace because he lived out the scripture just shared with you.

Still, this topic leaves us with questions too deep for words. Especially when we see people like Jim suffering so terribly. Will Jim's plight ever end?

In her book, *Having a Mary Heart in a Martha World*, Joanna Weaver writes; "never put a period where God puts a comma and don't put a comma where God puts a period." In other words, it's up to Him. He allowed Lazarus to die - looked like a period but turned out to be a comma when He raised him from the dead. Later, Jesus went to Jerusalem to die and His disciples protested. They wanted a comma, but He put a period there.

Weaver continues her examination of such things with this noteworthy insight; "While God is never late, I've found he's rarely early. That is why we must trust his schedule as well as his character." We must have total faith in Him!

In the same book Weaver quotes Ray Stedman; "The hardest problem I have to handle as a Christian is what to do when God does not do what I have been taught to expect Him to do; when God gets out of line and does not act the way I think he ought. What do I do about that?"

There is an old hymn of the church that answers that question; "Trust and obey, for there's no other way, to be happy in Jesus, but to trust and obey!"

The Lord allows bad things to happen so that we will be driven back to Him, seeking shelter and rest. He is our hiding place. When bad things happen to you, go to Him in prayer and read the Bible, searching for answers. Oh, great things will happen. Not even Satan himself can come upon us when we are with the Lord. When we seek Him out and trust and obey.

But what of those occasions when God seems to ignore us? How can we trust and obey when He won't answer prayers?

Stedman addresses a possible answer to this question too: "A delay in answer is not a sign of God's indifference or His failure to hear. It is a sign of his love. The delay will help us. It will make us stronger." By continuing to pray in faith, even when you have no clear response, your faith is increasing. You are being made stronger.

Jim's experience has made him stronger. The healing is underway, the lesson has been taught. I wonder if you were listening, if you saw the signs for what they were? That is the purpose of this life; to see God's hand at work, to recognize it, to accept it and to move closer to Him, deepening your faith.

The Apostle Paul knew well of such experience, too. While he was chained in prison he came to this conclusion about the good found in suffering;

*Remember Jesus Christ, raised from the dead, descended from David. This is my gospel, for which I am suffering even to the point of being chained like a criminal. But God's word is not chained. Therefore I endure everything for the sake of the elect, that they too may obtain the salvation that is in Christ Jesus, with eternal glory. Here is a trustworthy saying: If we died with Him, we will also live with Him; If we endure, we will also reign with Him. If we disown Him, He will also disown us; If we are faithless, He will remain faithful, for He cannot disown himself.* - 2 Timothy 2: 8 -13.

What problems we have here are tests of endurance to prove our faith in His loving salvation, already won for us. Therefore, don't be discouraged. Take what the Bible teaches you, the lesson learned from Jim's experience and know God's love for you is great. When we undergo trials and suffering and endure, we reign with Him!

Jim's faith has also revealed itself in his patience and obedience. Now he awaits the next step in his journey, completing the work God has for him. His example is stacked upon that of so many other faithful witnesses.

*"Therefore, since we are surrounded by such a great cloud of witnesses, let us throw off everything that hinders and the sin that so easily entangles, and let us run with perseverance the race marked out for us. Let us fix our eyes on Jesus, the author and perfecter of our faith, who for the joy set before him endured the cross, scorning its shame, and sat down at the right hand of the throne of God. Consider him who endured such opposition from sinful men, so that you will not grow weary and lose heart.* - Hebrews 12: 1-3. Instead of losing heart Jim has accepted his plight and we are to do the same. The reward is too great not to run the race.

Jesus taught of the eternal benefit found in suffering with this parable; *"There was a rich man who was dressed in purple and fine linen and lived in luxury everyday. At his gate was laid a beggar named Lazarus, covered with sores and longing to eat what fell from the rich man's table. Even the dogs came and licked his sores.*

*"The time came when the beggar died and the angels carried him to Abraham's side. The rich man also died and was buried. In hell, where he was in torment, he looked up and saw Abraham far away, with Lazarus by his side. So he called to him, 'Father Abraham, have pity on me and send Lazarus to dip the tip of his finger in the water and cool my tongue, because I am in agony in this fire.'*

*"But Abraham replied, 'Son, remember that in your lifetime you received your good things, while Lazarus received bad things, but now he is comforted here and you are in agony. And besides all this, between us and you a great chasm has been fixed, so that those who want to go from here to you cannot, nor can anyone cross over from there to us.'"* - Luke 16: 19-26.

Lazarus, the beggar, was put through quite a trial in his earthly life, but he found himself resting in the comfort of heaven while the easy life lead to hell and eternal suffering. Embrace your difficulties and know Jesus will comfort you on earth and much more in heaven.

The time to adjust your thinking of these things is now. If you wait and death should overtake you before you act it may be too late. Seek the glory of heaven in your suffering now and accept Jesus as your Lord and God. Look to Jim's example; he is God's servant calling you to believe.

## The Book of Job

Jim's experience has been likened to that of Job on more than one occasion, so perhaps a closer examination of Job's life would prove helpful. The intimate details of the book of Job are many, but I hope to abridge them in a way designed to illuminate Jim's connection to Job. Through this section I will seek to further connect Job's experience to you and me, because we have all endured parts of Job's suffering. However, few, if any, have endured all that Job did.

Despite his painful experience Job did not blame God, hate God or turn away from God. Can you say the same? I cannot. I have been confrontational and angry with God. When I turned to praising God, through Jesus Christ and the Holy Spirit, even in the midst of my suffering, I found indescribable comfort and joy. Jim told you of the same experience throughout this book. Listen to Job's account and hear the truth again.

The Old Testament book of Job identifies Job as *"blameless and upright; he feared God and shunned evil."* Job 1:1. Job had ten children and thousands of heads of livestock. His children each had a home and took turns hosting feasts for the other nine. When these periods of feasting were over, Job would send and have them purified - just in case they had sinned against God. In short, Job feared and obeyed God and was greatly blessed for it. He was a good man.

Then Job was tested. In the first chapter of Job we learn that satan had returned from roaming the earth and presented himself before God, along with the other angels. God pointed Job out to satan and how good he was. Satan's response was to challenge Job's faith in God by asking God to "stretch out His hand" against him. Satan said, when you do, *"he will surely curse you to your face."* Job 1:11

*"Very well, then,"* God replied, *"everything he has is in your hands, but on the man himself do not lay a finger."* Job 1:12

Satan responded by having enemies attack and kill Job's servants and steal all his oxen, donkeys and camels. Fire fell from the sky and burned up Job's sheep. Finally, Job's children were all feasting when the building fell in and killed all ten of them. Notice it was not God tempting Job, but the enemy, satan.

Upon hearing the news, Job tore his robe and shaved his head. *"Then he fell to the ground in worship and said: 'Naked I came from my mother's womb, and naked I will depart. The Lord gave and the Lord has taken away; may the name of the Lord be praised.'*

*"In all this Job did not sin by charging God with any wrong doing."*

Job 1: 20b-22.

Then Job was tested a second time.

On another occasion all the angels came to present themselves before the Lord and satan came with them to present himself before the Lord. God and the devil greeted one another as they had before; except God added a commentary. He said, *"And he (Job) still maintains his integrity, though you incited me against him to ruin him without any reason."* - Job 2:3c

Satan became angry at the thought of Job still loving God, so he challenged him again. *"But stretch out your hand and strike his flesh and bones, and he will surely curse you to your face."* Job 2:5

*"The Lord replied, 'very well, then, he is in your hands; but you must spare his life.'*

*"So satan went out from the presence of the Lord and afflicted Job with painful sores from the soles of his feet to the top of his head."* Job 2:6-7

During this time of misery Job did not speak angrily of or toward God. Instead he sat in ashes and scraped his sores. His wife must have been disgusted with what she was seeing because she said to Job; *"Are you still holding on to your integrity? Curse God and die!"*

*"Job replied, "You are talking like a foolish woman. Shall we accept good from God, and not trouble?" Job 2: 8-10*

Did you sense the power in Job's observation? *"Should we accept good from God and not trouble?"*

In the midst of this imperfect life, filled with hatred, disease, sin and lust - should we expect God to keep us from all trouble? After all, we wanted independence from Him and knowledge of the world. When Adam and Eve ate of the forbidden fruit, you and I were spiritually present. God has simply given in to our request. We wanted to possess knowledge and now we have it. Consequently, our lives are racked with pain and suffering. We decided to leave Him. I hope you now see the urgency in returning to Him. Not in death but in devoting your life to Him through works, study of scripture and leading the life Jesus taught us to live. We don't see this clearly now, but we will.

1 Corinthians 13: 12 - *"Now we see but a poor reflection as in a mirror; then we shall see face to face. Now I know in part; then I shall know fully, even as I am fully known."*

Our understanding of things in this life is limited, but we must rest assured that in the eternal life we will know all things. This life is a test to demonstrate the awesome creation of God - you and I. We can handle it, whatever it might be.

My uncle works for a company that produces rather large industrial machines of various kinds. One machine that sheds light on our study is the turbine they produce. He has told me of the time and cost involved in making these machines, but the company didn't sell them right away. The company, interested in the quality of their product, did some testing. They would run these turbines at very demanding levels for long periods of time. These tests were done at or in excess of the recommended levels of operation. The company wanted to ensure a quality product was being produced. I think God may be doing the same thing.

He has allowed us to undergo trials beyond our comfort zone so as to demonstrate the tenacity and strength of His creation. All the universe, Heaven and earth, looks upon God's people in wonder; especially those who endure illness, lost limbs, death of loved ones or other calamity and still give praise to God. When this happens, each believer stands as a light in the darkness: God's love is shining back upon Himself.

Jobs friend, Eliphaz, counsels Job after his suffering saying, *"Yet man is born to trouble as surely as sparks fly upward. But if it were I, I would appeal to God; I would lay my cause before Him. He performs wonders that cannot be fathomed, miracles that cannot be counted."* Job 5: 7-9

Jim is demonstrating the tenacity of God's creation by growing well and not giving up - even in the face of much adversity. Furthermore, he continues to lay his cause before the Lord and await the miracle. We know of God's miracles and wait for the day when Jim will be healed further. Still, we can see the miracle Jim has lived out by surviving the coma like state he was in and returned to tell of his journey and of God's love. We would all be well advised to lay our cause before God and await the miracles He will share with us.

Bildad, another of Job's friends, said to Job: *"Surely God does not reject a blameless man or strengthen the hands of evildoers. He will yet fill your mouth with laughter and your lips with shouts of joy."* Job 8:20-21 It is remarkable to see Jim laugh and praise God when just a while ago he couldn't even breath independently. He has lost all his earthly possessions but still has more than enough. Indeed God has done this for Jim, but how much more healing is to come? Time will tell.

It can be frustrating to endure such senseless suffering. Jim acknowledges that and so do you and I, if we've suffered. Suffering is a lonely and treacherous reality we all confront. Yet it remains very difficult to accept.

Likewise, Job responds to the explanation of his suffering with much frustration by asking,

*"Why then did you bring me out of the womb? I wish I had died before any eye saw me."* Job 10:18. He adds another profound observation; *"Man born of woman is of few days and full of trouble." Job 14: 1.* At this point the reader is certain of Job's frustration and the reality that we all will suffer.

The loss of his children and wealth and health has compounded his misery until he cannot stand any more. He wants the test to end and sees no end but the death of his earthly being. He shares a heartening insight into this otherwise dismal conversation. *"I know that my redeemer lives, and in the end He will stand upon the earth. And after my skin has been destroyed, yet in my flesh I will see God; I myself will see Him with my own eyes - I, and not another. How my heart yearns within me!"* Job 19: 25-27.

At this point Job has joined many of us in the realization that regardless of how this life treats us, how bad it gets, we have the promise of a better day. God will not forget His people and will come to us! What a great day that will be! So, if your life is pain ridden and full of trouble, ask your Redeemer to comfort you in preparation of His return.

Job continues his dialogue by seeking immediate Justice, even when he knows it's not likely found.

*"Even today my complaint is bitter; his hand is heavy in spite of my groaning. If only I knew where to find him; If only I could go to his dwelling! I would state my case before Him and fill my mouth with arguments. I would find out what he would answer me, and consider what he would say.*

*"Would he oppose me with great power?*

*"No, he would not press charges against me.*

*"There an upright man could present his case before Him, and I would be delivered forever from my judge."* Job 23: 2-7.

Job's argument here is much like we hear from others when they suffer; I don't deserve this! Jim told me people cry out this way, "God, help me!" But Jim took a different route; "I guess He wanted my attention. I've done a few things He's not too fond of," he said. Jim has accepted his plight knowing his Redeemer lives and rescue is at hand. So did Job, later, but he voiced what many of us wonder; "Why is God picking on me? Do I deserve this pain? Where is God's mercy?"

Indeed, all of these are valid concerns, but Job's conclusion is most revealing. *There* (Heaven) *an upright man can make his case and be delivered from the judge.* Job seems to know intuitively of God's plan to save His people. He wants to plead his case before God while Jim is patient and waits for the Lord's decision. The difference is that Jim knows Jesus as his personal savior. Jesus affords us the Holy Spirit who reveals God's love in our spirit. We know God's love because the spirit provides us with the fruits of the Spirit; love, joy, peace, patience, kindness, goodness, faithfulness, gentleness and self-control. Jesus asks us to persevere until His return and these spiritual fruits will prove we're on the right track.

Job is further reflective and longs for the days of better things. He desires a return to the days before his affliction. *"How I long for the month's gone by, for the days when God watched over me, when His lamp shone upon my head and by his light I walked through the darkness! Oh, for the days when I was in my prime, when God's intimate friendship blessed my house, when the Almighty was still with me and my children were around me, when my path was drenched with cream and the rock poured out for me streams of olive oil." Job 29: 2-6.*

Wouldn't we all enjoy a time machine to go back to better days when there was no hurt or heartache? Where everything seemed simpler and certain and we were at peace?

I noted a longing in Jim's conversation for the old days, when he was healthy and raising his children and active in the outdoors. This is a natural reaction to calamity. People accept change but that doesn't mean they don't long for something better, something familiar. We would all like to go back to a time when we knew the outcome was safe and predictable. This is a very human characteristic. God desires that we change and grow closer to Him, leaving worldly pleasure behind.

In this regard God is seeking to do more for us than provide comfort and a predictable future or relaxation. He is using hardship to propel us toward him. If we considered earthly pleasure and comfort something to be sought out how much more should we long for the place where there is no pain or suffering, only Jesus' presence? The Apostle Paul knew this well having been imprisoned and beaten and stoned for the Gospel. He wrote this to the Romans: *"And we rejoice in the hope of the glory of God. Not only so, but we also rejoice in our sufferings, because we know suffering produces perseverance; perseverance, character; and character, hope. And hope does not disappoint us, because God has poured out his love into our hearts by the Holy Spirit, whom he has given us."* Romans 5: 2c - 5.

As we persevere through difficulty our character is developed and in that we find hope, because we know God is with us. We can feel it. This is because the suffering has removed the worldly distraction and allowed us time to consider God's love and look for it. Love God by following Jesus' word and seeking to demonstrate the fruits of the Spirit hoping your faith is enough. Paul wrote of this to the Romans, too. *"For in this hope we were saved. But hope that is seen is no hope at all. Who hopes for what he already has? But if we hope for what we do not yet have, we wait for it patiently."* Romans 8: 24-25.

What are we hoping for? A better day? Jesus to return? Yes and yes! We hope for it because the Holy Spirit has alerted us to the coming of such things. We must wait on the Lord knowing that His timing is perfect. Our maturity and faith are developed and nurtured only in an environment where we see the weakness and short term nature of worldly pleasure and can seek out the Lord. Hope in the Lord and you will not be left wanting more, now, nor disappointed on the last day.

The pinnacle of Job's book comes when the Lord confronts Job. *"Then the Lord answered Job out of the storm. He said: 'Who is this that darkens my counsel with words without knowledge?*

*"'Brace yourself like a man; I will question you and you shall answer me. Where were you when I laid the earth's foundation?*

*"'Tell me if you understand.*

*"Who marked off it's dimensions? Surely you know! Who stretched the measuring line across it? On what were it's footings set, or who laid it's cornerstone - while the morning stars sang together and all the angels shouted for joy?*

*"Who shut up the sea behind doors when it burst forth from the womb, when I made the clouds its garment and wrapped it in thick darkness, when I fixed limits for it and set its doors and bars in place, when I said, 'This far you may come and no farther; here is where your proud waves halt?'"* Job 38: 1-11.

God continued quizzing Job about all the things He had done. *"Then Job answered the Lord: 'I am unworthy - how can I reply to you?'"* Job 40:4.

Jim has also surrendered his plight to the Lord. He said, "it's all in His time and He has all the power." So, what's next for Jim? We don't know.

*"The Lord blessed the latter part of Job's life more than he had the first. He had fourteen thousand sheep, six thousand camels, a thousand yoke of oxen and a thousand donkeys. And he also had seven sons and three daughters. The first daughter he named Jemimah, the second Keziah and the third Keren-Happuch. Nowhere in all the land were there found women as beautiful as Job's daughters, and their father granted them an inheritance along with their brothers.*

*"After this Job lived a hundred and forty years: He saw his children and their children to the fourth generation. And so he died, old and full of years."* Job 42 : 12-17.

My Zondervan NIV study Bible adds this commentary to the scripture text of Job 42: 7-9. "Despite Job's mistakes in word and attitude while he suffered, he is now commended and the counselors are rebuked. Why? Even in his rage, when Job challenged God, he was determined to speak honestly before Him. The counselors, on the other hand, mouthed many correct theological statements, but without living knowledge of the God they claimed to honor. Job spoke to God; they only spoke about God. Even worse, their spiritual arrogance caused them to claim knowledge they did not possess. They presumed to know why Job was suffering."

This commentary provides insight into the end of the book of Job 42: 12-16; "The cosmic contest with satan, the accuser, is now over, and Job is restored. No longer is there a reason for Job to experience suffering - unless he was sinful and deserved it, which is not the case. God does not allow us to suffer for no reason (ref. ISA 55: 8-9) - never for us to know in this life - we must trust in him as the God who only does what is right."

Since the book of Isaiah has been referenced, let's look at it. It contains a powerful scripture verse that is both revealing and thought provoking.

God tells the Prophet Isaiah; *"For my thoughts are not your thoughts, neither are your ways my ways,' declares the Lord. 'As the heavens are higher than the earth, so my ways higher than your ways and my thoughts than your thoughts.'"* Isaiah 55: 8-9.

I can consider no finer words to conclude our look at God's use of suffering as a tool to draw his people nearer him. We are simply not capable of thinking the things He thinks. He created us and we should be humbled by that alone, humbled to the point of worshipping Him. Suffering or no suffering, know that He is God. Christ is our sure hope of the eternal life to come. When you suffer, be assured that it is Jesus' suffering you are sharing in and, in the end, His glory you will also share.

One final note: It is important to differentiate between suffering as a believer and suffering ills you have heaped upon yourself. *"If you suffer, it should not be as a murderer or thief or any other kind of criminal, or even as a meddler. However, if you suffer as a Christian, do not be ashamed, but praise God that you bear that name."* 1Peter 4: 15-16

Examine yourself through meditative thought. Don't hide anything from God, He already knows. Admit your sins to the Lord, ask Him to forgive them, and know it has already been done. Then praise Him until your days are done and your hope becomes reality.

# EPILOGUE

*"Dear friends, do not be surprised at the painful trial you are suffering, as though something strange were happening to you. But rejoice that you participate in the sufferings of Christ, so that you may be overjoyed when His glory is revealed."* 1Peter 4:12-13.

I hope reading about Jim, his life and the GBS experience, has enlightened you as to his 'say what I mean, mean what I say' attitude. It may be more than an attitude; it could be a way of life. People may not like what Jim has to say but his perspective won't likely change. It hasn't over the life time I've known him. You will not change his mind with even a well choreographed debate, because he has thought through his position. He stands upon The Rock.

It should be apparent that Jim is a Christian. He will not back down from his defense of the gospel and his love of Jesus. Satan has tried to divert Jim's love of Christ to Jim, himself, in self pity. It didn't work. The result of GBS has been Jim's deeper love of the Lord and a more concentrated love at that.

Jim has shared with us the four truths he has learned from this experience. Those points have been illuminated for you. I wonder if you picked up on the other teachings; that all things are in God's perfect time and suffering is God's love revealed to you. Such lessons guide us to the realization that those things we dread the most are often opportunities to meet and serve Jesus.

The next time pain and disaster **land upon you,** recall this lesson and then do something extraordinary; seek Jesus. Give thanks that He loves you, praise His name and tell someone of His love; Believe He is and watch as blessings are poured out upon your head.

# *Appendix*

## Original Poetry

It is important to note that Jim did not use a pencil or paper, or computer or typewriter in writing these poems (His hands still fail him). Instead, he took advantage of the time he had and his mental fortitude and created these poems. He was reciting them to me much faster than I could write them down! This was all from his memory. Poems were gathered at the end of November 2010.

## The Best of Fall

### by Jim McKinley

Thank you, God, for the start of fall, for the honking of the wild goose call. The colors around are so bright; some are dark and some are light.
Leaves on the trees are starting to turn - soon they'll fall and we'll smell them burn. Thank You, God, for everything good.
Thank you, God, like we all should.

# Season's Blessings; A thank you

### by Jim McKinley

Autumn is gone and fall will be soon.
The sky is bright with the harvest moon.
The air is beginning to have a chill.
There's frost on the pumpkin in the corn field still.
Winter is coming, as we all know, the wind will bring
us glistening snow.
It's Thanksgiving now, this time of year.
The family gathering's we all cheer; all of this to God
we owe, for what we harvest is what we sow.

# Real Christmas

### by Jim McKinley

The tree in the mall is shining bright, decorated with
all the Christmas lights. Shoppers are scurrying to and
fro, carrying their packages all with a bow.
But, alas this is not what Christmas should be.
It's Jesus' birthday, don't you see!
Born in a manger, no room in the inn; the Messiah has
come to save us from sin. Shepherds came from fields
afar, Wise men also guided by a star. They have also come
from afar. The angels in heaven begin to sing. Hosanna in
the highest, Praise be the King!
Now, this is what Christmas should be:
God's greatest gift for you and for me.

# *Robin's Updates and a Journal.*

Jim's daughter, Robin, has taken care of the bulk of Jim's needs. She has arranged his insurance, medical and financial matters and much more I don't know of. I'm sure his son, Jeff, helped too, among many others, but I do not have knowledge of such things. What I can share with you are the following **updates** Robin shared with a number of us as things progressed. Not all the updates are presented here; Robin's computer died and mine did too, so we were only able to recover some of the updates. Nevertheless, I think the following notices offer you a glimpse into the serious drama as it unfolded. Note: I have not changed the wording or design of the e-mailed updates, so you may view them in a format as close to the original as possible.

A journal was also kept of the incidents as they occurred. Rather than create a separate chapter for the journal entries I integrated them into the **Updates** in chronological order. Many of the journal entries have no author assigned, so I will leave them anonymous. Quite a number I believe to be his daughter Robin's journal entries and will identify them as such. I have transcribed journal entries in the form they were written; there will be no editing.

Distinctions between e-mail **updates** and **journal entries** will be made only in the brief headings below.

**Journal entry;**

February 16, 2004

    Dr. Appt. - bronchitis diagnosis. Also, having tingling in hands and feet.

**Journal entry;**

February 17, 2004

    Difficulty swallowing. Called Larry who had difficulty understanding dad. Larry called ambulance and dad was taken to Mt. Nittany Medical Center (formerly Centre Crest Community Hospital). At first, it was thought that dad was having a slight stroke. Symptoms: difficulty breathing, swallowing, couldn't hold neck up, couldn't keep eyelids open. Blood pressure elevated. Loss of muscle control. Was coherent and communicated using thumbs up, thumbs down. Was able to pull self up and reposition himself. Was stabilized by being given medicine to prevent further stroking, to decrease blood pressure and calm anxieties. Stabilized. Jeff spent the night with him and "fought" with dad all night long. Dad was having difficulty breathing. In the morning, dad was sedated and he was placed on a respirator to open dad's air passage so he could breath.

**Journal entry;**

February 18, 2004

    Since dad was unable to have an MRI done yesterday (he couldn't lay flat comfortably to breathe) they scheduled another one today. The doctor's were still inconclusive as to whether or not dad had a stroke. Dad had the MRI in the morning and we awaited the results. It was a scary morning because he had deteriorated so much from the night before. It was thought he was having an evolving stroke that had affected his brain stem and it was feared there was nothing more that could be done for him. Many of family and friends were in the waiting room. Aunt Kate and her Pastor, Bo, stopped by and together we prayed. When the doctor's met with us around one, it was felt that dad did not have a stroke, but Guillian Barre Syndrome. Instead of Dad's immune system attacking the viral infection, it instead attacked his nervous system. Usually, GBS affects feet up, in dad's case, it affected him from the head down. The suggested treatment was Plasmapheresis, which was a filtering of the blood and antibodies. The nearest facility was at Hershey medical center. Arrangements were made and dad was life-flighted to Hershey by late afternoon. After consulting with the doctor's, dad was given a spinal tap to check his protein levels in his spinal fluid. They were only slightly elevated. Hershey was unsure of whether dad had a stroke or GBS. Robin, Jeff, Barb, Brent and Aunt Maxine were here. Ron Hoy stopped by in the evening.

## Journal entry;

February 19, 2004

It was a long morning waiting to see what was next. The neurologist team finally came in around lunchtime and determined that it was most likely GBS. They did not feel it was necessary to do another MRI. Instead they did an EMG to assess dad's sensory stimulation throughout his arms and legs. His arms and legs were affected, along with his face, neck, swallowing and breathing. The good news is that dad is alert, when he's not sedated, and aware and he's able to communicate with his feet - up and down for yes and left and right for no. Believing dad has GBS, the doctor's were ready to start treatment. They are not going to do the Plasmapheresis at this time because they want to start treatment as quickly as possible. Instead they are treating him with IVIG - a blood product with new antibodies to fight the GBS. He is receiving three bottles of treatment beginning this evening and continuing through Friday until completed. Then it is wait and see to see if it helps. He gets irritated from time to time due to saliva in his mouth, comfortableness from his ventilator and the up and downs of his blood pressure. Jeff came down and is spending the night. Robin and aunt Maxine were here for the day. Randy was here, too and gave dad a card.

### Journal entry;

February 20, 2004

Jeff spent the day along with aunt Maxine. Robin came down around 4:30 after work and Brent and Barb arrived around 8:00 to spend the night. The IVIG treatment was complete today. Dad's pupils were able to follow along a little when the doctor's checked them. The doctor's said dad is making little bitty baby steps, but the prognosis is good that he will recover and that most likely it will be short term rather than long term. Dad got a pedicure and foot massage today. His feet look a feel better. Also, good for the circulation!

### Journal entry;

February 21, 2004

Dad had help exercising his arms today! Now the IVIG treatment is done the goal is just to support dad, keeping him comfortable as possible. He is being medicated for his blood pressure and anxiety. He is sedated as needed to keep him comfortable and resting. Dad had lots of company

143

today. Barb and Brent had spent the night. Megan and Troy Miller stopped by around lunchtime. Aunt Nancy, aunt sue came and spent the afternoon and early evening with dad. Jeff came down in the afternoon. Even Doug McDonald stopped by for a visit. Dad received cards from the Yecina's and employees at Cannon. Dad was even given a Pink Cadillac convertible! Robin came down around 8:00 and was spending the night. Jeff was ready to go home but dad wouldn't let him. Jeff finally got out of here at 9:30 to go home once dad was sedated for the night.

## Journal entry;

February 22, 2004

Robin got to the hospital around 9:45. The neurologist had already been in. So he was the pulmonary team. Anthony Dunn was visiting Billy Lyons who is from Milesburg and is in a room two doors away. He says hello. Other visitors today were aunt Gail and Uncle Dale. They were chauffeured here today by Dave Grubb who also brought Chuck and Deb. Deb brought a framed picture of Dad, Dale and Chuck when they were making apple butter. Robin bought dad a card, an angel figurine and a Road Runner balloon. Also, having talked with Gail and Dale, I bought this journal/diary so we can have visitors sign in and write notes. Also, we can keep track of Dad's progress. The doctor's say it will be a slow recovery. Right now we might be looking at 6-8 weeks (?). He may end u with more IVIG treatments and he still could have the plasmapheresis done if we don't see improvement. Again, they say they just need to support him and keep him comfortable with the ventilator, monitor his blood pressure, feed him, etc. Today they put him an A- line in his left arm so they can monitor his blood pressure all the time (since

144

it fluctuates so much). They will also use this line to take blood samples when needed. This is so they don't have to poke him with the needles all the time especially since they are having trouble finding his veins.

Jeff arrived around 8:00 pm and stayed till 10:00pm. Dad had problems with his blood pressure and everything else was fine.

## Journal entry;

February 23, 2004

Jeff arrived around 9:30 am and they had Dad all cleared up. Shaved etc. Still having problems with his blood pressure. The physical therapist was in to see him and is going to have him wear boots on feet for support. They set the bed to vibrate his bed to loosen everything in his lungs so they can get them all suctioned out. The vibration is making him wiggle his toes. Jeff left about 1:20 pm. Maxine arrived around 11:00 am and is planning to stay the night if the roads are bad. Doctors were in about 3:00 - reflexes in legs were coming along and he was able to follow his finger a little with his eyes. He seems really tired but his blood pressure has been really high. He was sedated until this morning because he was upset and agitated from the weekend! His friend Darren from camp stopped in to talk with him and Jim responded but without much vigor. Darren said call him if you need anything, he is only about a half hour away. His number is; ----------. Robin called and talked to to Jim 4:50 - Tuesday 2/24/04. Stayed down last night. Nurse had me stay till he settled down about 10:00pm. Blood pressure still up around 200/106. Shoots up when do anything for him - Cutting down on assistance breathing from the trach tube!

## Journal entry;

February 24, 2004

Maxine arrived at hospital around 10am and left around 3:30pm. I arrived around 12:45. It's snowing outside today. It's a wet snow that lasted all day and left about a i inch accumulation. It was a quiet day. Dad's been sedated most of the day because of his blood pressure hovering around 200. The neurology team stopped by around 4:30. Dr. Reichwein feels it will be a couple more days before we see some improvement, though there has been some reflexes indicated in his legs. He says all that can be done at this time is to continue to support his breathing, eating, bodily functions, etc. and cross our fingers that there is no complications and no damage to dad's neuro "wires". They'll continue to monitor the blood pressure and breathing. Sam Burrauno called today to ask how you were doing and to let you know that "you are in his prayers and in God's hands." I left around 5:30 to head home, since the best thing right now for you is rest and no agitations!

## Journal entry;

Barb and Brent arrived @10:45am 2/26/04

Jim was sedated so we didn't get much response from him at first. They cut back the sedation started to get more response. Read Jim his cards from everyone! Physical therapy was in and worked legs and arms around 3:30. Seems very tired. We left around 4pm.

Thurs. Evening, Larry and Tina stopped in to visit. Jim was sleeping soundly. The nurse was here checking him over. Did give him a shot of medicine to lower his blood pressure, otherwise she said that everything else was looking good. She also said that he seems to be getting some more much needed rest, although she also said that they will be cutting back on the sedatives to see how he responds.

Thur. 9:20 pm

Larry has spoken to Jim for quite some time, told a joke or 2 and gotten a response or so thru Jim communicating with his foot. His blood pressure has definitely gotten better since we arrived around 8:30pm. Although you don't know me, you are in my thoughts and prayers.

THANKS TINA!

Jim wasn't a very good conversationalist tonight but at least he must be getting some rest. He did move his legs a lot of times. It was probably difficult to move his feet as they have them up against a pillow at the end of the bed.

Thanks to all of you who have visited and stayed with him, with all our prayers and His will Jim is going to be just fine. See you soon.

## Journal entry;

2/27/24

Jeff and Maxine were here- not responding very well- blood pressure down considerably 137/69 - still sedated pretty well. Chuck Grubb's wife and a friend stopped to visit for 1/2 hour or so. Jeff left about 4:20 after talking to Dr. Reichwein and etc. - Going to continue treatment the same for now and watching for changes from 14-21 days. Will decide next week if going to have to do plasma thing.

Robin arrived around 4:45. Sleeping beauty just kept on sleeping! Dad was given an X-ray to ensure that the respirator tube was in the proper place after being changed. Left hand red and swollen. Nurse said they will take the

A-line out and give his arm a rest for the weekend. Maxine and Robin left around 7:30.

## Journal entry:

2/28/04

Nancy and John, Chuck and Sue came down at 2:15pm. Jim was sleeping a good amount of the time but we did ask him a few things and he answered. Dan, the nurse came in and cleaned him and put lotion on his back and good smelling stuff. Nancy told Jim he must be going t party tonight. They took the A-line out of his arm.

Blood pressure came down quite a bit since we were here. 141/87 right now. Robin called and talked to her dad- he was just resting- looks peaceful! Left about 4:45pm.

## Journal entry;

2/29/04

Darren and Jack Miller came down. Jim seems to want to sleep. Asked him if he wanted the TV on said yes so I turned it on. Left around noon.

Robin and friend Kelly (from work) arrived around 12:00, missed Jack and Darren. Somewhat more alert than the last few times I was here. Blood pressure btw 135 and 175. An improvement. There's noticeable blood in dad's urine. They will try to determine if there's infection somewhere. Also, dad is swollen - fluids being retained and adjustments will be made to deal with that. May be given an additional IVIG treatment this week, but no benefit seems to warrant having the plasmapheresis done. There is talk that dad is getting closer to needing to have a tracheotomy done in the near future. Dan was your nurse today. He was very helpful and gave me some information in regards to Guillian-Barre Syndrome. I went home around 3:00. Take Care.

## Journal entry;

3/1/04

Got here about 11:15 - blood pressure was staying around 110/79- Normal temperature- Margaret was in with bunch of residents?

Dan is his nurse today and is being very attentive. Seems to be a lot of blood in urine and Beth (breathing) nurse sent sample of mucous to lab. Dr. Reichwine believes we will start seeing more improvement and that its about the end of the downward signs! Praise God! Had a really good bowel movement. Really don't seem concerned about urine because of normal amounts etc. Left 7:20 - 3/3/04 Got here about 10:55. Was going to move trach tube but still not decide at 3:30. Urine is normal colored with out gunk in it now. Praise the Lord! Blood Pressure staying pretty well down. Robin down about 3:30.

Barb and Brent arrived around 5pm 3/3/04. Maxine left around 5:45. Did not have trach done today. Will try again tomorrow. Occupational therapy was in today and worked hands, wrists and arms for almost 15-20 minutes. Dad indicated that there was some pain with it. Was sedated, but able to communicate at times. Brent talked to dad about people at work asking about him and wishing him well. Brent even told dad the latest sports news! Trach surgery is scheduled to occur sometime tomorrow morning - noon at dad's bedside. Robin left by 7:15.

Barb and Brent left around 7:45. We love you Jim!

# Journal entry;

3/4/04

Robin arrived by 9:15. Dad resting. BP 173/108. Trach has not been done yet. I haven't spoken to anyone about what's going on yet. Maxine arrived around 9:45 and by 10:00, dad's room was filling up with hospital staff. Around 10:15 the doctor's were giving dad his "peg" for his feeding tube. The trach would be this afternoon sometime. The doctor's had other surgeries to perform in OR first. The insertion of the feeding tube went well. Dad's sedated and resting. Around 2:15, the nurses came in to start preparations for the trach. We left the room around 2:40 and came back in around 4:30 after they were finished cleaning up. X-rays were taken. Now dad remains sedated and rests. Dad was given a shave today, but was left with a mustache! A new Look! It was a big day with lots going on. Dad needs the rest. Blood Pressure looking real good 119/74. Still out of it yet when I left at 6:45 nurse checked all of his signs and etc, earlier.

Thursday March 4th

Larry and I arrived around 8pm.

A nurse was working with Jim to try to clean up some residue from the trach. He seemed to be somewhat responsive to Larry communicating with his feet. There seemed to be some concern about bleeding from the trach. Dressing filled with blood quickly. The doctor was just in and told Larry it was not unusual to get bleeding after a procedure as he had. They said his oxygen level was good. Jim's color looks much better than last Thursday when we were here.

Jim – you need to wake up so I can meet you. My family and friends continue to keep you in their prayers.

Jim, lots of people keep asking about you. Lots of people have you in their prayers. Keep up the good work, you're looking much better and the nurses say you keep improving. The girls send their love, too. C'ya Later.

## Journal entry;

Friday March 5th

Jeff arrived around 9:30 am and nurses were cleaning up some. He had eyes partly opened and started wiggling feet when he saw me. He looks better not being on the ventilator. His blood pressure seems to be pretty good today.

## Journal entry;

Sat. March 6th Doug McDonald

I arrived at Jim's room at 2:00pm. He seemed to know that I was there. The nurse said he was sedated, but I continued to talk his ear off. I am looking forward to getting to camp with you Jim. So get better soon.

Doug

Robin arrived around 4:30. I must have missed Doug. I couldn't get in right away because the nurses were cleaning dad up and turning him. Dad's been in a real communicative mood. I read to him. He also wanted me to sing to him! He wanted me to sing hymns to him, but unfortunately I can't remember too many words. He got real excited when I mentioned the song 'Jesus Loves Me.' I sang it a few times and a few other songs. Then I shut up so dad could rest. He also wanted his feet massaged, so he got a little pampering, too! I left around 7:30.

151

## Journal entry;

3/7

Barb and Brent arrived about 9:30am. Stayed a little while and left about 1:30. Brent brought Jim up to date on the sports world and current events @ work.

3/7 Dale and Gail arrived to see improvement since the last time. Jim communicated some to us. Dale brought a picture of camp to hopefully cheer Jim up some. We arrived around 2pm. Jim seemed excited to see us. Talked to Jim about different things, his response was very good. GET WELL SOON OUR PRAYERS ARE WITH YOU.

## Journal entry;

3/8

Got here about 11:00 – really surprised to see he had his lower teeth in – seeing lots of signs of getting better – Praise the Lord! Kris (the occupational therapist) was in and gave him a good workout on his shoulders etc. Angie and helper changed bed and bather him, etc. Left about 6:50 (W.S.)

(found out later they were his own teeth – dah!)

## Journal entry;

3/9/04

Robin arrived around 4:30. One of the first things the nurse (Angie) said was dad was being moved to Holy Spirit (Select Specialty) in Camp Hill. Vent Rehab (long term acute care. What a surprise that it's so sudden. However, dad is stabilized and there isn't anything more that can be here now that he has the trach and feeding tube. Dad now needs the rehab "work out" to rebuild strength and regain mobility. Tried talking to dad, but he really wasn't very responsive today. Sleeping, I guess, since the nurse said he really isn't sedated much. I packed up dad's things. Left around 7:00.

**Journal entry;**

3/10/04

Maxine was with dad in Hershey this morning as he was being prepared for transport to Holy Spirit. Dad was supposed to leave Hershey around 1:00, but there was a hold up being the insurance company had not given authorization! Things were finally set for dad to leave by 12:30, but then they needed to wait for a respiratory therapist to travel along. They had to wait until 4:15. Dad finally made it to his room by 5:00. The nurses and respiratory therapist checked him over and got him settled. Dad was communicative tonight. He seems ok with the transfer now though he was definitely apprehensive. Dad wanted a foot massage with the cinnamon lotion. I also brought dad a CD player and some Cd's. He wanted me to sing hymns the other day, so I rounded up some Cd's – hymns, Christian, Roy Orbison and Ronnie Millsap. I want to look for a CD with 60's (oldies) music yet. He listened to a little bit of music tonight. The music should help comfort him and help pass the time. Todd was the respiratory therapist who worked with dad. He checked the trach, cleaned it, and suctioned. Dr. Evans is the director and assessed dad's situation with the vent/trach. We left around 8:00 to head home.

**Journal entry;**

3/11/04

Got here about 12:45 and they (the nurses) and Kathy the trac lady were in working on Jim! Turning him, cleaning out his tubes, mouth etc. Larry got here about 2:40 – Lonna from respiratory in about 3:30. Coming back in 10 min. to clean up his trac, suctions, etc. They had come up w/pad he can touch with his foot to call the nurse. Got new mattress that does the thing the bed did in Hershey! Larry left about 6:10 because he has to go to work. I left 6:30 – Shannon (therapist) came in and checked out arms and was asking him questions and got answers and so did all nurses, etc. all afternoon. Showing lots of positive signs – Dr. came in about urine and may use scope to make sure nothing is wrong w/bladder.

## Journal entry;

3/12/04

Robin arrived around 4:30. Lots of positive reports! Joe, the nurse, said dad was sitting up in a chair for several hours looking out the window. It was also reported that dad was tensing his muscles in his upper legs/thighs. Also, his breaths are breathing faster on his own than the ventilator. I know I didn't say that right! He is out breathing the ventilator! All are + signs. The therapists are giving dad a workout and he says he's up for it. He seemed tired. He communicated off and on at times. He listened to the Pat Boone Greatest Hymns CD. His feet seemed to move along with some of the songs! I left around 7:30.

## Journal entry;

3/13/04

Jeff and mom (Martha) arrived about 11:30 am. Dad's eyes are partly open and he responded to us by moving his feet. He was moving his eyes. He was able to follow the nurses light. His left eye is better than his right. We left around 2:00pm.

**Journal entry;**

3/14/04

    Chuck, Sue and Nancy arrived around 3:00pm. Jim was sleeping and not very communicative. After a little while he was wiggling his feet a little. The nurse was in and took his blood pressure – it was 112 over 71. Excellent!

**Journal entry;**

3/15/04

    Got here about 11:00 and the bed was giving his lungs a work. Phone rang but till I found the phone they hung up! Robin called later. Moved to room 507 – closer to nurses – put on a heart monitor because when they move him around his heart rate goes down but then right back up. They increased oxygen to 30% because the alarm kept going off. Left 6:00.

**Journal entry;**

3/17/04

    St. Patrick's Day. Robin arrived around 4:15. Had planned to come down on Tuesday, but we got snow. I talked with some of the staff today. Respiratory said they really haven't seen any changes at this pt. (I must have been misinformed the other day about dad breathing over the ventilator). Dad's insurance gave ok through 3/23. If no improvement with ventilator, dad will most likely go to a vent – supported nursing home. Doctor reports indicate that there has been slight improvements within a week, don't feel there would be any benefit to re-treating with IVIG of doing plasma –pheresis, however, short-term recovery is not expected. It's so hard when he's alert, but can't do anything. Dad's trac was replaced today and sutures taken out. Respiratory had to come in and adjust oxygen level. He also had been leaking air out of the cuff. Was readjusted. Nurses came in an gave meds while I was here also. Dad was communicative. We teased him saying he needs to use one foot for yes and one for no! He agreed but again used both! The nurse also put drops in his eyes. He may also be given an antihistamine for his post-nasal drip. I was also informed that dad had been treated a couple days ago for a urinary tract infection. Dad listened to a little music. I called Garrett and he spoke to dad. Dad moved his feet. I left around 6:30

## Journal entry;

3/18/04

Got here about 11:00 and they had Jim sitting up in a chair – I did his arms, legs and feet and he responded good. Some improvement in muscles in upper arms – Blood pressure good in am. Put him back in bed after about 2 hrs. because he wanted to sit up – His bed shook him up but didn't have much in his lungs when they suctioned him –Praise The Lord. Nun came in and prayed w/us. Did his feet, arms, etc. and moved them around a bit but his right hand was pretty tight but they had a splint on it cut off and on. Left about 5:30. (W.S.)

## Journal entry;

3/20/04

Jeff arrived about 12:00 and dad was sleeping. I tried talking to him but he wasn't very communicative! I talked to his nurse and she said he really hasn't shown any signs of improvement in the last few days. I asked if he wanted his Walkman on and he said no. I asked him if he needed some more variety of music and he said yes! They changed

156

his bed about 2:00 and now have him sitting up for a little while. It didn't seem to affect him much as his vitals go. I noticed dad moving his left thumb a little bit and I thought I seen him move his fingers a little.

## Journal entry;

3/21
Brent and Bar stopped in to visit with Jim.

3/21 John and Nancy arrived 11am. Jim more responsive than last week. He's moving left foot and leg. Twitches (?) in his left arm muscles. Seems like he is trying to open eyes. Told Jim lots of people praying for his recovery.

3/21 – 3:00 Larry, Tina, and Robin arrived. We missed all of dad's other company. Dad was communicating some, but the nurses said dad was drowsier than he's been. He received his respiratory treatment while we were here. We brought several cards that dad received in the mail and read them to him. Blood pressure 115/75. Left around 5:15.

## Journal entry;

3/22/04
Randy and I got here about 12:00. Jim was sitting up and opened his eyes some. Gave him a work out moving his arms, legs and fingers w/lotion (Vit E) Some movement on his own in fingers, arms and of course legs! Told him while he's lying here resting to tell himself it's mind over matter and try to will his parts to move and if they don't say I'll be back to that part later! With God's help it will happen! Left around 6:30.

## Journal entry;

3-24-04

Robin, Uncle Dale, and Gail came to see how our beloved fellow is doing. Jim, seems to be resting nice. Robin went to talk to Anne. Jim, you are in God's hands. Get well, Jim had a splint on left hand, to keep hand from tightening up into a fist, nurses check it every two hours. Replaced tube in Jim's mouth and cleaned it out. Cleaned and replaced new gauze near respirator. Sandra, CAN, was determined to come up with a call button dad could really use. I think they found one. She also cleaned dad up today – clean shave and hair washed. Dad had a new balloon in his room – miracles happen! The Miller's sent along pictures and notes made by the kids and a puppy with a heart that said hugs. Dad was pretty communicative – his toes, feet, and thighs were really moving at times. His eyes seemed to be more responsive too. He seemed pretty good all-in –all. We'll see you soon. Left around 6:45.

## Journal entry;

3/25

Larry and Tina arrived at 8:45pm. Jim was really moving his left foot. Was really kicking that left leg the entire time. Said that we didn't wake him up when we got here. He was sweating , must have told them he was hot as they had the fan blowing on him and he seemed pretty warm. Waiting on Kitty (the nurse) to come in and put on his hand splint and get an update on things. They have gauze bandages over his eyes. Want tp see why that is. The respiratory therapist was just in to check Jim, said everything looked ok, however Jim still isn't breathing on his own. I told him that's one thing he'd have to work on a little harder, however I'm sure he's doing the best that he can.

## Journal entry;

3/26

Pastor Dave and Judy Walker visited at 11:30 am. We shared some scripture with Jim (Isaiah 43:1-5; Habakkuk 3:17-18; 19a; Zephaniah 3:17; Romans *: 35-39) and prayed with him. While Jim doesn't appear to be responding to us, we know he can hear God's word. His church family at Fillmore UMC continues to pray for Jim.

## Journal entry;

3/27

Chuck, Sue and Nancy were here this afternoon. Jim seems unresponsive to me. Maybe he's mad at his sister Sue.

3/27/04 Got here about 11:00 and I did his feet, hands and arms w/lotion and did some exercises on his hands, arms and legs. Nancy got here about 3:00 right after they had taken him for Cat scan. Nancy went downstairs or somewhere and when she came back she said "Look who I ran into downstairs. Talked to Jeff and told him Jim's b.p. was going back up, that he was pretty stabilized. Left about 6:30. Douglas and Sam another guy Jim worked w/were here about 1:00.

## Journal entry;

3/28/04

Jeff, Robin, Garrett and Martha arrived around 2:45. Dad was fairly responsive to us. The respiratory therapist gave him a breathing treatment while we were here. Nurses said dad had a bath today. He needs a haircut. You could see the IV line that was put into the artery in his neck. I was told his other IV line (in his chest) wasn't functioning properly. I had gotten a call from a nurse Friday evening. They changed his IV line that evening. Also, Dad's blood pressure had been dropping. He was given dopamine for this. They said he was retaining fluids. Once he passed his urine, the blood pressure improved.. The CAT scan Saturday afternoon was to try and determine why he was retaining fluid and why his blood pressure had dropped. We gathered dad's things (he's supposed to be transported to a nursing home tomorrow) and we left around 4:30.

## Journal entry;

3/29/04

Dad was transferred to Sugarcreek Rest in Worthington near Kittanning. Dad was scheduled to leave Camp Hill around 10:00/ They left around 11:00 and arrived around 3:30. The ambulance crew got lost along 422 somewhere. Jeff and I arrived around 1:30. We met various staff and toured the place. Dad would like it around here ( the country outdoors, the pond) if he could see it. The respiratory therapist assures us they won't let him just lie in bed, they'll even take him outside if and when they can. Dad seems comfortable and relaxed. Very responsive. We left around 6pm.

## Journal entry;

3/31/04

Got here about 1: 15 – Terry (guy) therapist came in and Jim was pushing and pulling his legs up and down, was really communicating w/feet, pushing down against his hand, etc. Was trying to talk and made some sounds – they are going to sit him up tomorrow since he is adjusting and really trying hard! Terry told him "this is the time that is crucial because it will determine the way you will or will not get your body moving again." Really proud of the effort and progress he's showing! They changed his gown, etc. and when I came in he had foamy bubbles coming out his nose and mouth. Left about 6:45.

## Journal entry;

4/1/04

Jeff arrived around 2:00 pm and dad was sitting in a chair sleeping. I tried to wake him up but he is in a heavy sleep. His eyes seem to be getting a little more open. The physical therapist worked with him on his legs but he didn't respond much. Too tired I guess! Jackie, the respiratory specialist said that on Monday they will try lowering his oxygen to about 25 percent to see how he responds. I left around 4pm. dad didn't wake up. Must have been exhausted from sitting up.

## Journal entry;

4-2-04

Maxine got here about 1:30. Therapist had worked w/ him and seemed like he was really sleeping – Jackie, his respiratory nurse, and I sang him a couple of hymns Later. She had come in while I was trying to sing. Carl had Terry (therapist) come in and fill us in on his progress – Could see Terry and saw he had glasses – Moved eyes eyes from sided to side and up and down for yes and no- Waved his jaw up and down. Terry tried to get him to talk and his stomach was moving when he was trying. Is really doing better with his legs and feet moving. Jackie (Trac) replaced and cleaned him up good. He was slow in responding but he still had a temperature. Urine looks really orange (maybe from anti-biotics) Left about 6:00 – R.N. was going to check round red hard spot on right side of cheek, below ear!

## Journal entry;

4-4-04

Robin, Uncle Dale and Aunt Gail arrived around 12:40. Jim seems to be asleep, Robin washed Jim's face and mouth area. He responded to her loving touch. Urine is orange. Robin went to talk to staff. So good to see you Jim. We all love you. Jim, Robin and Gail massage your feet. Do hope it felt great. Robin clipped your nails. She is so loving and caring. She tenderly takes good care of you. Staff takes great care of Jim. Nancy, Sue and Larry arrived around 3:00. Robin, Gail and Dale left by 4:00. Nancy, Sue and Larry left too. They didn't want to get lost going home like they did coming here! And, so we can all eat dinner together. Nancy brought an Easter hyacinth. How pretty! See you soon dad. We love you!

## UPDATE

April 4, 2004

First of all, Jeff, Steve and I would like to say thank you so very much to everyone for their cards, prayers, gifts, etc. while our father, Jim McKinley had been hospitalized February 17, 2004 with Guillain- Barre Syndrome. We appreciate everything everyone has done to help us cope with dads illness and the responsibilities that go along with taking care of him.

Dad was hospitalized at Mt. Nittany Medical Center in State College on Tuesday, February 17th after being treated for bronchitis and having had tingling in his hands and feet on Monday, and then waking up Tuesday being unable to swallow. When he was admitted to the hospital, it was suspected that he was having a stroke. As the day progressed he deteriorated and by Wednesday, he was unable to breathe on his own and was placed on a ventilator. He had become paralyzed from the head down. He could not open his eyes, swallow, hold his head up, speak, support his upper body, use his hands and arms. His symptoms at that time did not make sense for a stroke and it was determined he had Guillain- Barre Syndrome. GBS is a rare disorder of the nervous system that causes rapidly progressing muscle weakness that in severe cases, can result in paralysis. With GBS, the body's immune system begins to attack the body itself.

Since being hospitalized, dad has spent 3 weeks in Hershey Medical Center, 2 ½ weeks in Select Specialty in Holy Spirit Hospital, and he is now at Sugar Creek Rest, a nursing home near Kittanning. He is on the sub-acute wing. He is at Sugar Creek Rest, because medically, dad is stable, but because of the severity of his paralysis and the fact that he's on the ventilator, he needed to go someplace where he could receive long-term care until he recovers. Unfortunately, for us, Sugar Creek is farther away than wed like (`2 ½- 3 hours), but it is the closest place he could go while he's on the ventilator.

Dad receives physical therapy/occupational therapy/ respiratory therapy Monday through Friday. He continues to show little bitty signs of improvement. Though his eyes are red and sore, they are open about halfway, starting to blink, and able to move them up and down, left to right. The muscles in his face and tongue have loosened up, though there is still some deformity. He is still unable to swallow.

In good news, though, the therapist mentioned that dad made a noise/movement on Wednesday as though dad was trying to talk. He's got a ways to go, but that was promising in regards to him being able to regain his speech. Monday, April 5, respiratory is going to begin to try and cut the oxygen level back on the ventilator. The goal of course is to wean him from the ventilator. All attempts at Holy Spirit to do so were unsuccessful. Dad has gained some strength back in his legs. He was able to push the hand of the therapist with his foot. The therapist, also mentioned that dads muscle spasms are from his nervous system starting to fire up again. Some days he's more responsive than others. Today he responded very little which is disheartening, but he tires very easily, due to his muscles being weakened from the paralysis. Dad uses his feet to communicate- up/down- yes and left/right- no. Thank God for his feet!! The doctors at Hershey indicated it could take dad 6 months to a year in rehab/therapy to recover. It will be 7 weeks on Tuesday.

The address is:

Sugar Creek Rest
RD# 2, Box XX
Worthington, PA 16262

Dads room number is 103. He does not have a phone in his room.

To get to Sugar Creek you can drive one of two ways: Interstate 80 West

Take PA-36 exit- exit number 78- Sigel/Brookville.

Turn left onto Allegheny Blvd/PA-36 S which becomes PA-28 S/66 which will run into US-422 W

Stay straight to go onto US-422 W. Do not take 422 Business. You will drive past Kittanning. Go through 2 stop lights (the second one is Bear St).

Approx 2.6 miles further you will see a Sugar Creek Rest sign on the left side of the road. Turn right onto a windy, country road. Follow the signs for Sugar Creek Rest (approx 6 ½ miles)

Or you can take 322, 220, I-99 US-22 (Ebensburg) and 422W (past Indiana). Do not take 422 Business. You will drive past Kittanning. Go through 2 stop lights (the second one is Bear St). Approx 2.6 miles further you will see a Sugar Creek Rest sign on the left side of the road. Turn right onto a windy, country road. Follow the signs for Sugar Creek Rest (approx 6 ½ miles.

A benefit dance for Jim McKinley is set for May 1st at the Milesburg Legion from 6-12 with the DJ starting at 8:00. There will be food provided from 6-8 pm. The food will be mostly appetizers. You don't have to be a member and all are welcome. There will be some 50-50 drawings. Cost: $5 person. All proceeds will be used to help pay bills not covered by his insurance and for all other expenses.

Please keep dad in your thoughts and prayers. His recovery will take time. Pray that he regains his strength so he can get off the ventilator and come home or at least go to rehab closer to home. Thank you very much for all the love and support we have all received. It is appreciated.

If you know anyone who would like to receive updates on dad, please e-mail Robin at -----or Jeff at -------. If you do not wish to receive these e-mail updates, please reply with remove in the subject line. Thanks.

Robin and Jeff

## Journal entry;

4/7/04

Wed. Barb and Brent arrived around 5pm. Eyes open but not very responsive. Brought Jim a CD to listen to "Hee-Haw Gospel Quartet." Jim must have woke up. He was moving his eyes a lot and he can "nod" his head now! Great ☺ The one nurse "joking" said she and Jim were having a disagreement and he was nodding his head. Told Jim about work and everyone there and gave him the Sports center updates! Left around 7pm! We love you Jim!

## Journal entry;

4/8/04

Randy and I got here about 2:00 – Kerry came in to show us how he could do his legs, etc. Terry brought her around to show how proud he was of Jim and the progress he is making! Communicating with his eyes now also – Movement in his arms and a little once in a while in is fingers – He is doing great! Left about 7:00.

## Journal entry;

4/9/04

Dale Benner and Dean Neal arrived 11:30am. Jim sleeping. Jackie said they had him medicated. Dean and I went to get something to eat, returned 2:15 pm. Jim was awake. Jim is moving more and Jackie said she was going to get him up and walking. Jim didn't think so. See you next time. Keep working.

## Journal entry;

4/10/04

Jeff arrived around 12:30. Dad was moving his eyes a lot and looks much better. He is being very responsive to everything I say. Moving his feet a lot. Robin and Garrett arrived around 2:15. Jeff left 2:30. Yes, dad quite responsive. Eyes open. Moving feet. Nodded head. Lifting leg. Brought dad some clothes, so he can get out of this darn hospital gowns. Urine looks back to normal again. Blood pressure 108/80. Oxygen level down from 30 to 27. Much improvement over the last two weeks! Happy Easter dad! We Love you. See you soon! We left around 5:00pm.

## Journal entry;

4/11/04

Brent, Barb and granddad arrived 10:45am. Happy Easter Jim. Jim very active with legs and nodding head. Left around 12:30pm

4/11/04 Tina and Larry arrived around 2pm. Jim was awake and moving his eyes quite a bit. He continues to move his feet and squeezed Tina's hand with his right thumb. We read to Jim from the Easter day of Our Daily bread.

## Update

April 12, 2004

This apparently has been a good week for dad. I spoke with nursing & physical therapy (Terry) this week. According to nursing and physical therapy, they say that dad has been quite active. They seem to feel he is having voluntary movements instead of involuntary ones, motion instead of just contractions in his muscles. The therapist feels this is a crucial time as the nerves begin to fire up; dad

167

needs to direct his body to do the movements he wants them to do. The therapist is seeing a range of motion- wriggling toes, left knee sliding, and bending of his legs, but mostly his left one. He is starting to nod his head, ever so slightly, but a nod nonetheless. This nodding was noticed by one of the nurses who said she was talking with dad about him needing a shave. He used his feet to indicate no. The nurse teased him, saying he was arguing with her about needing the shave and he nodded his head. They all have had positive feedback in regards to his progress so far.

Today, Carmen the charge nurse called. Dad met with the physician. Dad is being put on another antibiotic because he has an infection in his urine again. He's had a couple urinary tract infections since he's been hospitalized. They suspect this may be due to the catheter and will evaluate whether or not to remove it.

Jackie is the respiratory therapist who works with dad. As of Monday, April 5, she began working to cut back his oxygen level. He has been at 30 and they tried to cut him back to 25, just like the respiratory therapists had at Hershey and at Camp Hill. He has successfully been cut back to 27. His overall oxygen level is good, the problem is that his diaphragm has been weakened that he cannot support the pressure to breathe in or out on his own without ventilator. In time, we believe as the rest of his body gets stronger, his diaphragm muscles will too.

Jeff, Garrett, & I visited with dad on Saturday, and we saw for ourselves the progress he has been making. We actually saw dad lift his left leg an inch or two. We saw him nod his head, also. That was wonderful to see. His eyes were looking better, though still red. His eyes are opened more now and he's able to blink. He's beginning to use his eyes to communicate now, too.

We get frustrated some times when we are with him because we want him to respond to us and our many questions. Sometimes he's sleeping and/or tired. The therapist tells us that it just takes a little bit of time for him to "warm up"- we should ask him to wriggle his toes or something, give him a little rest and keep trying it again, till he's awake and ready. Sometimes he's really on a roll and we talk away. I really wonder what he'd like to say to us, though and can't. One day we'll know.

We would like to make a request. With it being springtime, it's soon time to mow grass. We would really appreciate some volunteers to take turns to help mow dad's grass. Jeff and I both work during the week, and with the time it takes to drive to see dad that only leaves the weekends for us to go visit dad. Our uncle Dale will get the mower tuned up for mowing and we will see that there is gas. There is approximately an acre of grass to mow (?) If anyone is willing to help with the mowing, we'd really appreciate it. Please contact Jeff @ 353-1791 or via e-mail jmck743@aol.com to work out a schedule to mow.

Just a reminder that a benefit dance is scheduled for Saturday, May 1st at the Milesburg Legion from 6-12. There will be food provided from 6-8 pm. The food will be mostly appetizers. At 9:00, the band "Gun Runnin Amish" will be performing instead of the DJ originally scheduled. This band plays a variety of music. You don't have to be a member and all are welcome. There will be some 50-50 drawings. Cost: $5 person. All proceeds will be used to help pay bills not covered by his insurance and for all other expenses.

Again, we thank everyone for their cards, prayers and support while dad continues his uphill battle to recover from his illness. We are please with the progress dad is making, though it's not as quickly as we'd like it to be. But, as long as his progress is positive, we are hopeful of a full recovery no matter how long it takes. Please continue to keep dad in your prayers, to work hard and to not give up.

Please keep Steve in your prayers, too. Dad has not wanted Steve to see him while he was in the hospital. Steve hasn't spoken with dad either. Steve obviously is not aware of the severity of dad's illness. We keep in touch with Steve regularly. At first he called every night. He was not happy when he heard dad was being transferred even further away from home. Strawberry Fields has kept Steve fairly busy.

To send cards or to visit, Dad's address is:

Sugar Creek Rest
RD# 2, Box 80
Worthington, PA 16262

His room number is 103. If you get a chance please go visit dad. He will know you and we're sure he'd appreciate the visit.

Robin, Jeff and Steve

## Journal entry;

4/14/04

Got here about 12:30 and Terry came in later and Jim really did a lot himself with his legs, eyes, jaw, etc. Really all were proud of you not giving up! And especially for trying so hard. Giving him antibiotics for U.T.I. again! Change trac tubing at neck where it fits in. Left about 7:30.

## Journal entry;

4/16

Didn't get here until 1:30 (because of other circumstances). Becca (occupational therapist) was working his arms and had him touching his head and hair – Terry came in late (physical therapist) had him doing his legs, eyes and moving his head up and down and back and forth. Sore on right ear still looks sore! John LPN said his butt was getting better too. I DID NOT CHECK IT OUT! Jim helped move his hands and feet when I was putting Vit.E on and exercising them. It is really great to see all the deliberate movement all over his body – Jackie had him breathing on his own a little too – He is really working hard! AND coming back little by little and sometimes big surprises! Left about 6:30.

## Journal entry;

4/18/04

Nancy, Sue, Larry and Robin arrived around 1:00. It' really great to see that you h ave improved so much this past week. Much better that your eyes are responding and that you are making an effort to talk to us. I'm sure that there are a lot of things that you would like to say to us, and will soon enough. It took dad awhile to wake up and warm up, but once he did, he joined in the conversation. He's using his eyes a lot more to respond, though he uses his feet and legs a little not as much as he used to. He did move his feet a lot when we spoke of the benefit dance coming up and "dancing the night away." It was as though he was dancing! We shared a lot of stories and had a nice visit. It was a beautiful day. We left around 3:30.

## Journal entry;

4/21/04

    Got here about 1:00 – really worked hard with his legs, jaw, head turning etc. Really gripped my hand several times hard! His eyes looked awfully red again but he was moving them up and down and back and forth. Left about 6:45. Praise the Lord for helping him come back!

## Journal entry;

4/23/04

    Jeff arrived about 8pm and Dad was getting a sponge bath by the nurse. He was wide awake and glad to see me. I showed him a picture of Kady and I and his legs really wiggled a lot and he was shaking his head yes. We communicated a lot tonight. He is looking a lot better. I plan on staying till around 10pm!

## Journal entry;

4-25

    I got a wonderful surprise yesterday when Robin called to say that you said your first word. Robin is sure great on keeping us informed, and Jeff too. And then we got an even nicer surprise when we got here today and saw you get out of bed and in a chair. It is great seeing you make such improvement. Larry, Gail, Robin and Garrett arrived around 1:00. Dad was sitting up in the chair. It was the first time any of us had seen him sitting up. It was great. We passed the afternoon by Garrett telling jokes. Jacque had a CD player in his room. The CD was Mercy ME. Jacque and Robin sang "Ican only imagine" while Garrett held pap's hand and dad moved his legs and feet. It was an awesome moment as we Praised God for all His blessings and the healing improvements dad makes each day and each week! Dad was placed back in bed while we were here. He really looked good with his new haircut – no more curls and freshly cleaned up. Eyes red, but not mucousy (?) like before. He used his eyes, head and feet to communicate. We left around 3:30.

## Update

April 25, 2004

We are so excited. Each week it seems we see new progress. Granted they are little steps in the whole scheme of things, but to us they are giant leaps considering how far he has to come back from. We have seen the following just in the last two weeks:

Dad's eyes are looking much better. He can open and half close his eyes. He's not really blinking his eyes yet and therefore they are still red and need eye drops during the day and eye patches at night. I was worried that he wouldn't be able to see, but it appears as though he can. At times it seems he is staring at you, trying to focus. He will acknowledge seeing you, but how focused we are to him, we're not really sure. At some point he will be evaluated by an eye doctor.

He is now able to open and close his mouth some and move his lips as though he's trying to speak. He's able to support his head a little more and actually move it up and down and left to right. This is really great having another way to communicate yes and no. He is using his eyes to communicate yes and no, also.

Dad is having movement and spasms in his arms now. Dad needs to concentrate on his mind telling his body parts what movements to make. In doing so, the therapist indicates that dad is able to move his ankles and his feet up and down ~ I ½ feet; he can draw his legs up and push them out. Dad's sister, Maxine, said that dad was finally able to grip her hand this week, and Jeff said he felt it too.

As dad regains muscle control, it is clear that his right side has been affected more than his left side. It is taking longer to come back, but he is making progress.

Unfortunately, dad has made no progress with the ventilator this week. Dad's oxygen is great; it's just that his diaphragm has been weakened from the paralysis that he is unable to support the air pressure to breathe in or out. There is concern that dad may never be able to be weaned from the ventilator to breathe on his own again because of this. I am told that it may be possible for dad to supported by a portable oxygen tank at some point if he were able to go to rehab or home. I just can't see dad living like this, but we'll live with whatever is meant to be. Please keep praying about this.

Today my uncle Larry,a Gail, my son Garrett and I went out, to see dad. Dad was sitting up in a chair when we got there. He has been positioned in a chair before, but this was the first time we have seen him sitting up in a chair and it was great. After about an 1 ½ he was tired and ready to be placed back in bed. Also, Dad finally got a haircut after 10 weeks in the hospital. He really looks good, especially when he's clean shaven!

While we were visiting dad today, Garrett kept dad entertained with his silly jokes. Also, Jacque, the respiratory therapist, set up a CD player in dad's room and we listened to a CD of <u>Mercy Me</u>, a Christian Rock group. When the song "I Can Only Imagine" played, Jacque and I sang along while dad moved his feet and legs. It was a really great moment.

Actually, you could say we were celebrating yesterday's miracle of dad speaking his first word "yes". Speech therapy has only been working with dad 2 or 3 times so far, so this was a huge breakthrough.

In other good news, dad is finally ready for Steve to visit him. Jeff and I will be taking Steve out to see dad next Sunday, May 2nd. Steve is so excited. This will be the first time Steve has seen dad and talk with him, since he's been hospitalized. I hope all goes well.

Thanks to those who offered to help mow dad's yard. Jeff mowed dad's yard this past week after he and Brent spent time the week before getting all the stones out of the yard. Between Jeff and Brent mowing, they'll probably be able to keep up with the yard. But, if there's ever a time anyone wants to take a turn, just contact Jeff @ 353-1791 or via e-mail jmck743@aol.com or contact Brent Hockenberry.

Just a reminder- the Benefit dance for dad is this coming weekend: Sat, May 1st from 6-midnight at the Milesburg Legion. Pork/sauerkraut, hotdogs/rolls, chips/pretzels are being served from 6-8pm. Anyone interested in bringing covered dishes to share- appetizers, casseroles, snacks, desserts, etc. are encouraged to do so. DJ Halestorm will be there from 8 (?)- 12. When we told dad about the benefit dance he started moving his legs and feet as though he were trying to dance! Attached is a sign if you wish to print it out and post it somewhere. The sign can be opened with Adobe Acrobat Reader which can be downloaded for free if you don't have it.

Hope to see you there this Saturday night!

Thank you again from all of us for all the thoughts, prayers, and cards on behalf of our dad. We appreciate all of your love and support. We are so grateful to God for all the blessings and improvements we continue to see in dad. Please continue to keep us in your prayers.

Robin

## Journal entry;

4/30

Got here about 1:00 and had them change him because he smelled like his bowels had moved. He said he felt better too afterwards. Got to talk to him on the phone from polling place on Tuesday. Joey (occupational Therapist) gave his hands good work out. Working hard to get body parts moving again. Left about 6:30.

## Journal entry;

5/1/04

Brent and Barb got here around 3:00pm. Jim was doing well moving head and moving mouth. Was sleepy. It was really warm in the room. We opened the window, but it was still quite warm. Maybe we will bring a small fan down for Jim. We left around 7:30.

## Journal entry;

5/2/04

Robin, Steve and Leslie and Jeff and Kady arrived around 1:45pm. Dad not moving too much, but was glad to see us. We clipped his nails and Robin massaged his feet. We brought him a nice basket of flowers that were donated to him from a lady that works with him. The benefit dance was a huge success. We raised over 2,00 dollars to pay for some of his medical bills. We left about 3:30. He communicated pretty good today!

## Journal entry;

5/4

Jim was really trying to talk and really worked hard for Becca and Terry. Eye Dr. was in and said he wouldn't have 20-20 vision, but so what? Who does? His right eye is better than the left but is still coming along. Got here 1:00 – Left 7:00. Really proud of his progress!

## Journal entry;

5/7/04

Got here about 1:00 – Jim kept trying to talk and moved his mouth counting when I was doing his arms, hands and legs and feet. Joey (Therapist) tried confusing him with counting but it didn't work! Doing great, Jim! Left around 7:00.

## Journal entry

5/8

Nancy and Sue arrived about 1:00. Jim seemed glad to see us. The nurse put a different pair of glasses on him. Were much better and didn't not rub his face. Nancy got him a cross for his window and a card. Brought him a goldfish plant for his window and a pair of short p-j's.

5/8/04

Dear Jim

Chuck and I was here to see you. Chuck told you that we got done butchering the hogs and told you to get better because October is Apple Butter making. I promised to have you a slice of ham, eggs, home fries at butchering if your good. I'll do it at Apple butter making. Kenny, Davey says hi. We love you with all our hearts. Get better.

Love, Chuck and Deb

Hey baby-

Scott and I where here to see you and I wanted to know if I still was your baby and if we were going to go for pizza when you get out of here after we butcher. I love you very much. See you soon.

Love, Kim and Scott, Harley and Cole

We visited with the Grubb's for a little while in the waiting room. They were glad to see Jim and he responded to them with head gestures so we know he was glad to see them, too. They really care about Jim!! We do too. Was good to see Jim and see him responding 'yes'. We left about 3:45 pm.

## Journal entry;

5/9/04

Larry, Tina, Robin and Garrett came to see dad today. We arrived around 1:15. A beautiful day. A really nice breeze coming through the window. Dad seemed comfortable, except for his crossed legs. He was very alert and communicated very well with his head, eyes, mouth and feet. His eyes looking much better now they are being treated. The goggles don't look too bad and if they help – great! He's really trying to talk – we need to learn to read lips. Garrett brought some stuffed animas to keep dad company- Sponge Bob, a frog, and a fish. We brought a picture of Garrett holding a fishing rod. Maybe one of these days, Garrett and dad can fish in the pond outside. We also brought some shorts and a t-shirt. Can't wait to see him out of the gowns! Jacque says they'll have to get him outside now that it's warmer. The fresh air, warm sun and outdoors have got to help him feel better. Staff are very positive about his progress and prognosis. Love you dad. Hang in there! Keep up the good work! We left around 3:15.

## Update

May 10, 2004
Benefit Dance-

Thank you so much to everyone who came out to the Benefit Dance on behalf of our father, Jim McKinley, on Saturday, May 1st at the Milesburg Legion. It was like a family reunion with so many family members and many, many friends of our dad and us. There were 270 people signed in at the dance. Approximately $2400 in profit was raised which will be used for medical expenses. A great time was had, with great food and great music all evening long. A special thank you goes out to Ed Bennett, Heather Cole and the Milesburg Legion for their support of the benefit. The legion provided the room and the food. Calvin & Lori Stark paid for DJ Halestorm who played a wide range of danceable music.

Did anyone see Kenny Chesney at the legion? Kenny Chesney played at the Bryce Jordan Friday evening. There was a limo in the parking lot and it is rumored that he came into the legion that evening. He was to have been on the dance floor surrounded by lots of women, unrecognizable in his baseball cap. I think it must have been Kenny singing the song Green, Green, Grass of Home. What do you think?

Steve's visit to see dad-Prayers were answered and my brother Steve and his wife, Leslie, finally got to visit with dad. This was the first Steve had seen or spoken with dad since he was hospitalized. Jeff, Kady (Jeff's daughter) and I took Steve and Leslie to see dad on Sunday, May 2nd.

Steve was so excited. He called me several times last week to thank us for taking him to see dad. All went well with the visit. Leslie was hesitant to get close to dad at first, but she got near him and talked with him about how well she is taking care of Steve. Dad responded by moving his head and feet.

### Progress-

When I visited with dad this weekend, he seemed quite alert. He was responding and communicating a lot with his eyes, head, mouth and feet. He was opening and closing his mouth as though he's trying to speak. We need to learn how to read lips! He apparently is beginning to make noises when working with speech therapy, but because of the trach, the airway is normally closed off to the vocal chords. The staff is looking into using message boards to help dad communicate. When someone is pointing at a picture dad can nod his head and eventually, once dad regains use of his fingers and hands, he can point.

Dad was seen by an optometrist this week. After consulting with an ophthalmologist, it was determined that dad has cornea ulcers on his eyes. Contributing factors were that he cant close his eyes; his eyes are dried out because he is not producing tears,; and there is mucous/pus/infection. These ulcers can perforate his cornea and cause permanent scarring on his cornea. There is some scarring damage already. He is being treated with artificial tears, antibiotics, steroids, eye patches, and now swimgoggles to keep air from drying out his eyes. The eye doctor feels confident that in time these will heal with treatment and hopefully, surgery wont be necessary. I thought his eyes were much better after only a couple days of treatment.

In speaking with Jacque, the respiratory therapist, the pulmonologist saw dad on Friday, April 30th. Though there has been no change with the vent yet, he is confident, that dad will be able to weaned at some point in time. Jacque also mentioned that physical and occupational therapy have been working with dad twice daily for approximately one hour each time. They are real pleased with how hard dad is working and trying to get well. Its got to be so frustrating, when your body just isn't strong enough to do what you want it and need it to do. We are continued to be reminded that this is a slow process, but he continues to show positive progress.

## Websites-

I finally had some time to do some internet browsing for information on Guillian-Barre Syndrome. There are many websites with GBS information. I am thankful to see that dad has and continues to receive the appropriate treatment and care needed to help recover. Time is the biggest factor. If you haven't done so already, you may want to check out the following:

- www.um-jmh.org/HealthLibrary/ORN/Guillian_Barre.html
- www.gbsfi.com/overview.html
- www.emedicine.com/pmr/topic48.htm   Very thorough and detailed.
- www.nhgri.nih.gov/11009202
- www.rnmag.com/be_core/

## Visits-

If you get a chance to, please consider going to visit dad. Unfortunately, it is pretty much a day trip. He's been visited by many family members, but I'm sure he'd appreciate the company seeing some of his friends, too. Thank you Chuck, Debbie, Kim, and Scott for visiting with dad last weekend (and Aunt Nancy, Aunt Sue, Uncle Larry and Tina). Feel free to give us a call if you'd like to carpool (especially with the price of gas these days!)

Thank you for your continued prayers on dad's behalf.

Robin

## Journal entry;

5/16/04

Jeff arrived around 12:30 and dad was sitting up watching TV. Probably listening mostly. He was very responsive and pretty hot. I removed the blankets from his feet and put a cold rag on his head. He liked that.

Larry and Tina arrived at 2:15. Jim was listening to a ballgame. He was wearing his swim goggles and seemed to be moving his head quite a bit. Jim looked good in his face.

We know God is with him. You continue to look better each trip out, of course you always were the better looking brother. Seemed to be more comfortable and moving around more today, keep up the good work Jim so we can get you home again.

## Journal entry;

5/19/04

Got here about 1:00. Was really a mess since trac had apparently leaked and dried on left side of his face, hair, pillow, etc. was still leaking and making everything wet. They had changed his bed but hadn't washed him for heaven knows how long. The black guy from midnight shift helped clean him up. His eyes looked better, not nearly as red. Left about 7:00.

## Journal entry;

5/23/04

Robin and Garrett arrived around 11:45. We missed dad last week, so it was great to see him. He was clean shaven and looking good. His eyes are looking much better. Medication is working. Sugar creek called yesterday to say the eye doctor was in to see him. We brought pictures of my fishing to Lake Ontario in New York. I also brought a card from Russ Shroyer. Then lots of company arrived. Barb and Brent arrived around 12:45 and Nancy, John, Chuck and Sue arrived around 1:00.

Hi Jim – was good to see you. See slight improvement every time we come. Slow but sure – we'll take every little bit of progress we see. Before you know it you'll be down looking at the geese and swans. Your family loves you and can't wait until you are well again.

Hey, Jus your little sister. Looking good and very much responsive. Was moving his head and trying to talk. Told him we were down looking at the baby wild geese. We told him we would take him down to see them when he's able to go outside. Sue!

## Journal entry;

5/26/04

Looking better except for swelling in arms and hands. Got here about 12:45. Really had a hard rain for a while. Left about 7:00.

## Journal entry;

5/30

Larry stopped in for a visit, must have been tired, you were sleeping for a long while. You are looking better each time, keep up the good job of working on getting better and out of here. The nurses were in to check on you and said that everything looked good, and said that they continue to see steady improvement, says it will just take a little more till you are up and around and taking Kady fishing! Lots of people continue to ask about you and how you are doing. We all continue to pray for you and a quick recovery. See you for your birthday.

## Journal entry;

May 31-04

Jeff, Robin, Dale and Gail arrived to see you with your eyes opened wider, your head moving quite a lot more, Jim your in God's gracious hands, he will make you stronger each day. We love you, will be glad to take you home. The guys look forward to taken you out to camp again. God Bless you, Love You.

Jim McKinley **Update** #5- May 31

For those of you who don't know, dad's 62nd birthday is this June 7. Please feel free to send him birthday cards at Sugar Creek. The address is:

Sugar Creek Rest
RD# 2, Box
Worthington, PA 16262
Room 103.

I don't know if any of you have had a chance to look up any information on Guillian-Barre, but it can take months to a year, or longer to get back to where dad was before the illness struck. At this point there really has not been any major improvement, but yet it seems he's come along way since when he was first hospitalized. The respiratory therapist says he has taken a few breaths on his own, when they are cleaning his trach. And hopefully, a few breaths will lead to a few more breathes on his own. Every little step is a step in the positive direction, no matter how little the step. The eye doctor continues to check on dads eyes. He makes adjustments in treatment from time to time, but they appear to be improving. He gets recurring urinary tract infections with his catheter, and the nurse called me again Saturday to inform me he was given another antibiotic to treat this.

My brother, Jeff, Aunt Gail, Uncle Dale Benner, and I went out to see dad today. He was lying in bed, but he seems more comfortable than he had before. The biggest improvement we have seen in the last couple of weeks is that he has regained a lot of strength in his head and neck. He was lifting his head up and moving it from side to side a lot. He turns to you to listen to what you say. He moves his mouth and lips as he tries to talk to you, but of course he cant. Not yet anyway. The ventilator/trach is the biggest obstacle to this. We've yet to see any change in his arms and hands. I've been told that he will try to grasp your hand, but I haven't felt it yet. I did however, feel a twinge and movement for the first time in his thumb. I believe it will all come back in time. We just have to be patient and be hopeful in the meantime.

My brother, Jeff and I plan to go see him soon on a week day so we can touch base with his doctor and therapists to get an update on his condition and prognosis. We try not to focus on a time frame to get better and come home, because it is unpredictable. We can only focus on improvements one day at a time.

Please don't give up on the prayers on his behalf. Consider sending him a card for his birthday. And, if you

185

get the chance, please go visit. I know it is a long day and the price of gas is expensive, but we welcome carpooling. It makes the trip a little easier. Just call or e-mail us if you'd like to go out sometime.

Thank you for your e-mails, cards, prayers and support. It is so very much appreciated and needed for perseverance and hope.

Robin

## Journal entry;

June 1

Saw they had put in an IV shunt for infections (don't know where). Getting 2$^{nd}$ anti-biotics. Right hand really swelled! Talked a bit!

## Journal entry;

6/5/04 Saturday

Brent and Barb arrived around 2pm. Jim was looking good moving head. He was moving fingers slightly on left hand. Happy Birthday Jim! We left around 6pm-

## Journal entry;

6/6/04 Sunday

Sam Hilliard arrived around 11:30 am with Doug McDonald, Dale Bennar and Dean Neal. Jim is looking a lot better then last I saw him at Camp Hill (Holy Spirit).

Dear Jim

If I would have tried to come here without Dale I probably would have ended up in Phillipsburg, Jus like camp!! Real pretty out here, you have a nice view. Get well soon.

Jim your going to have to get well soon, I don't know how many trips I can make with these guy's. Jim was very active today. Moving his head and feet, I think he was glad to see Doug, Dean and Sam. Dale

Hi Jim. It was good to see you again. Too bad its not at camp. We could play a game of spades. Connie and her sister will be up to see you soon. Dean

June 6, Nancy and Sue arrived around noon. It's a gloomy kind of day; but the sun has finally come out. Wait until you can go outside Jim, you will like it very much. There is a nice pond and lots of green grass. The wild geese are everywhere. You seem very responsive today and are moving your shoulders and head. Have a very "Happy Birthday" and we'll celebrate more next year.

Jim, you have some very good friends. I think Doug was especially glad to see you. We look forward to seeing you every time we come. It is like God's country up here and you have to get well when you are in God's country!

Love You! Happy Birthday!! We celebrate next year in

Moose Run. - NY

### Journal entry

6/7/04

Happy Birthday, Dad! Jeff and I are so glad to be able to be here with you today. We brought you flowers and balloons. We spent a lot of time talking with the various staff who are working with you. We were able to see the movements you make when working with physical therapy. Progress is slow, but steady. We are with you for as long as it takes, every step of the way.

## Journal entry;

6/12

Brent and Barb stopped to see Jim. Arrived about 2pm left around 4pm. He seemed to be a little tired did respond a little.

## Journal entry;

6/13/04

Larry, Tina and Robin came out to see you today. It's always good to see you.

It's a fairly sunny day, today. Jim had just got his haircut. He was really moving his head. It is so wonderful to watch Jim react to his family. My family's prayers are and will continue to be with you. Hopefully Jim, you will be able to be up and about and get outside. I know God is with you throughout all of this. (changed writer)

I think Tina is anxious to get to talk with you one of these days. I'm sure she will like you you, actually I don't know anyone who doesn't. It's great news that you are making progress on breathing on your own. That is real encouraging news. Get off that ventilator and you'll be able to move a little closer home. See you next week. (changed writer)

Looked over the journal from when dad was first hospitalized. In 1 week he will have been hospitalized for 4 months. It seems like it has been so much longer. But, looking back, we have seen a lot of improvements. We remain hopeful for a complete recovery however long it takes. The respirator assistant said you were breathing18 breaths of your own this morning. I had heard you were taking a few breaths on your own but I wasn't expecting 18 breaths. Everything is up and down, good days and bad days, but still continue progress in the positive direction. Keep on hanging in there! You can do it! You have lots of love and support believing in you and encouraging you and praying for you. Take care.

## Journal entry;

6/19

Dale came out with Mr. Wilson. Another nice day up here. Jim looked like he was warm. Didn't respond a lot today. Wish you a happy father's day. Next year we'll do it somewhere else.

## Journal entry;

6/20/04

Jeff arrived about 1:30pm. Dad really moving his head and toes around. He looks good. I talked with Jackie and she said he is making progress with his breathing, but it is slow. She said one time he had a high 28 breaths per minute on his own. But it is very inconsistent and she thinks it's because therapy wears him out. I take that back. She said when therapy works with him that makes do things on his own instead of lying there and being lazy. She also said he has no infections right now and the pneumonia is gone. Well, Happy Father's Day from all of us and We love ya Dad!

## Journal entry;

6/22/04

Gram Mitchell's Birthday. Unfortunately it was not a good day. It was quite a scare actually. Apparently, around 2:15, staff put dad in the recliner chair and he went into cardiac arrest. He was taken to Armstrong County Memorial

Hospital. The news and situation did not sound good. Jeff, Dale, Larry, Sue, Nancy got to the hospital around 8:00. We were very surprised and perplexed when we arrived and saw dad. He was laying there in the bed. When the nurse came in, she started talking to him. He was responding and moving his head! We could not believe our eyes. Barb, Brent, and Maxine arrived later in the evening and stayed till around 1:30 am. Dad had a C/T scan (chest x-ray) done around 12:30 am.

## Journal entry;

6/23/04

Jeff, Robin and Maxine spent the night 6/22. It was a short night. He had more tests run in the morning. His heart appeared to be fine. All the tests that were run were inconclusive. His hemoglobin blood level had dropped and he was given several pints of blood.

## Journal entry;

6/24 – 7/2

Dad remained in the hospital through July 2nd. He had lots of tests run. I believe it was God's way of getting dad the medical attention he needed. He was seen by the pulmonologist, neurologist, eye doctors and GI doctors while he was in the hospital. He had C/T scans, GI scope, colonoscopy, a port line (for antibiotics), thoracecntises, and bronchioscopy to name a few. The biggest problem to deal with was the pneumonia and fluid in his lungs. The doctors were also looking for where he might be bleeding (blood level dropped). Other than the left lung, every thing else seemed to be inconclusive. He returned to Sugar Creek on Fri., 7/2. Garrett and I visited with him a little before he was transported. He didn't want to go back and I asked if he wanted to go somewhere else and he said no also. He wanted to stay right where he was.

## Journal entry;

7/28/04

Jim was transferred to Ebensburg.

## Journal entry;

8/20/04

Pap was trying to talk. He was making a little noise. He moved his head, shoulders, and feet. When he was trying to talk he would move his lips over and over. He was shifting his body. Pap says all the good baseball players should go to the Pirates so every year they win the World Series!!! Good to see ya, we love you, see you soon. Love, Garrett and Robin.

## Update #9

August 25, 2004

Dad was transferred to Ebensburg on July 28th. Ebensburg is ~ 1- 1 ¼ hours closer to home than Kittanning. We are so grateful that he was able to get closer to home, especially before winter settles in. Already, he has had a lot more visitors than he had while at Sugar Creek. This is appreciated, because the more visitors, the more able to keep dad's spirits up to keep hanging in there. There is no doubt that faith in God and the prayers also keep dad from giving up. None of us could hang in there without our faith and prayers.

Dad was having some difficulties when he was first transferred to Ebensburg. He was running a temp and was placed back on antibiotics for a short while, but everything seems to be much better now. The pneumonia has cleared up also so I am told. He has had the catheter removed, also, and this should help minimize the urinary tract infections he was getting.

Dad seems to be handling the move pretty well. The staff at Laurel Crest seems to be pleased with how well he's doing and the progress he is making. They do get frustrated at times in trying to communicate with him, but with patience, we are all able to have some understanding in trying to meet his needs.

A team meeting was held on August 10 with the various specialties who are working with dad. He continues on the feeding tube, but once he can swallow again, they will be able to reintroduce foods in time. He is receiving physical therapy again at this time. Physical therapy works with his legs. Within the few weeks at Laurel Crest, he was able to work up to 20 reps per exercise. Occupational therapy works with his arms. He still is unable to move his hands and arms. You can feel the impulses move down his arm and into his hands, but only his thumb can move at this point. You can feel a slight grip in his hand also. The arms are the slowest to come back so far, which seems weird because these were the last to go when he first became paralyzed. He has regained strength in his neck and shoulders and is able to shrug. He is also starting to wriggle from his waist, to indicate he needs repositioned. I was told that he would regain millimeters a day. We are encouraged, however, with every bit of progress he makes. He is also being seen by speech therapy. Because of the difficulty of communication, they will work hard to get him to speak while on the ventilator. To do this, there is a cuff attached to the trach, which air is let into the vocal chords so he can speak. Letting air into the vocal chords, however, decreases the air into his lungs and the oxygen saturation decreases. He was able to tolerate ~ 10 minutes when speech therapy first started working with him. When I was with him on 8/16, he tolerated 20 minutes. The goal is one hour. The day I was with him, I actually heard him speak and he said the alphabet. This was so exciting. I'm not sure how he's doing right now. The only other area addressed at the team meeting was his eyes. I'm sure many have wondered whether he can see or not. Dad had developed cornea scarring due to dad's inability to blink and his eyes dried out. He has been seen by several eye doctors and he is to be consulted by an eye doctor in Ebensburg also. Over the months he's had drops, antibiotics, ointments, etc. to help clear up some of the problems with his eyes. He's also worn eye patches. Dad can see images, light, etc., but without clarity. I was told that at this time he is legally blind. I am told that there could be the possibility of cornea transplants, but there are certain criteria that need to be met first. He probably will not be considered for a transplant until dad is closer to recovery. To be honest, at this time it wouldn't do any good for a transplant since he still is unable to blink, his eyes would probably continue to dry out and could end up with the same problem again.

I want to say a special thank you to the employees at Cannon Instrument Company where dad was employed. The company picnic was held in July and a 50/50 raffle was held to benefit dad. The money raised was used to purchase a stereo system for his room. He had a headset, but this really didn't work very well. So, now he can listen to music to help pass the time and without hurting his ears and head. There are several CD's in his room- country, Christian, and gospel. I recently added a collection of 60's rock and roll. We were listening to Rockin' Robin one day, and he had his whole body rocking, dancing, and shaking to the music!!!

I am so grateful for the special moments we are sharing with dad when we are able to visit. God is no doubt at work in this situation and we patiently wait dad's healing. We are thankful for all the blessings and progress we see as each day goes by and are hopeful for his full recovery, sooner hopefully than later.

God Bless!

Robin

## Journal update;

8/31/04

At 10:30 pm last evening, I got a phone call. Dad was being taken to the hospital. He had blockage ("mucous plug") from the drainage and difficulty breathing. He spent the night @ UPMC Lee Hospital in Johnstown. Uncle Larry rode along with me. It was an interesting trip. Dad was transferred back to Laurel Crest around 2:30. Seems to be resting comfortably. Finally.

(Recall the event surrounding his Angel's visit)

## Journal entry;

9/5/04

Garrett and Robin came out to visit. A beautiful day to drive and see how dad is doing. It was a rough week for him. I called Friday to check on h im and they said they almost had to take him to the hospital again for another mucous plug. They are going to give him humidified oxygen to see if that helps and suction him more often. We read from the Bible, listened to the First Baptist Church tape "The winning Team" and listened to the music. We turned on the Pat Boone Greatest Hymns CD. He really seems to like this one!

### Journal update;

9-9-04

Dale and Dean arrived 2:30 PM. Jim very active and tried to talk a lot. We thought Jim looked good and had good movement. Jim said he was ready to take on Dean and Jeff at a game of spades. Jim looked real good The best I've seen him in a long time. It makes me feel good.

### Journal entry;

9/19/04

Robin and Garrett came for a visit. Dad looking good. Respiratory "showed" us how they communicated with dad, by having him tap out the alphabet with his foot. Dad had movement in his right hand and thumb and tried to sit up. Regaining strength slowly, but surely. We listened to some of the Steelers football game and Ronnie Milsap CD.

### Journal entry;

9/22/04

Sam Hilliard came to see Jim with Doug McDonald. Jim looks a lot better than the last time I saw him. He's moving his head, shoulders and feet. I guess it will just take time. I pray for Jim often and always will. God Bless, Sam.

## Journal entry;

9/24/04

Jeff arrived around 7:30 PM woke dad up. He has a roommate again. She likes the TV loud. She better wear a sweater cause Dad likes his A/C! He was hot so I adjusted his air conditioner. He also wanted his arms propped up. He is looking good!

## Journal entry;

9-26

Dale and Gail arrived around 1:13. Jim looks great. Dale gave Jim the updates of camp. Be glad when the fellows can give him a Big Camp Party. With God's Grace you get stronger each day, Jim.

9/26 Robin arrived around 2:00. Lots of company today and this weekend. Looking good. Seems comfortable. Lifting head, jiggling arms, coughing for respiratory when they are suctioning and spelling out several words to communicate. We see the progress. He needs to be encouraged that he is making the progress. He is really leaning on God to help him get through this.

## Journal entry;

9/27

Larry and Tina arrived around 8:30pm. Jim's eyes were covered with patches so we couldn't see the eyes. He seed fairly responsive but didn't move his body much. Jim really seems to be responsive to the conversation and definitely knows what's going on and what's said. He even corrected me on a couple of things. I was glad that you weren't sleeping since we were late getting here. You seemed to be comfortable and relaxed, looking even better. We're glad to see that you continue to make progress. We keep praying for you to make a quick recovery which I think will be soon seeing how far you've come along these past few weeks. Keep up the good work and we'll hope to see you next weekend.

### Journal entry;

10/4/04

Tina and Larry arrived around 745pm. Jim was sleeping when we arrived. His color in his face looked really good. (Just like he had been out in the sun) We know God continues to be with you and that you continue to work at getting better. Well you were resting comfortably and sleeping very soundly as our talking and even the feeding beeper going off didn't wake you. We waited and waited but you were sleeping soundly so I guess you missed out on a lot of news and catching up. Well maybe we'll catch you awake and talking this weekend. We love you and miss you, and continue to pray for you!

### Update

October 13, 2004

It seems a lot has happened since the last e-mail update I sent out. Things seem to be moving along smoothly now with signs of improvements each time we visit.

For a couple of weeks in August, dad seemed to be uncomfortable and having difficulties breathing, but we couldn't figure out what his problem was. On August 30, I received a phone call that dad was being taken to UPMC Lee Hospital in Johnstown. Dad was having difficulty breathing. It turns out he had a mucous plug blocking his trach. The plug was at a place where it was difficult to suction from his mouth and from the trach. The only way to get to the plug was by taking him to the emergency room. He was in the emergency room from around 11:00 pm till 5 am. He was then sent to a room and then sent back to Ebensburg in the afternoon. He almost went back to the hospital again that Friday for the same problem. After the second incident, respiratory began giving him humidified oxygen and suctioning more often. These changes in dad's treatment seem to have made a big difference with his breathing and there haven't been anymore difficulties with the mucous plug. Another thing that may be helping with this is that dad is now able to cough while staff is suctioning to help loosen anything in his trach. You can't hear him coughing, because of the lack of air in the vocal chords, but you can see his chest move as he tries to cough. This helps loosen the mucous and respiratory is able to suction it out easier.

Physically, we've seen some changes in his movement. We haven't seen much change in his legs, but we are seeing much improvement in his upper body and arms. He is now able to shake/jiggle both of his arms. He is now able to move his right thumb and we are able to feel him squeeze your hand with his right hand (Praise the Lord!). And, when you walk into his room or talk with him, you can see him leaning forward from his head/neck as though he's trying to get out of bed. Believe me, if he could, there would be no holding him back! When you ask him, he doesn't always feel that he's getting better, but we absolutely see the changes.

One of the best miracles we've seen is in our communication with dad. Speech therapy has been working with him so he can begin to talk while on the ventilator. On August 29, Jeff & I went to visit dad. Respiratory left air out of the cuff and into his vocal chords. Dad said "Happy

Birthday" to Jeff. This was the first time Jeff heard dad speak. Another way we have learned to communicate with dad is with words. Staff has worked with dad so he can communicate words by tapping out the alphabet with his foot. It gets very frustrating trying to understand dad's head nodding and guessing all the time what he needs beyond the obvious things. When this happens, we will spell out words by saying the alphabet and he moves his foot when you get to the correct letter. Thank goodness he's a good speller! The first time I saw this demonstrated was with one of the Respiratory therapists. She was finished suctioning him and was getting ready to leave. He indicated that there was something he needed but we couldn't figure out what it was. He spelled out the word "Show" as a way to demonstrate this method of communicating. That same day he spelled out "Savior" to me and the word "hunter" for Garrett (Garrett will be turning 12 in December and be able to go hunting this year). Dad still nods and "talks" (even though we can't read lips), but when we just can't figure out what he's trying to say, we resort to the foot and alphabet method to spell a word.

Visits with dad have gotten much easier than when he was first hospitalized. I don't cry as much as before. I still do my best to visit with him every week. It's a lot easier now that he's in Ebensburg. He is also getting "new visitors" who haven't seen him since he was hospitalized. Actually, for many people, it is very difficult seeing dad in the condition that he is in and difficult for dad, too. However, he is really coming along (it will be 8 months already on Saturday-10/16) and he is happy to receive visitors. If transportation is a problem, please feel free to contact me and we can ride together. Right now, I typically visit with him on Sunday after church, but I go at other times, too, depending on my schedule.

Just a reminder that his address is as follows:

Laurel Crest Manor

429 Manor Drive

Ebensburg, Pa 15931

He is in Room 115B.

I am so excited thinking about the day when dad is well and able to come home again. This will be a wonderful day of celebration thinking of all the family and friends who will be waiting to celebrate with him. We know there will be so much to talk about from this journey we've all been on as a result of his illness. My aunt asked my dad if he ever asks God "Why me?" and he shook his head no. We are all getting through this because of God. There is a purpose in it and we will all be better because of it. His favorite music CD to listen to is Pat Boone's Gospel Hymns. I put this on for him every time I visit and I get ready to go home. One of the nurse's said that she tried to put another music CD on for him to listen to and he only wanted Pat Boone!!! He also enjoys when we read from the Bible, read devotions from the Upper Room and Guideposts, and pray. One day at a time he continues to get stronger and regain use of his body. Thank you God!

Robin

## Journal entry;

10/17/04

Nancy arrived about 10:30 AM. We played the spelling game until he spelled that he wanted to talk so the nurses 'took the air our'. He said he doesn't like the computer – he would much rather 'talk' to people and loves having visitors. He asked me to do him a favor. He asked me to put a note up that if he is sleeping when you get here, please wake him. I told him he needs the rest. But he said he would rather visit with his family than rest. He said he includes 'us' in his prayers. Imagine that – he's praying for us!! Amazing the progress he is making! Was really good to see you and to be able to communicate with you! WE love you very much and pray for your continued recovery. Left about 1PM. (very cold, blustery day! The air conditioner froze up and he asked the nurse to turn the fan his way.) Nurse says they get lots of snow here!

10-17-04 Robin, Garrett, Dale and Gail arrived around 1:45. The nurses said Jim would like to talk to us today. God Bless him. He could speak to us. He had a taste of apple butter the nurses okayed it. He sure enjoyed it. Just a dab on his lips. Later they suctioned it out. But he still could taste it. Jim looks so good today. What a wonderful surprise he is praying for us. He is in our prayers everyday. God Bless, take time to get well we can all wait for you.

Jim got to do his absentee ballot. Voted, yes. Very important to him. Robin sure gives her dad a lot of loving care. Jim received a foot massage. He sure smiles at that.

## Journal entry;

10/20/04  Jim looking great. No patches and able to talk! Got Jim new stereo, but there was no plugs so maintenance will hook it up for him! We plugged it in for a little while so we could listen to the tape of the service from Grace Baptist in Tyrone. Pastor Roy. Jim really enjoyed it and Kelly's niece sang a song on it he really liked it. So I will bring him more at his request! The Lord is working miracles! We also read the Bible verses! It was a great visit! We love you Jim!

## Journal entry;

10/24/04

Jeff, Larry and Tina arrived around 12:30pm. Jim was looking good. It was great to see the patches off his eyes and he was able to talk to us. What a blessing and how far he has come. It was so nice to actually visit and converse with Jim. I was anxious to get up here and hear Jim talking. He was off the vent for about 45 mins. Before he needed it back. The nurse said that he is getting stronger everyday. It's great to see him making progress. Jim gave us advice on how to vote and said that he had done so already.

## Update

October 24, 2004

Just a quick update, but the news was too great to wait!

On Sunday, October 17th, my aunt Gail, Uncle Dale, my son Garrett, and I went to visit dad. It was one of the best visits we had in a long time. It is such a thrill to see the improvements each time we see him.

Dad's eyes are blinking again, and therefore, he no longer needs to wear patches on his eyes during the day! He is still given eye drops regularly and wears the eye patches at night, but after 8 months he is able to see us even though I'm told he is legally blind. At some point he should be able to be given cornea implants. He continues to be monitored by an eye doctor.

The other exciting news is him being able to talk to us! Speech and respiratory have been working with him to allow air into his vocal chords so he can speak. He is tolerating this more and more. I visited with dad again on 10/23 and we carried on conversation for at least 45 minutes. Now it's expected that staff will deflate the air in the cuff in dad's trach any time anyone visits with him. This is great! We are always telling dad that everyone is praying for him, well my aunt and uncle were surprised to hear dad reply that he prays for all of us, too. And, his prayers are being answered!

Also, while we were visiting with dad on this day, we were talking with him about making apple butter the day before. Every year, dad, my uncle Dale and other friends make apple butter at their friend, Chuck's place. Dad's presence was sorely missed and unfortunately, Uncle Dale had to receive all the "ribbing" this year, instead of dad. Anyway, as a surprise, we took some apple butter along when we visited dad. He has been on a feeding tube since he was first hospitalized. Until he regains his swallow reflex (speech therapy evaluates his progress with this), he is unable to eat anything. He has not lost the ability to taste which we noticed. Sometimes nursing staff and respiratory wipe out his mouth with flavored sponges- ie. lemon and mint. Well, we gave him a taste of the apple butter, and he licked his lips and rolled his eyes and head! It was heaven to him!!!

A special prayer request right now would be for dad's legs and a bed sore. Dad's legs seem to be stiffening up. He needs to get up out of bed and into a wheel chair so his legs can get into a different position. Also, dad continues to be battling a bed sore. I'm told it is decreasing in size, but it makes lying uncomfortable.

Wednesday, November 3rd will be the next team meeting on dad. I will be attending and meeting with the various therapy departments. I am excited for this meeting, knowing how much progress dad has made and looking forward to the months ahead. I'll keep everyone posted.

Robin

## Journal entry;

10/26/11

Jim was very talkative. It is great to hold a conversation with him. We listened to the church service tape from Grace Baptist, Tyrone and I read from the daily bread. We brought him Alan Jackson's greatest hits he asked for it the last time we were here. He told me the Red Sox were going to sweep if they won game three!

## Journal entry;

10/31/04 – Halloween!

Sue and Nancy arrived about 9:30 am. Jim right away wanted a nurse so he could talk . There wasn't anyone at the desk, but we got the nurse about 20 minutes later. He talked to us for about 1 hour and 20 minutes before he said his mouth was dry. He stayed off for a while longer while Sue read to him. He hasn't lost his sense of humor – and he asked us lots of questions about family and things close to home. He is amazing, how much he's improved. It makes you feel good to be able to visit with Jim now that we can communicate with him!

## Journal entry;

11/13/04

A midweek visit. Today was dad's IDR (Interdisciplinary Review) mtg. Great progress since August. Vision-eyes look great –blinking, can see, just not sure how much? To be evaluated at some pt. Speech-improving. Cuff deflated for over 2 hours! Will try giving him pudding within a week to see what he can swallow. PT/OT to reevaluate so he can get into a wheelchair. Muscle tone is good. Concern is in the joins – tightened due to calcification? Lifting arms off the bed from the elbows. OT worked with him while I was here. Kicking legs. Working hard and proud of him. Shared election results. Dad mentioned Doug and Sam's visit last evening. Red Sox won World Series.

## Journal entry;

11/24

Sonny Bitner and his son and sister Isabel visited for an 11/2 hr. Sonny was visiting home from Colorado, an old friend! Robin arrived later and spent the evening talking about birthday's and Christmas. Happy Thanksgiving, Dad! Love Ya.

## Journal entry;

11/25/04

Barb and Brent arrived around 9am. Happy Turkey day Jim! Brought Jim turkey banner from work (Cannon) he liked it!

So we hung it on the bathroom door. Jim gave me a workout as I worked his arms and legs! We read the books and had good conversation. Jim seems a little more stuffy today needed sucked out a few extra times. We left around 2:30pm.

11/25

Larry and Tina arrived around 5:30pm. Jim was awake and had a big smile on his face when he saw us. Jim was talking up a storm. He wanted to hear all the news. You wished us Happy Thanksgiving first thing, hated to talk about the big meal we just had in front of you. We'll take you out for a big meal as soon as you're able. You are talking much better which is good as I feel bad when I have to ask you to repeat yourself. Caught up on news, sports, weather and other topics. Great to see you again, see you next week. Lots of Love and prayers.

## Journal entry;

11/26

   Dale and Gail, Ray and Martha Conner visited Jim. Snow on the mountain. Jim's room looks great for Christmas. Nice tree in the corner of room. Arrived 3:17. Jim and Dale catching up on hunting bear stories. Jim sure can tell us what's going on now. What he ate, everything about Ronnie in the hospital. Jim was concerned. We told him he has to get well. Dale and Jim catching up on butchering at Chuck Grubbs. Jim sure enjoyed the stories from Grubbs. Wonderful to hear Jim get excited over the stories. You are in our hearts and prayers. We all love you Jim.

## Journal entry;

11/29/04

   Sue and Nancy came about 6:30pm. To tell Jim about Ronnie's passing away. He wished Ron had been good until he could get out of here to see him. Jim seemed to take it well; but I'm sure he'll think about Ronnie a lot later.

## Journal entry;

12/10/04

   Max and Randy were here and we spent some time with Uncle Jim and helped with some therapy. Jim's making very good progress. With the therapy he has a twitch in his fingers but cannot move more than just his middle finger a little but therapy will take time for the other hand. Max and I spoke of hunting and weather, Christmas and of family.

## Journal entry;

12/12

Larry and Tina arrived around 415pm. Jim's color was very good. Was still full of things to say. Had us fill him in on all the news on the home front. You filled us in on news we didn't know about. Said today was bad day with phlegm buildup, and a little uncomfortable with that at times. Told us about seeing the specialist on the 20th. Seemed anxious to see what he has to say. Tina brought some fudge and other goodies for the staff and a card for them from Jim. She also brought along a new logbook for when this is full. Jim said to put it in the drawer. We stayed till you started getting tired. We love you and miss you a lot and are continuing to pray for you.

## Journal entry;

12/19

Dad had a Dr. visit with the neurologist on Mon. 12/20, so Maxine and I came out Sunday evening to visit and spend the night since his appt. was @8:00 am.

## Journal entry;

12/20

Arrived bright and early (6:45) to follow dad to the neurologist apt in Johnstown @ 8:00am. This was the 3rd attempt to schedule this apt. So, we weren't going to miss it for anything. Of course, today was the coldest and windiest day we've had so far this winter! At least we didn't have to contend with falling snow. Dr. McGeehan met w/ dad. He seems positive about the healing progression. His recommendation is that he receive physical, occupational, speech and respiratory therapy everyday. He will follow up with dad in 4 months. It was nice seeing dad in a t-shirt and shorts! Real clothes. Of course, he really had to be bundled up in blankets for his trip to the doctor's apt. I was able to visit dad for a couple of hours after apt. Lots to talk about. Will see him on Christmas Day!

(Santa) Dale and Gail arrived with a bag of presents, poinsettia, Christmas tree, stockings and holder, nativity scene. Talked about hunting season.

## Journal entry;

12/23/04

Jessie and Ashley brought real Christmas tree. Patty helped carry in presents Jim ordered for everyone. He seemed satisfied with them.

## Journal entry;

Dec 25th (Christmas Day)

Barb and Brent were here to see dad. Brent brought a video he made from work. Dad really enjoyed it. He burned a CD for dad. Jeff and Kady brought presents for Dad. Kady performed a violin concert for Pappy. He was very impressed! He looks good!

12/25 Larry and Tina arrived around 430pm. Jim looked good and seemed to be talking better. He had some company today and had lots of goodies. We brought a few gifts for Jim. Jim was glad to have visitors today.

12/25 Robin and Garrett arrived around 6:30. Dad said Christmas for him was better here in the nursing home than at home! 4 Christmas trees, 2 nativity scenes, a stocking, lots of Cd's, stuffed animals, flowers, and electric razor, etc.! Correction – It is not that Christmas is better in here, it's just that he got more gifts! Merry Christmas Dad, we love you!

## Journal entry;

12/29

Sue came about 1:45. Jim was very talkative. He showed me all his presents and told me how very thankful he is for everyone coming to visit. The therapists were here and worked his arms and legs. He told me about Katie's concert for him.

## Update

January 13, 2005

Happy New Year! I apologize for not writing an e-mail update before this. I hope you understand that with the holidays things were busy. Many times I felt I should write an update, however, I just could not bring myself to write one. I have been prompted recently by several people, including dad (!), and it is indeed time to write. Since the last e-mail the end of October, the 2 biggest miracles we had seen over recent months, was having dad able to see us and talk with us again. It was hard on us, but we can only imagine how difficult it was for him. It was almost 8 ½ months that dad was unable to see us or talk with us. Once he began blinking again, the patches were able to be removed from his eyes. Images are blurry, but he can see us. Having dad be able to speak to us has been such a blessing! Speech and respiratory had been working with dad since August to allow air into his vocal chords so he can speak. I visited with dad in October and we carried on conversation for at least 45 minutes and now he can speak to us for hours. This is wonderful Dad had an appointment with a neurologist on the coldest day in December! We had tried several times to schedule this appointment and finally on December 20th it finally happened. The appointment was in Johnstown and dad was taken by ambulance. For the first time in 9months he actually was wearing shorts and a t-shirt- no hospital gown! Of course, he was bundled from head to toe in blankets and only his face peeped through! The neurologist was optimistic about dad's progress. His main recommendation was that he must receive physical and occupational therapy daily. The progress is slow, but his healing takes place millimeters a day. He has regained movement in both arms and he is now beginning to move the tips of his fingers. He continues to progress in the positive direction with minimal complications at this time. The doctor is in the process of gaining visitation privileges to Laurel Crest and he'll be able to monitor dad's progress monthly. Dad's next IDR- Interdisciplinary Review meeting will be held on January 26. At this meeting dietary, social service, speech therapy, physical therapy, occupational therapy, recreational therapy, and respiratory therapy are represented to discuss and review dad's plan of care. This meeting is held every 3 months. Christmas was very special this year. Dad said he received more visitors and gifts than he ever would have received had he been at home. Of course, the gifts weren't what was important, but the visits from family and friends are. We all know how precious time is with each other in times like this. Though dad was confined to his bed, his mind is still clear, and now that he can communicate with us- watch out! Actually, it was very important for him not to forget his family and friends this Christmas and be able to contribute however he could. Many thanks to our family and friends who helped dad be apart of the holiday even from his bed. Together everyone made sure that Christmas cards were sent out from him; his room was decorated; holiday music CD's were played; gifts were bought for us-his children, grandchildren and even his roommate; and the Laurel Crest staff were recognized for all they've done.

Our hope for this New Year is that dad comes home! We anticipate his home coming and we can't wait! We know this experience has touched so many people's lives and we can't wait to celebrate this journey and his healing. My prayer request right now is for dad to regain his strength and be able to sit up and use his arms, hands, fingers, and legs again. Dad's joints have stiffened up and I pray that with continued therapy he will regain movement again. He is still on the ventilator, too, of course, but the neurologist feels that he will indeed be able to be weaned once he regains his upper body strength. We can never thank all of you enough for all the love, support, gifts, and words of encouragement we have received over this past year. We are so grateful and know that God has watched over each and every one of us during this time. Dad's spirits especially are very good considering the circumstances and it is through his faith that he is sustained through this experience. Thank you so much! God Bless you and your family in this New Year!

Robin

**Journal entry;**

1/16/05

Missed dad, so made a trip out to visit even though it was snowy. Not too bad, just had to be careful. Enjoyed visiting with dad. Took down the Christmas cards and the rest of the decorations. Complaining of his hip hurting.

## Journal entry;

1/20/05

Randy and I got here about 3:00. Roads were fairly good and mostly bare. They were feeding him through his tube every so often and not constantly! He said they weren't doing therapy again because they couldn't see any improvement but he is moving his arms, etc. Had a good visit and left about 7:30. Caught up on his guideposts.

## Journal entry;

1/21

Arrived about 10am. Jim says his eyes are 'fuzzy' today but he looks good. Good to see him – I haven't been out for a few weeks. He showed me how he can move legs and arms. Improvement every time I see him.

1-21-05

Dale and Dean arrived around 4:45. Went and visited with Russell before we got here. Jim looks good his color was real good. Had to wait for the nurse, so Jim could talk we can't read lips.

## Journal entry;

1/26

Came out for Dad's IDR – Inter disciplinary review mtg. Feeding tube every 4 hrs. instead of continuous. PT continued, esp. to work with hips. Neurologist on staff beginning in April and will monitor dad monthly. Speech therapy exercises to strengthen tongue and swallowing – experimenting with pudding as tolerated. Spoke with a nurse re: concerns. Also, will try to get dad a new chair so he can interact with others and participate in activities. We talked and I read Guideposts.

## Journal entry;

1/28/05

Jeff came up to see Dad. Therapist worked him over real good. Dad was in a lot of pain. But he knows he has to do it to get better. He looks good. He said he was thinking about a Brody's hamburger.

1/28/05 – Just missed Jeff and Jim told me too about the hamburger bit at Brody's! Brought in Jessica's pictures on the front of the L.H. Express! Jim said they are not doing therapy but his fingers and arms are more flexible and he can move his arms if you lift them up. Bill, the respiratory therapist nurse hurts his throat when he changes the tube part. Apparently he is pretty rough! Read him his Guideposts.

## Journal entry;

1/29/05

Sam H. and Doug McDonald stopped to see Jim. He seems to be doing well. Stayed and talked for about 1 ½ hr. Be back soon. Sam H.

His sisters came up soon after we got there, they gave me (Doug) a hard time of course. I had a good time seeing Jim. Doug.

1/29 Sue and Nancy came to see Jim an Sam and Doug were here. Jim said to ask Doug if he got lost in Philipsburg. We had a good laugh! We brought him the Punxsy groundhog! Looked terrific and very good to see him.

1/29/05 Ron and Maxine came and Sue and Nancy left. Ron was trying different ways and different antennas. Maintenance was bringing up a ladder to help. Eyes were bothering him especially the left one. Found 'Focus on the

Family' 97.3. If you just press FM and tuning will go to the next program at station.

## Journal entry;

1/30

Larry and I arrived around 330pm. Jim was listening to music when we arrived. He looks good but he said his eyes are bothering him. The nurse did come in and gave him some supper and put eye drops in his eyes. Tina and I helped with some exercise moving his arm. He said he has more mobility in the right arm. Tina playednurse and massaged his feet, put lotion on them and on his lips and changed his pillows. Had a nice visit!

## Journal entry;

2/6

Robin, Garrett and Ryan made it out to see dad. It's a beautiful sunshiny day. Dad sang Happy Birthday to me! Such a miracle knowing a few months earlier he couldn't talk. I see dad has ha a lot of visitors lately!

## Journal entry;

2/8/05

Jim called me his scratching machine. He had a bath today and they didn't rinse him enough so he's itching all over! He says he has feeling in both hands and he is getting more movement all over.

## Journal entry;

2/13/04

Sue and Nancy arrived 10:15. Jim looks good and wants to know all the news from home. We told him not much is going on – so he told us all the news he had – both good news and bad. He has good spirits!

Jim is going to church at 2:00. He wanted a note written so everyone would know where he is. He says he has been up in his chair several times. Looks very good and is in very good spirits

2/13 Dale and Gail came to see Jim around 4:09pm. Larry and Tina visiting Jim. Jim was joking around and laughing. Jim you look great. I told Jim, "I'm trying to make him a quilt." I know, Jim is never cold. I told him if he can struggle back with all he has been through, I surely can make my 1st quilt ever. It is a struggle for me. But to give him the gift would be an honor. With God's grace Jim is getting better and His guidance for me to make a special gift for a special friend of our family. God bless you Jim, we are all praying for you. We love you, Jim.

### Journal entry;

2/19/05

We surprised dad with a late night visit. Garrett and I brought Steve and Leslie! They were so excited to see dad and vice versa. Dad was getting worried because we arrived later than planned, but we stopped at Red Lobster for supper. We had to make this visit and were concerned about the potential for snow expected tomorrow. Everyone talked up a storm. Dad looked good. He said he was up and out of his bed and room 4 times this week. He talked about getting out and attending church service last Sunday. He really enjoyed the pastor and the sermon on "love." Health issues – X-ray because of some trouble with his lung.; but everything is ok. He also mentioned his ventilator support -breaths per minute has been cut from 12 to 10. Great!

## Journal entry;

2/26/05

Barb, Brent, Anastasia came to see Jim. He looks good. Got a haircut, was very talkative, swapped some jokes and caught him up on current events @ Cannon and back home in the State College area!

## Journal entry;

2/27/05

Beulah and Harold came to see Jim. He was so glad to see them. Had a nice chat. Sue and Chuck were here also and visited with Jim. Looked good and seemed like he's coming along extremely well. Jim is going to church at 2:00. If anyone comes later, please go up or wait for him.

2/27

Maxine and Randy were here with Jim. Maxine went up to church with Jim.

Larry and Tina arrived at 2pm. Went to church with Jim. Jim looks good. It was good to see him sitting up. He was very talkative. He was cracking jokes.

Jeff and Jennifer were here to see Jim also.

## Journal entry;

3/6/05

Robin and Garrett came out for a visit. Sunny, but windy outside. Dad's color looks great along with his haircut. Some difficulty with his breathing lately, so his cuff is kept inflated unless he has visitors. Also complaining of dizziness and a headache, so he's been given medicine. We looked at and read his cards. We also talked about the happenings going on.

## Journal entry;

3 9 05

Max and Randy came to see you Jim, while the weather was good enough to come. Jim had rehab when we came and it had been hard because the night before Jim had not slept well and had a bad headache but was feeling somewhat better today. Best wishes from Max and Randy.

## Journal entry;

3/13

Nancy and Sue came up since it wasn't snowing. Partly sunny. Jim looked good.

Jim seems tired today! He's going to church at 2pm. Jim had good color, but seemed tired and talked slowly.

3/13/05

Robin visited and was able to go to church with dad. Did some pampering nails and massaged feet. Brought a thank you card to Craig and his family – they gave dad his old tv and paid for 6 months of cable! I'm told the 1ˢᵗ channel dad wanted to watch was ESPN.

## Journal entry;

3/14/05

Larry and Tina arrived around 7pm. Jim was sitting in the dark but seemed glad to see us. He had to have his tube fixed so he could talk to us. We filled him in on our trip to camp this past weekend. We left around 9:30 pm.

## Update

Jim McKinley- Update #13 March 16, 2005

How quickly time passes by. Here we are 2 months since the last update and a full year and a month since dad first

217

entered the hospital on February 16, 2004. Never would we or could we have imagined that something could happen to dad that would completely change his life and ours. Never would we or could we have imagined that we would be taken on such a journey where we would have seen and experienced so many things.

What a year- 7 hospital stays, Life flight, at least 8 ambulance rides; many miles, doctors, nurses, specialists, etc.; insurance, financial, and legal dealings. Looking back now, it's hard to believe how we stayed sane with all the scares, stresses, responsibilities, etc. but we did, no doubt thanks to God. Things are calmer now, but not without unexpected things cropping up from time to time. And, we experience totally different feelings now as we consider the continued road ahead for dad. He continues to improve at a slow and steady pace, however, fears/doubts are setting in thinking about how far he still needs to go. The whole time we try to remain positive, being grateful for how far he has come.

He's continues to be completely bed ridden and dependent for all his care at this point. However, the staff is now getting dad into a reclining chair and sitting him out in the hallway near the nurse's station on occasion. He's even gone to the church service on Sunday afternoons a couple of times. I went with him this past Sunday. That's got to be motivation to keep working to get stronger and come home. Speech therapy continues to work with him to strengthen his movements for speech and swallowing reflexes. He is receiving bites of food several times a week, a couple of bites at a time. Recently, he's been given mashed potatoes and gravy. I'm sure it tastes so good to have a little bit of food. He remains on the feeding tube, though he no longer receives continuous feedings. He gets feedings on a normal dietary schedule- morning, noon, afternoon snack, and evening.

The biggest change we've seen recently is with his respiratory. The ventilator settings have been adjusted to 10 beats per minute instead of 12, meaning his diaphragm muscles must be getting stronger- 2 beats closer to weaning. Recently the trach cuff has been kept inflated, not allowing oxygen into his vocal chords, except when he has company. Apparently, It bothers him by drying out his throat and making it difficult to talk. He has mentioned several times recently that he's had difficulty breathing at night. There doesn't appear to be any reason for this. There hasn't been trouble with pneumonia anymore or anything else that I'm aware of at this time. I'm not sure if maybe he gets into an uncomfortable position and it puts pressure on his lungs or something. The staff seems to think it is anxiety. He's had scares and they feel he gets anxious thinking something may happen. He insists angels have been watching over him and helped him with the breathing when he's had trouble.

The eye doctor has been in to see him recently. Dad says he is seeing fairly well out of his right eye, but not left. Sometime in the future, we anticipate him having cornea transplant surgery to remedy this, since the loss of vision was due to illness and eye treatment. Fears seem to be affecting dad at the moment- not being able to breath; thinking he won't be getting out this year; and he feels he's losing ground and less movement in legs. He was kicking his legs while in the chair during the church service on Sunday. I think reclining in the chair should help him be able to kick and strengthen his legs more so than lying flat in his bed. He does have a long way to go to be able to sit in an upright position, but I think this is primarily due to lying flat for so long, and therefore, his joints have tightened, making it very difficult to bend. He complains of pain in his hip the most and thinking maybe something is wrong there. He did mention that physical therapy is checking into x-rays.

His next appointment with the neurologist is April 20. The doctor is in the process of gaining visitation privileges to Laurel Crest and he'll be able to monitor dad's progress monthly. I think this will be a plus in monitoring dad's progress. His next IDR (Individual Department Review) team meeting is also scheduled for April 20. We all work to keep his spirits up and positive, to hang in there and have hope. His faith and prayers have done much to sustain him during his illness. However, as you can see, there are healing concerns physically and emotionally (fears) at this time. I ask for continued prayer on behalf of dad. Thank you so much and God Bless!

Robin

## Journal entry;

3/17/05

Happy St. Pats Day! Barb and Brent visited with Jim. Brought Jim a big clock. Talked about what's been going on.

## Journal entry;

3/18/05

Jim had mashed potatoes, ham and Mac and cheese – said everything tasted good. Brought his stand to put pictures, flowers, etc. on. Left about 7:40.

## Journal entry;

3/19/05

Jeff and Kady and Jennifer and Jessica stopped in to see Dad. He looks good. Kady putting on a concert for him with her violin. Really happy to see Kady making progress with her violin. He was very talkative.

## Journal entry;

3/22/2005

Paul, Douggie and Sam came for a visit. Jim had us cracking up with his jokes. Jim and donna wanted to know where Sharon is!? She stayed in Texas with the warm weather! Jim really looks good. It's been a month since last visit and he has good improvement. Hope to see him home soon. Sam H.

I told Jim to keep getting better so he can get to camp and fry some potatoes. Douglas

## Journal entry;

3-25-05

Dale Benner, Dean Neale and Jim Wilson came to see Jim. He looked really good and talked a lot. Told him everyone back home missed him and was praying for him. Gail Wilson sent her best wishes and hopes Jim can come visit us soon.

Jim said he likes dress down day because of jeans on the nurses. He looked good and moved his arm when you helped him.

3/25/05 Lots of visitors today and in the last week. Robin and Garrett just missed everyone by about 20-30 min. I guess we spent too much time in Wal-Mart. Glad to see dad. He looks good and was very talkative. He was showing us how much he could move his arms around if we lifted them up. Impressive. Just needs strength to lift them on his own. He said he had chicken nuggets and asparagus today. We read through the many cards he received. Thanks to Maxine for the stand, it's perfect. Also, thanks to Maxine, Nancy and family and Jen for all the flowers. And thanks to Mrs Wilson for the candy. Thanks to Dean and Connie for the book, "In the heart of Hope." Thanks to Barb and Brent for the clock. Garrett and I left around 7:00 so Garrett could watch his March Madness! Before we left, dad read the book, "In the Heart of Hope" to us. The first book he read in over a year! Way to go dad! Things are looking up! Love you much! Robin and Garrett. Happy Easter!

### Journal entry;

3/26/05

Well it was a very busy day for Jim. He got a ride in the ambulance again. He had to have one of his tubes taken out, it had gotten infected.

We arrived around 2pm and Jim got back to Laurel Crest around 2:30pm. He said he had a bad headache and he felt upset in the stomach. They gave him some Tylenol for his headache. He was running a little fever also. He wanted his air turned on full so he wasn't able to talk, but we wanted him to rest anyway. He looks very tired! I hung an Easter Bunny on the door that I had people from Cannon sign for Jim. Jim was feeling better when we left his temperature was down. He needs to get some rest so we left around 5pm.

## Journal entry;

3/27/05

Happy Easter! Jeff and Jennifer and Jessica arrived around 11:00. Dad was trying to sleep but not having much success! He really isn't feeling good today. Hot and tired and a slight headache. He was sneezing. Must be Jennifer doing it to him. Really having trouble with his swallowing. He needs rest. We brought him some exercising equipment when he is ready to start working out.

3/27/05 Larry and Tina arrived around 3:30. Happy Easter. We shared news and updates with Jim. He seemed content to listen to stories. Sorry to hear you were not able to attend church today. Next week...hopefully.

## Journal entry;

3/30/05

Sue came up today. Was anxious to see Jim. He was tired and had a little trouble swallowing. We moved his arm up and down and around. Shared news of the day and all the recent happenings. Take Care Jim – we love you very much! Sue.

## Journal entry;

2 Apr 05 George came by. Jim is a lot better than I imagined. I really miss him and hope/pray that his recovery speeds up. It would be nice for him to be able to go out and enjoy life. May the Good Lord look after him. I love ya brother... George.

4/2/05 Pastor Duane Bardo and Terry, Fillmore Church's new pastor and his wife. May God continue His Blessings on you Jim! What a wonderful witness you are! We are looking forward to the day you come back to Fillmore! God Bless!

4-2-05 OH Jim I'm so glad to see your improvement since August! God is good. We love you and pray and await the day when you will give your witness of God's grace to Fillmore. Love, Dora and Jack

4/2/05 Jeff and Jennifer and Kady and Hannah arrived to a full house. It was nice to meet some of the many friends Dad knows. He looks a lot better than he did last weekend. He is very talkative.

4-2-05 Judy, Rhonda, Ashley were here. Jim talked the whole time, didn't stop. Sure was glad to see him. I think he looks great. He was happy to see us.

4/2/05 Uncle Jim, I hope you get better soon, Ashley.

## Journal entry;

4/7/05

Surprised dad with a visit during the week. The neurologist was in to see him today. He was quite impressed with your improvement in strength since the last time he saw dad in December. He was pleased to hear dad speak also. De. McGheehan now has privileges here at Laurel Crest and will come out monthly to see patients. He will evaluate dad every 3-4 months. Had a lot of catching up to do. He looked great – he was just cleaned up. May have a dermatologist look at dad because of break outs on his back. Is now getting Cortisone shots in his hip as needed. I was here when physical therapy came in. Had a great visit!

## Journal entry;

4/8/05

Brent, Barb, Anastasia came to see Jim. He was doing well! We didn't stay long, Mom's knee was hurting from her surgery!

## Journal entry;

4/10/05 – Sue and Nancy here today. Jim is anxious to get up for church. Looks good! He likes to catch up on what's going on at home.

(Continued) Caught Jim up on the news and heard his. Was good to see him and give him a big hug! Sue

4/10/05 Larry and Tine arrived around 315pm. Jim was not here but was up at church. We went up to church and they took him outside for about 5 minutes. Jim thought it was hot out. He looks good, color is good and he's talking much better than our last visit. Jim told us he had hotdogs and baked beans to eat on Saturday. He is supposed to get a tray tonight for dinner. Jim had a cheeseburger, mashed potato, pudding, and something we couldn't tell what it was.

## Journal entry;

4/13/05

Met dad @ UPMC hospital in Johnstown around 3am. He had another mucous plug earlier and went into distress. He was taken to the hospital to be checked out. We got back to Laurel Crest around 5:30 am. We rested off and on. He had physical therapy and nurses aides cleaned him up while I was here. We then talked a while. I left around 10:30 because he needs his rest. Was complaining of upset stomach, too. He had thrown up a couple of times. He was given medicine to settle his stomach and help him rest. Take care and see you soon.

# JOURNAL #1 ENDS

## Update

July 7, 2005

I bet you are waiting news of how dad is doing? I apologize for taking so long. It seems as time passes, I'm finding I'm getting busier and able to get back to my own life- that I don't need to devote as much time being on call for dad and his affairs. I am able to relax and trust God in his healing process as dad is healing in his own time. I think he's made a lot of progress in the last couple of months.

Within the last few months, dad is able to eat pureed food. Dad has been getting 2 meal trays a day. I'm told he needs to eat 75% of each meal before can be taken off the feeding tube. He's at 30- 50%. My understanding is that within the last couple of weeks he is now getting 3 meals per day- he is now getting a breakfast tray. For breakfast, he says he is getting oatmeal and egg beaters, oatmeal and egg beaters, and oatmeal and egg beaters! For lunch and dinner he is getting an amazing variety of foods- some good, some not so good. He has eaten mashed potatoes/ gravy, chicken nuggets/asparagus, ham salad, macaroni & cheese, etc. I'm sure he is enjoying the variety of flavors very much. We will feed dad his meals anytime someone is visiting at the time his tray is served. What he doesn't eat, he likes to offer to us- I think this is so he can tell the staff he ate more than he really did!!! We have even brought in some outside favorites for him. My aunt, Maxine, brought in one of his favorites, Clem's Ribs, for him to eat one evening. Fortunately, the dining staff, was helpful and pureed it so he could enjoy it. He was quite appreciative. Now we need to work on getting him a taste of Red Lobster! He's also asking for sausage gravy from a restaurant in Snow Shoe.

We've seen some great improvements physically, especially in his upper arms. Physical therapy continues to work with his legs. He also sits up in a geri (?) chair and is able to sit in more of an upright position where he can move his legs and feet. If we lift his arms, he can move them from side to side and wriggle them. As of 5/14, he was lifting his arms from his shoulders. He is also beginning to move his fingers and thumb and is starting to be able to turn his wrists. He has very little fine motor skills at this point and unfortunately, occupational therapy only works with him on an on-again off-again basis according to the gains he makes. Fortunately, my brother Jeff's girlfriend, Jennifer, has worked with physical therapy and when she visits she helps him with exercises. She has also brought "tools/equipment" to "exercise" with when any of his family/friends visit. In addition, he does his own exercises when therapy isn't working with him and we aren't visiting.

Since March he has been in and out of the hospital a couple of times. On March 26, he was taken to the hospital to have the port in his chest removed. The port was placed in his chest last June when he was having difficulty with pneumonia. He was running temp because the port had became infected. On April 7, he was taken back to the hospital because he had another mucous plug and again was having difficulty breathing. He has been to the dermatologist twice because of a skin rash (eczema) on his back. He is still having problems with his hips from time to time and sometimes needs to take pain medicine for this. He has an eye doctor appt scheduled for July 21. He will be fitted for glasses at that time. He has regained some vision, but the cornea scarring has affected his vision and things are blurry.

Socially, dad is making the rounds and getting out of his room on occasion. He is going to church in the dining hall on Sunday afternoons. The service is at 2:00 in the dining hall if anyway would like to join him sometime. We also had a surprise birthday party for him this year with since basically he missed it and couldn't enjoy it last year. He knew we were up to something for his birthday, but he was totally surprised to have a birthday party which we held in the dining room. Many immediate family members and friends attended. He was able to have some birthday cake mixed with milk.

A special thank you goes to my Aunt Gail. She presented dad with her very first homemade quilt in honor of dad. The quilt represented dad's life and illness. It was beautiful. It was quilted in the barn raising pattern since dad grew up on a farm in his younger days. There was blue/gold for Bald Eagle Area where he grew up and went to high school. There was a pattern with fall colors and leaves to represent when she began making the quilt. Many colors and patterns represented his illness and the healing from God during this time. Unfortunately, I do not have pictures at this time. If I get some, I will attach in an e-mail. She is considering entering the quilt at the Centre County Grange Fair this year with dad's blessing. For Father's Day, dad was given a DVD/VCR player. I was thinking this would be a great way for anyone who may have home videos that they could bring along when they visit to share with dad the happenings going on in our lives. My son Garrett plays sports and I thought maybe I could videotape some of his games for dad. He is missing out on a lot in our lives. This is one way to keep him included. And, once he gets his eye glasses in the next couple of weeks, he'll be able to see the tv screen a whole lot better. I want to thank dad's roommate and family for giving dad his tv and paying for cable service for several months. Dad really seems to be enjoying being able to watching sports. Dad really looks out for his roommate and they've developed a special bond between them. Dad is talking and making friends with staff. He commented to me one day that he "thinks they (the staff) really like him". He is learning about them and their lives. There is a reason for everything- this time in his life (touching so many lives)! Dad has such a sense of humor.

Laurel Crest sponsored a Sr. Prom in May. The hallways and dining room were decorated with a Disney theme. It was incredible the effort that went into decorating. Unfortunately, dad was unable to attend and the reason he gives for not attending was that he had "no date". I get more excited about his progress and recovery as time goes by even though dad is verbalizing that he probably won't be home this year, either. He's come along way, but he's got a long way to go. However, we continue to be encouraged by his continued process.

Thanks to everyone who send cards faithfully, visit and inquire about his progress. Dad has a wonderful network of family and friends and we are forever grateful for everything everyone has done for all of us during this time. Take care and God Bless!

Robin

# Update #15

September 7, 2005

I had to let everyone know that I received some good news today. After weeks/months of dad asking about being weaned off the ventilator and being told that the weaning process would be the last thing in his healing process, the pulmonologist and attending physician at Laurel Crest have agreed to have dad go through some weaning trials to see if he is ready to begin weaning. I told dad at my last visit that it seemed that things were at a stand still, so this was unexpected and welcome news. The weaning trials will most likely occur at the Select Specialty Hospital in Johnstown. The case manager is in the process of trying to make arrangements and will let me know as soon as they have been made. We have no idea how long this will take. He could be at Select Specialty for a couple of days and it be determined that he's not ready. Or, he could be there for several weeks/months until he is weaned. The weaning occurs in stages. We just have to wait and see at this point. Please, please keep dad in your prayers at this time. This is a big step, one of which we hope can get him closer to home. I will keep everyone informed as I hear more.

If anyone attended the Grange Fair, I hope you had the opportunity to go into the Grange buildings. My aunt Gail entered the quilt she made for dad. The quilt won a first place premium ribbon! He was very pleased and honored that she made the quilt for him and he encouraged her to enter it at the fair for everyone to see. There was a picture of dad and a write up attached to the quilt describing the colors and patterns and how they represented dad, his life, his illness, and his healing. Included here is the rough draft of the write up for the fair. Attached are pictures of dad and the quilt from his birthday party in June. I hope you can see the pictures.

I know dad has been in many of your thoughts and prayers over this past year and a half. We are all so appreciative of this. He still has a long road ahead of him and we hope you continue to lift him in prayer. Thanks so much and God Bless!

Robin

## Update #16

September 14, 2005

Dad was transferred to Select Specialty at Conemaugh Hospital in Johnstown, PA today. When I called this evening around 9:00, he was all settled in, had his medication, and his doctor had already written up his orders. They said he arrived near 5:30 pm which was only a couple hours after they called me and told me that they had gotten the ok from his insurance company to be transferred. They sure move quickly once you cut through the red tape.

He will be evaluated in the next couple of days by respiratory, physical, occupational, and speech therapies. With his insurance, his progress will be monitored on a week to week basis. We should know within the next week, whether the weaning will be possible at this time. Laurel Crest will hold his bed for up to 15 days until they know for sure how he's handling the weaning trials.

The address is as follows:

Select Specialty
1086 Franklin St
Johnstown, PA 15905
He is in Room # ...
Please keep him in prayers. Thank you.

Robin

# Update #17

October 9, 2005

Dad has now been at Select Specialty at Memorial Hospital in Johnstown since September 14th (3 ½ weeks already). In this amount of time, we are very pleased with the progress he has been making. During the first week, the doctor cut back the ventilator's settings from 10 respirations per minute to 8 per minute, and now he is at 4 respirations per minute. (This is the number of respirations that the respirator makes per minute, the rest of the time dad takes his breaths on his own). He was at 12 respirations per minute when he was first hospitalized last year and he had been at 10 respirations per minute most of the time while he was at Laurel Crest. Within the second week, the doctor began taking dad off the ventilator and putting an aspiration mask with oxygen over the trach tube. This began with 5 minutes, 4 times a day. Then each day that he is successful, the time gets increased. It went from 5 min, to 10 min, to 15 min, etc. As of Saturday, he was off the ventilator 1 ½ hours, 4 times a day for 6 hours during the day and breaks in between for him to rest. Dad breathes on his own without the help of the ventilator during this time. The oxygen is to keep the air humidified so it is easier for him to breathe. Dad says he feels a whole lot better without the ventilator. This week he'll work up to 2 hours, 4 times a day and keep working till he is off the ventilator all day, and eventually all night. When he can do this, then he'll be able to come closer to home. I am really hoping that he'll be closer to home by Christmas. I believe it is possible, since things are going so well to this point.

He is having a few complications since he entered Select. When he first arrived, he was having chest pains. He was given EKG and EKG Doppler(?) tests the first couple of days he was there. Everything turned out ok, though they still have him on a Nitro patch for his heart. He was having headaches from the patch, but this seems to have lessened. He remains on the Nitro patch at this time, because the doctor feels it will help keep his heart regular so as not to add any additional strain due to the weaning. (something like that?). If the doctor feels it's necessary, we are fine with it, especially since the headaches have subsided.

The other complication is with his meals. He still receives three meal trays a day, but he is barely eating 10-20% at a time. He was placed back on the feeding tube supplemental feedings throughout the day. A lot of the problem seems to be the texture of the pureed food. He is to receive honey thick pureed food, but it is no where near the texture he was receiving at Laurel Crest. I've spoken with the nurses several times and the case manager, and he was supposed to be seen by speech and dietary in regards to this. So far, there has been no noticeable change. I hope this can be straightened out soon so he can get back to eating more and get off the feeding tube.

Just as a reminder, the address is as follows:

Select Specialty
1086 Franklin St
Johnstown, PA 15905

He is now in Room # 446. Dad changed rooms within the first week he was at Johnstown. He is in the last room on right after you go past the nurse's station.

Directions to go visit are:
219 S to Johnstown from Ebensburg ~ 14.4 miles - Merge onto PA 56 West ~ 4 ½ mile - Take Bedford exit

toward PA 271/PA 403 ~ .3 mile - Turn slight right ~ .1 mile - Turn left on PA 271 ~ .2 mile Hayes St - Turn left on PA 403- Napoleon St- Go .9 mile - Stay straight to Franklin St ~.2 mile Last hospital building on right. Parking garage $2. Parking lots- availability depends on day/time of week. Cards and visits are most appreciated by dad!!

Like I said earlier, I'm praying for dad to get back to Centre County by Christmas. The case manager is making contacts with some local facilities at this time. If anyone has any recommended long-term care placements we could consider please let us know. She mentioned Centre Crest and Brookline. I really don't want Centre Crest. We are definitely looking at Health South at this time; however, since they are a rehab facility, I'm not sure he is physically ready for the demands of the rehab. It would be great, but I don't know. We would consider Mifflin County, Philipsburg, and Lock Haven areas, in addition to State College (our preference).

I'm so glad to be able to share good news of his progress. One day at a time, he is getting closer to coming home. Please pray for guidance in finding the best facility for him and continued prayer and thankfulness for his continued healing. Thank you.

God Bless!
Robin

## Update #19

November 2, 2005

Dad will be back in Centre County tomorrow (Thurs 11/3)!!! Praise the Lord!!! We are just so thrilled at this news! It was looking as though he was going to be transferred to a facility in Altoona (which of course is closer than where he's been), but I received the news today that he was accepted at Health South in Pleasant Gap. He will be leaving Johnstown in the morning and should be at Health South around 10:30. My brother's girlfriend will be checking in on him around 12:30/1:00 and Jeff and I will be stopping in to see him right after we get home from work. He will of course be evaluated over the next 2 days and will most likely begin his therapies on Monday. He will have to be able to tolerate the therapies for a minimum of 3 hours a day and I was told that he will probably receive up to 5 hours. If this proves to be too much he would have to go long-term care again. However, at this time, all the facilities locally either have waiting lists or do not accept trach patients. I'm glad they are going to give rehab a try at this point. I'm sure it will be a challenge for him, but I hope he will be able to make some real improvement in regaining his mobility. He will receive physical, occupational and speech therapies and I don't know what else at this time. Dad is completely off of the ventilator (as of Wed, 10/26), but he still has his trach and receives oxygen. This will be monitored and hopefully the trach will be able to be removed at some point. A smaller trach has been inserted since he came off of the ventilator. And hopefully, dietary can get the consistency of his food straightened out so the feeding tube can be cut back. He was placed back on the continuous feedings with the feeding tube because he had been eating very little from his meal trays. For some reason, Select Specialty had difficulty pureeing his food to a consistency that he could swallow.

I just spoke with Select Specialty and they said dad is apprehensive. He's been apprehensive every time he's gone to a new facility- new staff, new routines. He's been at 6 facilities to date. You'd think he'd be used to it! Just kidding. The staff at Select Specialty in Johnstown has been especially great and friendly, even though he has been there for only a short time. A rehab facility will be quite different from every place he's been to so far. He has a lot of work ahead of him. But again, just like these last 20 months, he has had lots of support and prayers to see him through each step in this process.

We are just amazed. I remember at the beginning of September saying to dad that it seemed that nothing was happening. I would not have imagined that he would be back in the area in 2 months time! It happened quickly and expectantly. It has been 20 months already. It will be a relief not traveling the time and distance to visit dad. Now it will be much easier to stop in and see him practically whenever we want along with his many family and friends. Visiting hours are encouraged after 3:00 during the weekday and of course all day and evening on the weekends. The address is:

Health South
Nittany Valley Rehabilitation Hospital
550 W College Ave
Pleasant Gap, PA 16823

I do not know his room number at this time.

I can't wait for work to be over tomorrow so Garrett & I can go see him! God has been so good at seeing him through all of this and answering everyone's prayers of healing and bringing him closer to home!

Robin

## Update #20

12/11/05

Dad has been back in Centre County for 6 weeks already!!! Praise the Lord!!! We are so happy having him back in the area and so are a lot of his other family and friends! He is doing so well, too. He has made so much progress in the last 4 months it's incredible. It is such a relief not traveling the time and distance to visit dad. It is so nice stopping in to see him practically whenever we want along with his many family and friends. All of the cards and visits are much appreciated. He has seen some faces he hasn't seen since he first got ill. This is great!

He has made a lot of progress while at Health South. We are so grateful for his care and the progress he has made there which has allowed him to remain in rehab longer than most typical rehab stays. The staff working with him has been wonderful. His case manager, Linda Gray, has said that dad is "their best patient". Nursing staff and the physical therapists "fight over him" because they all want to work with him. We are impressed with Health South also, because they have been very proactive- they are always looking ahead and anticipating his needs and if something doesn't work, they keep trying something else till they find something that will. Linda has been wonderful in updating insurance weekly with the gains he has been making and has indicated that the insurance company has been impressed with the gains he's been making also.

His progress thus far includes:

Respiratory- Dad is completely off of the ventilator (as of Wed, 10/26) and he is no longer receiving oxygen. He still has his trach and a smaller trach had been inserted since he came off of the ventilator. Dad has improved in

237

being able to cough and he is being suctioned less often. This will be monitored and hopefully the trach will be able to be removed at some point.

Speech- The therapist has worked with dad on oral-facial (tongue, jaw and oral) movements. He has a soft voice. They feel some of this is due to the fact that he can't open his mouth very wide. He can open to 1-2 fingers and the goal would be to be able to open his jaw to 3-4 finger width. There was concern about the joints in his jaw and he was to have a dentist to evaluate this. He does have swallowing control and the therapist has worked to upgrade the consistency of his food. Speech works closely with dietary. He has made improvement in what he's been able to eat. He still receives supplements from the feeding tube at night, but it has been discontinued during the day since he has been eating more from his meal tray. He really likes the food at Health South. He is given a variety of food and he can choose what he'd like to eat each day. He still eats between 10-20 % of his meal, but it is an improvement over what he was able to eat at Select Specialty. He still receives a meal tray of pureed food, but the consistency has changed from honey-thick to nectar-thick. He is now able to tolerate thin liquids and is able to "drink" milk from a spoon and eat ice cream again!

Physical and occupational therapy have done a lot in working with him. They have worked him hard and he has made great gains from 20-30 degree movements to 40-70 degrees in range of movement in his arms, elbows, shoulders, hands and legs. He is now able to lift his arms by himself, not always gracefully, but he can do it. He has been on a tilt table at 62 degrees adding muscle stretch and weight in his legs. They have also been having him assessed for wheelchair accessibility. They are still looking into this, but his hips are making this difficult for him.

This has all been a challenge for him, but he is making some real improvement in regaining his strength and mobility. However, there are limitations that are preventing him from making more independent gains, primarily his hips and vision. His left hip has much scarring, calcium deposits, and arthritis. His eyes, we mentioned earlier, have cornea scarring and he is now legally blind. Dr. Allatt has been very proactive and has been consulting with orthopedics and ophthalmologists. He has been seen by Penn State Orthopedics/PSU Family Medicine and he has an appointment with the Eye Care Center in Hershey on December 30th to determine if he'd be a candidate for corneal implants. He, also, has a lot of pain in his tailbone at this time. It's been bothering him since he left Johnstown. This makes him very uncomfortable lying in bed and sitting up in therapy. Please continue to pray for these health issues.

Dad is scheduled to be discharged on Monday, 12/19 from Health South. He will still have the follow-up appointments with the orthopedic and eye doctors so it would be wonderful if he can remain nearby. Linda Gray has been making contacts with many facilities in preparation for when he is discharged. She has contacted many facilities in Centre, Clinton, Mifflin, Union, and Clearfield counties. Many will not take him because he still has a trach or else they have no beds available. At this point, a facility in Clearfield would take him in a heartbeat. We **really** don't want him to go to Clearfield. None of us seem to have a good feeling about this. The attending physician at Health South has been in consult with dad's family doctor about getting him to Centre Crest so he has access to doctors for his follow up appointments. We weren't real interested in Centre Crest either, but it turns out they won't take him because they feel they can't adequately provide for his needs. Today, we made some phone calls to several other facilities. One is Hearthside in State College. It used to be University Nursing Home and we were told that it wasn't a good facility. However, it is now under new management and starting Monday, Jen (Jeff's girlfriend) will be drawing blood there Monday through Friday, so we would have a connection to keeping an eye on things. Steve and Leslie could walk there to visit dad when they'd like. Of course, it would also allow for family and friends to continue visiting as often as they have at Health South. We also made a phone call to Brookline in Mifflintown. I called a former co-worker who used to work there and she had very good things to say about their therapy and activities. They don't have a bed available, but they will by Monday. They did inform me that they are considering several applications at this time. So, there is hope to keeping dad relatively in the area. Please pray that God will open the door for the right facility for dad at this time.

In other news, you may have heard that dad and Barb's house is up for sale. Yes, this is true. Due to unfortunate circumstances, they could no longer maintain the house until dad was well enough to come home. The house is being sold through Prudential if any one knows anyone who may be interested in buying it.

I will e-mail when I know for sure where he is going next. At least he can get settled in before Christmas. Hopefully, he will be nearby. It is essential that he be accessible for his follow-up appointments. Having family and friends visiting regularly also helps to maintain dad's spirits and hope.

Yes, we have had much to be thankful for this year. He has had lots of support and prayers to see him through each step in this process. God has been so good at seeing him through all of this and answering everyone's prayers of healing and bringing him closer to home! May we continue to have faith and trust God with dad's continued care and healing.

Merry Christmas to you and your family. May you have a blessed holiday!

Robin

## Update # 21

December 23, 2005

Dad was transferred to Mountain Laurel in Clearfield today. We really didn't want to see him leave the county, especially at this time of the year, but insurance dictates that his time was up and time to go to a different level of care. I made many phone calls to try and have him placed elsewhere closer to home- either facilities wouldn't take him because of the continued trach care or they had no male beds available. We got spoiled with him being in Centre County.

Health South worked really hard with him and insurance to keep him there as long as possible and they were successful. He was there longer than most people stay in rehab. We are very pleased with the work they have done with him and he is at a really good place for continued therapy. They were very proactive at assessing his needs and working with him. I believe they were a very important part of preparing him for the next steps in his recovery.

In meeting with several people in physical and occupational therapy yesterday I believe they will pick

241

up where Health South left off and continue working with him with his range of motion and strength. I believe we will continue to see great strides in improvement. These past 4 months have been proof of that. However, I don't believe he'll be in Clearfield for a long period of time. I believe he will be in and out of several facilities this year as the doctor's proceed with taking care of some of his other medical needs- vision and hips- and as he continues to heal and regain strength and mobility.

Thursday, before leaving Health South, the therapists had another wheelchair assessment done with dad. They and Dick's Homecare brought in a wheelchair rep from Tennessee to fit dad with a wheelchair to meet his needs- tilt, standing, maneuvering. They found one. Dad drove it through the hallways of Health South. Everyone, including dad was impressed with how well he did. The Dick's rep was impressed with the improvement in dad since his last wheelchair assessment a few weeks ago. Now we await the process to go through insurance approval and ordering which they anticipate to take 4-6 weeks. I do hope all goes well with this. This wheelchair is a huge factor in dad's step toward independence.

Please pray for dad's trip on Friday, Dec 30th to the Eye Care Clinic in Hershey. He has a long trip in a med-van transport and he does so by being on a litter. His tail bone is very bothersome and this will be difficult for him. Though we'd like to put this off a little longer, we feel we do need to make this trip at this time if we want to get his eyes corrected to where he can have good vision again. We feel to postpone this trip, we may lose the window of opportunity to have it taken care of- things are in motion thanks to Health South and their doctors. They will perform very extensive tests to determine whether he is a candidate for cornea implants.

**His address at this time is:**
**MOUNTAIN LAUREL NSG & REHAB CTR**
700 LEONARD STREET
CLEARFIELD PA 16830
He is in room 122 if you want to write or visit him.

Really, it is not very difficult nor that far to get to Mountain Laurel. It is a couple of miles off of I-80. The easiest is to take I-80 to the Clearfield exit and take a left at the stop sign. Follow the road to Rt 322 and turn left toward Philipsburg. Go to Leonard St (not far from the mall and immediately past the PA DOT building). Turn left on Leonard St. Go straight, then turn toward the right. Mt Laurel is the building on the right. Go in the front door, sign in as a visitor, turn right and go to the nurse's station, then turn left. He is in the first room on the left and in the bed next to the window. Visiting hours are 24 hours per day.

Thank you for all the cards and visits. Dad is so appreciative of all the love and support shown to him during his recovery and so are we.

Merry Christmas to each and every one of you and your families. Have a wonderful, peace-filled holiday. God bless each and every one of you.

Robin M. Zubler

*"There are only two ways of spreading light - to be the candle or the mirror that reflects it."*

Edith Wharton

# Update # 22

**February 20, 2006**

   Dad is still in Mountain Laurel in Clearfield, but they just moved him to another room/floor. He now has a private room and it is room 224 on the second floor. To get to his room, you need to walk straight in through the main entrance door, walk straight and into the dining room. Take the elevators on the left to the second floor and when you get off the elevator turn right and go the end of the hall (next to the last room on the right). We are glad to see he is still getting visitors even though he is not in Centre County at this time. He really appreciates the cards and visits to keep his spirits up. To get to Mountain Laurel it is a couple of miles off of I-80. The easiest is to take I-80 to the Clearfield exit and take a left at the stop sign. Follow the road to Rt 322 and turn left toward Philipsburg. Go to Leonard St (not far from the mall and immediately past the PA DOT building). Turn left on Leonard St. Go straight, then turn toward the right. Mt Laurel is the building on the right. Visiting hours are 24 hours per day. His address at this time is:

   MOUNTAIN LAUREL NSG & REHAB CTR
   700 LEONARD STREET
   CLEARFIELD PA 16830

   We really didn't want to see him leave the county, but there weren't any facilities in Centre/Mifflin/Clinton Counties that would take him because of the continued trach care or they had no male beds available. We got spoiled with him being in Centre County. We are in the process of trying to get him back to Centre County and into Hearthside in State College. This used to be the University

Nursing Home, but it is now under new management and the chain-owned company is in the process of renovating. My brother's girlfriend, Jennifer, works there and she has been speaking to many of the staff there about dad. I've also visited and met some of the staff also. We are still waiting for the staff to receive trach care training and then they will consider taking dad. I really want to see him back to Centre County. The other advantages of Hearth Side is that their attending physician is also on staff and has connections at Health South. This would be great for follow-up and continued care that he received while he was there.

As for dad's health, it is still such a slow process and unfortunately he has some aggravating health issues that hinder his progress; One of his hips, which will require some surgery at some point, and his tailbone. His tailbone has been bothering him since he left Laurel Crest. These two problem areas make things difficult for dad to sit up for extended periods of time and cause difficulty in therapy. Dad does his best to push through the pain though, especially when therapy is working with him. We are pleased with the therapy department at Mt. Laurel. They have been working with dad to sit up at the edge of the bed and to stand up (with support of course!). Occupational therapy works with his upper body and he continues to make small gains in his range of motion.

We are still waiting to find out if insurance will pay for a wheelchair for dad. Health South and Dick's Homecare brought in a wheelchair rep from Tennessee to fit dad with a wheelchair to meet his needs- tilt, standing, maneuvering. This wheelchair is a huge factor in dad's step toward independence. I do hope all goes well with this.

Dad made a trip on Friday, Dec 30th to the Eye Care Clinic in Hershey. He had a long trip in a med-van and he handled it fairly well. Dr. Rossen-Wasser performed extensive tests to determine whether he is a candidate for cornea implants. According to the doctor, dad needs three procedures: a cornea transplant, cataract removal, and a lens replacement. The doctor will start with dad's left eye, since his right eye is his better eye. I have several appointments scheduled at this time- dad needs to go for follow up testing and measurements and then the plans are for dad to have surgery at Holy Spirit in Camp Hill (both are currently scheduled for the middle and end of April)- however there are some logistics to be worked out first. There are also several follow up appointments over the next year which fortunately will be able to occur out of the State College office. He is going to have to receive very good eye care at whichever nursing facility he is at.

I will let you know if/when we are able to have him moved back to Centre County and any updates to the pending eye surgery. Please continue to keep him and his health in your prayers. I just read an article in the Lewistown Sentinel about a gentleman who developed Guillain-Barre two days before Christmas and has since recovered (thank God for him). However, it was very frustrating to read this article when I see my dad still struggling to regain all that he had lost due to this illness. Yes, he is a long way from where he was 2 years ago, even a few months ago when he was still on the ventilator, but I just want to see a miracle and see him make faster gains! (I'm sure he does, too!).

Thank you for your continued prayers and support. We greatly appreciate it.

God Bless!
Robin M. Zubler

# Update #23

Dad remains at Mt. Laurel in Clearfield at this time. We have tried unsuccessfully to get him back into Centre County since he still has a trach. However, there is some work in progress to make this happen, though, it won't be an easy road for dad.

When dad was at Health South, he had an initial consult with Dr. Shebondy, of Penn State Orthopedics. Dr. Allatt stated that without some type of surgery being done on dad's hip, he won't progress in therapy. Dad, however, was not ready for surgery at that time, but he definitely is now. Earlier this year, dad was having a lot of difficulty and pain with his hip. Fortunately, we were able to determine the medication he was receiving at Health South (an anti-inflammatory) and this has helped tremendously in alleviating a lot of his pain. In the meantime, we have been in touch with Dr. Shebondy whose office is coordinating appointments to enable dad to have medical clearance for hip surgery.

There are several appointments that have to occur before dad has clearance for surgery. Good or bad (travel-wise), the appointments get him out of Mt. Laurel for a little while and he gets the added benefit of some fresh air and sunshine. He just made a trip to Health South yesterday to meet with Dr. Ratner, a pulmonologist. Apparently, he had quite a "reception" while he was there. Actually, if he gets the ok for hip surgery, he will be going back to Health South for a little while. We are thrilled at this prospect. And, he will not be going back to Mt. Laurel. Hopefully, other options will open up for him once he leaves Health South and he will stay in Centre County. Anyway, before

Dr. Ratner gives clearance for surgery, he wants several tests done first. Fortunately, these tests will be done on Monday, May 8th at Clearfield Hospital. We would have had to wait until July if these were done at Mt. Nittany Medical Center. He will be having a chest x-ray, a stress test, and some blood work done. After Dr. Ratner has this info, he will be able to give his "go ahead" for surgery, though he will need to have some other "breathing/trach care" things done before surgery. He did say this can be done at Mt. Nittany the day before surgery. Then, he needs to be given a medical (heart) clearance from the doctor at Mt. Laurel. Once Dr. Shebondy has these two clearances, then he will see dad again and make a determination of what level of surgery will be required- partial (removing extra bone from his hip) or more extensive (hip replacement- though this probably won't happen at this time). Dad will also have to meet with anesthesiology and then he'll be good for surgery. This will occur at Mt. Nittany. How soon, I'm not sure, one appointment and step at a time. There are risks involved, of course, but I believe in God's timing with all of this, and am optimistic that all will go well.

Please keep dad in your prayers- though I know you already do. Thanks so much. I'll keep you posted when we have a date for surgery.

Robin

## Update #24

**July 11, 2006**

July 25th, dad will be having surgery on his hip at Mt. Nittany Medical Centre. Dr. Sherbondy, from Penn State Orthopedics, will be performing the surgery. He will be removing extra bone that has grown on his left hip making movement difficult and painful. Dr. Allatt at Health South stated that without some type of surgery being done on dad's hip, he won't progress in therapy. If all goes well, Dr. Sherbondy will consider surgery on his other hip at some point if this particular surgery proves to be beneficial to dad's overall health and movement.

This is what we've been working towards the last several months. He has made several trips to Centre County for pre-surgery appointments since April. He has had blood work, x-rays, etc., and he met with anesthesiology and a pulmonologist to ensure he would be able to handle surgery.

Dad will be admitted to Mt. Nittany on Monday, July 24th. Dr. Ratner, the pulmonologist from Health South will be changing his trach in preparation for surgery. Then his surgery, will be on Tuesday. We do not have a time yet, and won't know until the 23rd or the 24th. He will remain at Mt. Nittany several days. While he is there, he will be receiving a dose of radiation to hopefully stop the bone from growing back. He will then be transferred to Health South again (yeah!). How long he'll be there, we don't know, however, while he is there he will be receiving physical therapy and probably will have another wheelchair assessment. Also, Dr. Ratner will be looking into removing the trach and the feeding tube altogether (another yeah!). These are huge steps in dad's progress. Then he'll only need to focus on mobility and strength, hopefully.

Dad will not be going back to Mt. Laurel. It has been a very frustrating 6 months. If all goes well at Health South with the trach and feeding tube removal, there should be no reason why dad won't be able to stay in Centre County once and for all.

There are risks involved, of course, but I am optimistic that all will go well. That's where faith in God comes in. We would not have been able to make it through all of this without faith, though, that's for sure. Please keep dad in your prayers. All of the prayers on his behalf mean so much. We are forever grateful. Thank you.

On another note, this is a special request from me. My computer got fried during one of our recent thunder storms and I had to replace my computer. We were able to recover some of my files, but not the updates that I have written throughout dad's illness and progress. I am pleading for help from anyone who may have saved these updates. I promise to back these files up this time if I am able to recover them. I have received copies of updates #21, 22, and 23, thanks to two of my cousins (thank you very, very much!). If anyone has any of the previous updates, I will be eternally grateful. I was hoping to put them together into a "book" for dad.

And, I forgot- one more request. Dad is eligible for Medicare beginning August 1. Unfortunately, he will be losing his COBRA insurance benefits at that time. We will need to enroll dad in a medi-gap/prescription drug policy. If anyone has any recommendations for us to consider, please let me know.

Anyway, I'll let you know how things turn out and where dad goes from here. I am anxiously waiting.

Take care and God Bless!

Robin

# Update #25

**August 5, 2006**

I have lots of great news to share since the last update before dad's surgery and his "return" to Centre County!

On Monday, July 24th, dad was admitted to Mt. Nittany Medical Center . Dr. Ratner, the pulmonologist from Health South changed his trach in preparation for surgery. The rest of the day dad just hung out and had visitors. On Tuesday, July 25th, dad had surgery on his hip. Dr. Sherbondy, from Penn State Orthopedics, performed the surgery. He removed extra bone that had grown on his left hip making movement difficult and painful. Dr. Sherbondy indicated that all went very well and dad actually had increased movement in his left hip from about 20% prior to surgery to ~60-70% following surgery. A couple days following surgery, dad received a dose of radiation to help prevent the bone from growing back. Dad remained at Mt. Nittany longer than expected, due to loss of blood and fluctuating blood pressure, but this worked out for dad's benefit (the best news yet!) because while he was still in the hospital Dr. Ratner removed dad's feeding tube on Monday, July 31 and his trach on Tuesday, August 1st!!! These are huge steps in dad's progress. Now, hopefully, he'll only need to focus on gaining strength and mobility.

He finally left the hospital yesterday, Friday August 4th and went to Health South. How long he'll be there, we don't know. I'll know more once Dr. Allatt has met with him and the therapists have done assessments so they can come up with a treatment plan. He most likely will be receiving respiratory, physical, occupational, and speech therapy and he will probably have another wheelchair assessment.

Now with the trach and feeding tube removed, there should be no reason why dad won't be able to stay in Centre County once and for all. We are looking at trying to get dad into Centre Crest. When we were considering Hearthside, it was because we were desperate to try and keep dad in Centre County, but they never got their trach training and therefore dad never made it there, probably for good reason.

In the last update I mentioned that I was requesting copies of previous e-mail updates because I had to replace my previous computer due to storm damage. Thanks to some of my cousins and dad's friend (thanks Monica, Kathy, Chris, and Ilene!), I was able to recover all but updates #6, 9, 10, and 11. I am most appreciative!! If anyone has any of these other updates, I will be eternally grateful.

Anyway, things really are looking up for dad right now. We are most grateful to God for all this progress in dad's recovery. We continue to look forward to great things happening for dad and we are especially grateful that dad is back in Centre County!

Dad's address at Health South is:
    Health South Nittany Valley Rehabilitation Hospital
    550 West College Ave
    Pleasant Gap, PA 16823
Dad is in room 328 in the West Wing.

Take care and God Bless!<br>Robin

# Update #26

September 11, 2006

Just wanted to let everyone know the latest on dad since he "returned" to Centre County! As of Wednesday, Sept. 6, he left Health South and is now in Centre Crest in Bellefonte. This is where he will most likely stay until he is ready for assisted living or able to come home (we hope!) This has been a long time coming for him to remain in Centre County to stay. It has been 2 1/2 years! He has come so far and we are so proud of him and thankful to God!

Before leaving Health South, a representative from Dick's Homecare and the physical therapy department completed another wheelchair assessment. We are now waiting to see what will happen with financing. They were looking at a motorized, tilt/lift wheelchair. I hope things go well with this because this wheelchair would provide dad with a lot more mobility and independence.

I want to send a special thanks to everyone for their assistance in helping me to recover all of the e-mail updates that have been sent out these last 2 1/2 years since dad has been in. And, yes, I have backed them up on a CD. I was able to recover all of the updates! These updates tell quite a story of the progress of an extraordinary man who refuses to give up! Of course, we refuse to give up on him, also. I am eternally grateful to those who "saved" these e-mail updates!

A special event occurred on Sunday, August 27th when dad attended the McKinley family reunion. This was the first time he had seen many of his family, especially nieces and nephews since before he got ill. Many pictures were taken to capture the "happy" reunion. See attached. We look forward to many more opportunities where dad can get out and socialize with many of his family and friends at more special events like this.

Anyway, things really are looking up for dad right now. We are most grateful to God for all this progress in dad's recovery. We continue to look forward to great things happening for dad and we are especially grateful that dad is back in Centre County!

Dad's address is:

Centre Crest
Bellefonte, PA 16823

Dad is in room 242.

Take care and God Bless!

Robin

*"There are only two ways of spreading light - to be the candle or the mirror that reflects it."*

- Edith Wharton

## Update #27

**October 24, 2006**

Well, dad has now been at Centre Crest in Bellefonte for almost 2 months since he arrived after leaving Health South on Wednesday, Sept. 6. He has adjusted very well and the staff has adjusted to him just as well.

Dad's address is:

Centre Crest
Bellefonte, PA 16823

Dad is on Keystone Hall in room 242. He is, however, on a waiting list for a larger room, but he'll remain on the same floor and hall.

Physical therapy has been working with dad since he went to Centre Crest. They worked with him in his room until recently when a wheelchair became available and he can now have therapy downstairs in the therapy department. They have him sitting up at the edge of the bed and doing range of motion exercises. He is also using some weights to help build his strength. We've noticed that he is gaining some additional mobility in his hands and now able to bend his wrists more.

I found out that Dick's Homecare has received the paperwork from Health South for the wheelchair. This information has since been passed on to Centre Crest's therapy department. They are to apply for a grant to purchase a a motorized, tilt and space wheelchair. This will greatly improve his independence. All staff will have to do is get him into the wheelchair and then he'll be able to get out of his room to "wander and explore."

Future medical needs- Dad continues to have follow up appointments with several doctors. He has met with Dr. Sherbondy for follow-up from the surgery on his hip. He's also had follow-up appointments with Dr. Ratner, the pulmonologist at Health South, who had dad's trach removed. Dr. Ratner has made a referral to Dr. Engreft, a head/neck surgeon for a consult to have dad's trach closed shut. This appointment is scheduled for Monday, October 30th. This is a good thing to help reduce dad's risk of infection. In the spring, we hope to explore the possibility of the cornea transplant on dad's eyes. This had been put on hold since dad had the surgery on his hip.

Another special event occurred on Saturday, October 21st when dad was told we were taking him out to dinner. Instead , he was "surprised" with a "Welcome Home to Centre County" celebration/benefit in his honor at the Milesburg Legion. It was a great evening with so many family and friends welcoming dad home and to celebrate his road to recovery and amazing journey. We look forward to many more opportunities where dad can socialize with his family and friends.

If you know of anyone that is on this e-mail list, but who is not receiving the updates, please have them check their junk mailbox. The updates may be coming in as Spam due to so many names and addresses on the distribution list.

Take care and God Bless! Praise be to God!!
Robin M. Zubler

*"There are only two ways of spreading light - to be the candle or the mirror that reflects it."*
- Edith Wharton

## Update #28

August 20, 2007

I am so sorry it has taken so long to send an update on dad. I can't believe I haven't sent an update since before Christmas. Since dad has been back in Centre County at Centre Crest, things seem to have settled down for him and our family has been able to pick up with our own lives more. It is so much more comforting knowing he is nearby and so many more family and friends can check in on him. And, if he does need anything (such as coke, cheese and candy bars!) we are right nearby.

Things have gone very well at Centre Crest. Things have gone so much better at Centre Crest than they have at any other facility. The staff that work with him really have been great. Dad has had "angels" at each place he's been at, but as a whole, things have just gone so much better here.

Right before Christmas dad had surgery to close the trach opening and all went well. It is so nice not having a reminder of his trach anymore and no longer the risk of infection either. Now he can continue to work on improving his physical mobility. He does receive occupational therapy and he continues to make gains in his physical strength and ability. Little by little we are able to see him do things with his fingers and hands that he wasn't able to do before. He told Garrett (my son) the other day to give him six months and he's expecting to be able to feed himself again. Therapy has worked very well and very hard with dad ever since he's been at Centre Crest.

Besides his physical needs, we are still working with doctors to help dad regain his sight. We were expecting him to have eye surgery in May, but the eye doctor wanted him to see two other eye doctors/specialists first. He is now scheduled to have his eye surgery (cornea transplant) this Wednesday, August 22nd. It will take place at Holy Spirit Hospital in Camp Hill. He will have a post-op appointment the next day in Hershey, and then several follow up appointments over the next few months/year. Please keep him in your prayers. This is a complicated procedure and dad is a high-risk patient for infection and rejection. However, this is what dad wants. He figures his eyes can't get much worse than what they already are. Dad has had many obstacles to overcome these last 3 1/2 years due to the Guillian-Barre. Though it has been a long road to recovery, he has amazed many people throughout this process. It's not easy, but God is good. Patience, perseverance, faith and hope has seen all of us through this and most certainly will continue to do so. We believe in many more miracles to come.

It is so nice having him back in Centre County. We are even able to take him to some family outings now. The holidays were great in comparison to the last couple of years. We took him to Christmas Eve service at Fillmore Church and we brought him to my new home on New Year's Day to watch the Penn State football game. He was able to go to his niece Monica's wedding in June. He even made it to the Camp Picnic on August 4th. We were planning for him to be able to go to our family reunion this Sunday, also, but unfortunately due to his eye surgery this week, he will probably have to miss it. He was able to attend last year, though. It is wonderful being able to include him in these things.

As for activities, dad usually has therapy Monday through Friday and he gets up for church on Sunday afternoons. He listens to tapes, some of which the nursing staff have brought in for him. On TV, he's usually keeping up with the sports. He's a Steelers & Pirates fan ( though he doesn't have much faith in the Pirates these days because every time the watches them, they lose!). The rest of the time as he lies in his bed, he spends a lot of time in prayer. He prays many prayers for his family and friends. He also makes sure we or the recreation staff help him send cards to those who are having birthdays or to those who are sick and/or having difficulties in their lives. These things are dad's way of keeping in touch, giving back and caring for his friends and family. He's even written two letters to the editor of the Centre Daily Times on behalf of the physical therapy department and the nursing staff at Centre Crest. And most importantly, he enjoys visits from family and friends very much. There is no doubt that God has a plan and a purpose for dad and he is using him while he is in the nursing home. He has touched so many lives through all of this. He will have a story to tell/book to write of his experiences.

God has taken care of dad and we are thankful for his healing and recovery. We continue to believe and patiently wait for a full recovery. We are grateful every step of the way. And again, please continue to keep dad in your prayers for his surgery on Wednesday and healing in the days/ weeks ahead that he may regain sight again.

I hope all is well with you and your family. Take care and God Bless.

Robin M. Zubler

*"There are only two ways of spreading light - to be the candle or the mirror that reflects it."*
- Edith Wharton

## Update #29

### August 2007

All went well with dad's surgery on Wednesday, August 22nd. The surgery took about 2 1/2 hours and he was in recovery about 1 1/2 hours. The doctor (Dr. Pramanak) said that things went better than expected. He remained at Holy Spirit until the next morning because his post-op appointment was at the Central PA Eye Institute in Hershey. He will have a follow-up appointment in 2 weeks in Hershey. At that time, the doctor will remove the stitches in his eye lid. His eye should take 6- 12 months to heal. His next appointment then will be in October and will be in State College (as will all other future appointments). Dr. Pramanak said that he will be seeing dad every 6 months for the rest of his life. If all goes well with his left eye, then the doctor said they can consider options/surgery on dad's right eye.

Thank you so much for your prayers for his eye surgery. Please continue to pray for healing and restoration of sight without complications.

Robin M. Zubler

*"There are only two ways of spreading light - to be the candle or the mirror that reflects it."*

- Edith Wharton

On Sun, Sep 21, 2008 at 2:57 PM, Robin Zubler wrote:

Where has the time gone by? I did not realize it has been since August 2007 that I sent out the last update. An update clearly is long overdue. Things have settled down since dad is back in Centre County. Though it doesn't seem like "huge" changes occurring in dad's physical healing, he continues to progress and is able to do more than he had before. The medical concerns aren't as urgent as in the past and therefore is not the main focus of his life at the moment, but more of his gaining independence and being able to engage in life.

## Health

Dad continues to have follow up eye doctor appointments for his left eye- the one in which he had the cornea transplant. The doctor says his eye is healing really well. He did have three procedures to keep his eyelid closed more to protect his eye from drying out. In the next few months the doctor may be able to open his eyelid again. His vision has improved greatly from having the transplant. He was seeing 20/200 in his eyes when he first began the eye doctor appointments and he is seeing ~ 20/50 at this time. At some point, the doctor will be looking at his right eye and maybe doing surgery on it, but not until his left eye is fully recovered. He did say it was a two-year process and it has been one year since the transplant.

To address dad's physical needs, he continues to receive on-again/off-again therapy (this is dependent upon "his gains"). When he is showing improvement, he receives PT/OT therapy, when he plateaus, he receives restorative care (range of motion). This is nothing new throughout this whole process. Currently, he is receiving PT and OT. For those who don't see dad on a regular basis, they are "surprised" at how much movement he is able to do. And, so are we as we think about what he wasn't able to do not so long ago and what he is doing now. The goal is still for him to be able to feed himself. He is able to raise his arm much higher than before. PT is actually standing him up. They support him and he leans against a walker, but he is able to stand supported for a couple minutes he said.

Dad is gaining more movement in his fingers and his hands. One thing that helps with his dexterity is the jumbo TV Remote control that his sister Maxine and nephew Ron got him. Dad keeps this on his lap and he is able to turn on/off the TV, adjust the volume and change channels. It is a struggle, but it is working and helping. (And, he doesn't need to depend on others to turn the TV on and off for him).

Finally, after about 2 years and numerous "assessments" at Health South, dad finally has an electric wheelchair, a "Cadillac" in dad's terms. Many thanks to Ken Neff, social services; Office of Long Term Living; and PA Medical Assistance, for making this happen. Dad was using a wheelchair, that believe it or not, he was able to get himself around inside Centre Crest. This electric wheelchair, however, has allowed him to be able to go in and outside of Centre Crest without being as dependent upon the nursing staff. They just need to get him in and out of the chair, and then he can go, go, go. With the nice weather, he can go out front and watch people come in and out and he's able to go out back to the garden area. Yesterday, he went out for the "Butterfly release." He still uses the other wheelchair when he goes to appointments and when we take him out on visits.

## Activities

Dad is becoming quite an active resident of Centre Crest. I remember a couple of years ago when it was such an effort to get him out of bed. There was a time when I could only dream of him enjoying the outdoors and sunshine and participating in the different recreational activities that were offered in the different facilities. If some of you remember, one of the first activities he insisted on participating in once he was able to get out of bed, was Sunday services. Now, he is "finding" a life for himself in Centre Crest. He is a member of Resident Council, he goes to Sunday church services, he participates in book club, and attends various special events. Also, it turns out he knows many of the residents and he goes visiting from room to room, or hangs out at the nurse's station or sits out front of the building. So, he no longer gets out of bed once a week, he's out of bed everyday, maybe not as early in the morning as he'd like sometimes, but a good part of the morning and afternoon! Thank God for this!

Dad has now had four roommates since being in Centre Crest. Two, unfortunately, have passed away and one has gone back home, but he keeps in touch with dad. His current roommate is a former Undine buddy. It is great seeing him have roommates now that he can communicate with, hang out together, and most importantly, reminisce with.

Not only is dad getting out and about in Centre Crest, he is getting out and about in the community! It is becoming much easier to get him in and out of a wheelchair and vehicle, so we've been able to take him more places. What had been a once or twice a year outing the last two years, has now lead to more frequent outings, ever since last Christmas Eve.

Since being at Centre Crest, the pastor and some congregation members at Milesburg Presbyterian church have been visiting more frequently. Some of you don't know this, but the Milesburg Presbyterian Church is where we attended while growing up. To me, it is like going home every time I attend church there. Anyway, Pastor Barbara has been visiting dad, reading the Bible and saying prayer. On occasion some of the church elders attend and they have communion together. This really means a lot to dad and to me, also. Because of their visits, we made an effort to attend Christmas Eve Service last year with dad. And, he talked us into attending Pastor Barbara's Ordination early this year, too. We are also grateful to the pastors from Wingate, Fillmore, and Axemann churches who have also visited (I hope I'm not missing anyone), read the Bible and said prayer, too. We all know how important dad's faith in God and all the prayers (his and others) have played in dad's continued recovery. We truly believe dad would not be here today with us, without God, our faith, and our prayers.

This summer started by taking dad to the Last Cruise Car Show in Bellefonte for Father's Day. Dad loves his "older" cars and this was one of the last things dad and I had done together before he got ill. So, this meant a lot to me to be able to take him this year. Attached are some photos of that day. Jeff, Steve, and I, along with our families spent the day with him. There was only a little bit of rain that day and that's when we decided to eat at the Bellefonte Wok.

In August, dad got out at least twice. We took him to the Camp Picnic. This was the second time we've taken him to camp. Everyone knows how much dad loves camp! I am so glad we are able to take him out there for the afternoon. He was having such a good time telling stories with the guys, I really hated having to take him back to Centre Crest. We also took him to the McKinley Family Reunion again this year. This was the third year we've been able to take him- the first time we had to take him by ambulance transport. Thank God we know longer have to do that anymore.

Since September began, he's been out three times so far and we are planning another trip this Sunday. Dad had been planning a road trip most of the summer. He wanted to visit several people he doesn't normally get to see since he's in Centre Crest. I took him out on Saturday, September 6th. We left Centre Crest at around 11:30 am and we did not return to after 7:00 pm that evening. I had no idea all the places and people he had in mind to see! He held up better than I did! It was a wonderful day, quality time, I'll never forget. We even had Miller's hoagies, Middleswarth Barbecue chips, and chocolate milk for lunch! Unfortunately, not everyone was home that day, so Jeff got the honors to take him out the next weekend. Dad was invited to the wedding of one of his nurse's. This seems to be becoming a regular occurrence!

So, on the way, dad and Jeff stopped at the homes of a few more friends. I hear they had a good time.

Thanks to the many visitors that stop to see dad. I know it is hard sometimes to go into a nursing facility or to see someone you care about not able to do things you remember. Dad may be physically challenged at this time in his life, but he is still the person many of you remember. His memory is good, he has a great sense of humor, and he has brought inspiration to those around him. We would also like to thank those who bring in the homemade dishes from home. Dad's appetite is just fine these days and I don't have to worry about him starving from nursing home food because of all the goodies everyone brings in!

And, finally, I'm not sure how many know this or not, but a good friend of dad's from camp, Paul Funk, has begun to write a book about dad's illness, his healing and his faith. Paul has been gathering much information, and believe me, we have lots to share. I overwhelmed him with the journals that have been kept and all of the updates! He is interested in speaking to some of you that know dad well and whom can attest to his faith and God's healing. We may be asking if you would be willing to speak or e-mail him with anything you'd like to share. Please keep Paul and this endeavor in your prayers, because I believe God has a story to tell here with all the people that have been "touched" through dad's illness so far.

In my eyes, dad has come alive again. Though at this time, he is still unable to use his hands to feed himself, etc. or to walk yet, he is at least living and enjoying as active a life as he can. And, no doubt, God is using him right where he is today. And, no doubt, we believe the day will come when he will come home again.

I hope you find that this update was worth the wait. We are reminded, and dad especially, that things happen not in our timing, but in God's.

Robin M. Zubler

*"There are only two ways of spreading light - to be the candle or the mirror that reflects it."*

- Edith Wharton

From: Robin Zubler
Sent: Sunday, December 07, 2008 9:39 AM
Subject: Prayer request

Dad (Jim McKinley) has been in the hospital since Thursday, December 4th. He has gall stones and is also jaundiced due to a blockage. Fortunately, he is not in any pain, though he had not been feeling well in the stomach since Thanksgiving. The doctor's have taken blood tests, ultrasounds, sonograms, a CAT scan, and an MRI so far in order to determine where the blockage is. His urine color is improving along with his color (slightly), though his blood levels of bilirubin have not. He has been receiving an IV and a clear liquid diet since Thursday to try and keep his system flushed out. He is expected to have an ERCP procedure done tomorrow (Monday 12/8) afternoon. They will be taking a scope down his throat, through his stomach & into his intestines to look for the blockage. Dad is a bit anxious about this, though it seems to be a necessary procedure. Most likely they will be removing his gall bladder before he leaves the hospital. He's expected to remain at Mt. Nittany Hospital through the beginning of this week- my best guess at this point would be around Wednesday, but I'll know more tomorrow.

Thank you for your prayers.
Robin M. Zubler

*"There are only two ways of spreading light - to be the candle or the mirror that reflects it."*

- Edith Wharton

## Update

From; Robin Zubler 12/8/08

Dad finally had the ERCP procedure done this afternoon. The GI doctor said the procedure only took 20-30 minutes & was successful. He found 6-8 gall stones blocked in the dual bile duct connecting to the pancreas and gall bladder. He opened up the duct further to allow any other stones to pass through, hopefully, without any further difficulty. However, after the procedure dad was having some difficulty from the intubation and the anesthesia. He was having some difficulty with his breathing and they called in the ear, nose, throat doctor that had stitched dad's tracheotomy. There was concern that if he had continued difficulty with his breathing they might need to place a breathing tube down his throat or even do another tracheotomy. As time passed, he seemed to be breathing better. His oxygen levels were good. The first time I saw him, he seemed a little rough, but after he went to ICU & I got to see him again, I felt more comfortable leaving for the night. He will be in ICU until tomorrow morning & the doctor's will check on him again. I'm sure they'll do more blood levels to make sure the bilirubin is stabilizing & his breathing is good.

I'm not sure yet what they'll do about the gall bladder, but we're certainly glad that the ERCP is done. Dad was quite concerned about possible complications and really did not want to have the procedure done. And right before the procedure a woman from the Pleasant Gap UM Church came in with a goody bag that included a pamphlet with some prayers for when a person is in the hospital & the anxiousness one may feel about the uncertainness of the procedures/surgery/doctor's. It reminded of God's faithfulness that he is with us in all circumstances. That helped a lot- God's perfect timing right when dad needed it most. However, dad's anxiousness was confirmed with the breathing complications afterward. But of course, again we need to have faith in God to see him through. And like I said, he was definitely seeming more like himself before I left.

Thanks so much for the prayers and the well-wishes. Please say a few more prayers that they're aren't any more complications.

Robin

## Update

12/9/08

Dad is out of ICU and has been moved to Room 387. In speaking to the GI doctor this evening, dad is doing very well and eating solid food again!. There doesn't seem to be any further complications due to the breathing difficulties last evening. At this point I'm waiting to hear from his general practitioner to find out whether they will release him or whether they will keep him in and take out the gall bladder since it is full of stones.

Thanks for the prayers, well wishes, love & support!

Robin

## Update

12/19/08

Jim McKinley ended up in the emergency room Tuesday night, 12/16, after having nausea & pain earlier in the evening. He was admitted & early Wednesday afternoon he had surgery to remove his gall bladder. All went well with the surgery and he had no complications from the anesthesia like the last time. He stayed in the ICU overnight and was moved back to room 353 yesterday afternoon. The doctor expected him to remain in the hospital 5-7 days. I would expect him to most likely be able to leave by Monday. When I spoke to the nurse this morning, he is no longer on morphine for the pain. He's still a little uncomfortable, but that is to be expected. Hopefully, he'll be feeling much better real soon.

Robin M. Zubler

# *Personal Accounts*

*It is with great appreciation that I share these insightful reflections. Thank you Judy, Jim and Sue.*

## Judy Hefty

Paul,

I will attempt to tell you some memories of Jim. It is accurate as much as I can remember. I hate to admit my memory is not as good as it once was.

Jim and I attended elementary school together at Central City School. It was a school that had four classrooms. I think it was fourth grade when I first met Jim. I remember many recesses when boys and girls played softball. He was among those who enjoyed playing this game. We graduated from this school in eighth grade and started at Bald Eagle Area High School in ninth grade. He lived at the bottom of Moose Run Road, close to Milesburg, with his parents and several brothers and sisters. When he was a teenager he started working for my father, Irvin Watson, on our farm. He and my father had a good relationship. I know he had to be a hard worker to satisfy my father. I also know he enjoyed driving the tractor.

Jim's father died before he graduated from Bald Eagle Area High School. We both attended the same high school and graduated the same year in 1960. I remember my father gave him a wrist watch for a graduation gift. Jim continued the relationship with my father and mother even though he did not work on the farm any longer. He joined Middle Branch Hunting Camp and went fishing and hunting with my father and the other members. He was a faithful friend to my parents. He married and had three children but he and my father remained buddies. After his divorce from his first wife he eventually placed a trailer on a portion of land on my father's farm. He remarried and lived in this trailer. There was a fire that destroyed this trailer and he put a new trailer on the same spot. The second marriage ended in divorce and he was single for many years. He married Barb after dating her for many years and they built a very nice home on the lot where the trailer had been.

Over the years Jim was very involved in volunteer work. He was a member of the Advent Historical Society and worked hard with others restoring this old church to its appearance of 1849. He became friends with my Uncle Merril Watson and they worked together restoring the church. He was on the reunion committee of our high school class of 1960 for many years. I know he mowed the grass at the Advent Church and The United Methodist Church he attended in Wingate.

If my father needed help he could always count on Jim to help him. After my father's death Jim was a faithful friend to my mother. He helped move my mother to her new apartment when she moved off the farm. He lived in the Watson farmhouse for several years before he married and built his home. Mother could count on him to care for the property. When she sold the farm and purchased a home in Boalsburg Jim was there again to help her move.

I know Jim was a good neighbor to those who lived near him. He was always willing to help others. He gave gifts to my parents over the years. I remember one Christmas he brought a gift to my son's family who lived next to him. He had a genuine concern for people.

I know Jim is an encouragement to all he encounters in his daily life. He listens to the workers at Centre Crest tell him their problems and they know he really cares. He has offered good advice to many and their lives are better because they listened to him. Whenever I would visit him to encourage him I would discover he encouraged me. He loves and trusts his Lord Jesus Christ and is thankful for everyday things most of us take for granted. I appreciate his positive attitude and grateful heart.

Judy (Watson) (Armstrong) Hefty
Bellefonte, PA

## Jim Keenan on Jim McKinley

I met Jim McKinley somewhere during the mid to late 1970's.

I had been coming to camp middle branch with my father in law Merril and his brother I. T. Watson since the early 70's for a week of fishing in early June.

I started hunting in 1979.

Jim McKinley, Dale, Bobby Watson and I hunted the second week of the antlered season for a couple of years.

Probably 1981 the four of us hunted the clear cut behind tall pines on the Monday of the second week. I remember Dale had the scout and rode us up to the bridge there that day. Bob and I tramped the laurel towards coon run/swamp branch while Jim and Dale were our spotters out there somewhere. Not much of a hunt that day – no deer, however, after a nice dinner at camp we four got cleaned up and headed for Renovo for Monday night football.

Now this was back in the day when you were allowed to spot deer with a light right through the season as long as you didn't have a weapon in the truck. So, the four of us pile into my jeep pickup, which was new at the time, that's how I remember it was 1981. Now Jeeps are narrower than regular trucks and Dale and Jim are a little wider than regular people but we all managed to squeeze in there. Now, I was working the wheel, Bob's shifting gears, Dales along for the ride and Jim's got the light out the passenger's window. Up coon run across swamp branch, up past the Alamo to beech creek and out to the hard road. That's when we came upon the phantom four point. You say what?

Yes, well the next thing I see is Bobby holding a .357 magnum. Well the deer went up on the bank on Jim's side of the truck, so Bob hands Jim the gun and Jim hands Dale the light.

Now, I had never poached a deer, but I figured this is as good a time as any. It's still early, like 7:30 pm and we're about the only ones around and we're not far from camp. So, go ahead, Jim, and shoot this buck!

Well, Jim draws a steady two handed bead on the deer, which is chewing on some laurel slightly above the truck and maybe 20 –30 feet away. POW. Deer just stands there chewing on the laurel. POW. Deer takes a couple steps and stops. POW. Jim shoots the third shot. Deer takes a couple more steps but continues to chew on the laurel bush. Now Jim's out of the truck. Two handed shot #4, deer takes a few steps away from the bush and Jim heads up the bank. When he gets to the top he fires #5 and the deer trots away. Last shot less than 10 feet away.

Now, I know Jim's been hunting and fishing all his life, so he must be a pretty good shot even with someone else's gun. But after all the noise he just made we figure we better get moving. Jim's back in the truck and up the road we go. Now, we hadn't gone more than a couple hundred yards when a black bear crosses the road right in front of us. Pretty neat. Jim's still wondering, like Dale and I, what was up with the deer. Continue to the top of the hill where we come upon a porcupine.

Jim, being frustrated over missing the deer yells, stop the truck. I'm going to kill that S.O.B. Jim never did like porky pines. There right up there with rattlers in his book (endangered species especially when you see them). So, I stop the truck. Dale hands me the spot light and I've got the truck angled with the high beams on and the spot light on the pin cushion with legs as he goes up the bank on the left side of the road. Jim has a flash light with him and he grabs a 4x4 out of the back of the truck. He proceeds to go after the porky pine. Now, this is the second bank on the side of the road he scrambles up in about ten minutes time, with cowboy boots on. But he gets up there and catches up with the porky pine. Now we got the spot light on Jim and the high beams. Jim's got a firm grip on the 4 foot 4x4 and he takes a mighty swing down on the porky pine and connects. It was just about this time when the flashlight broke and went out, so we decided to help him by turning out the rest of the lights on the truck and the spot light. Now, Clinton county at night is probably one of the darkest places in Pennsylvania and at this point also one of the loudest cause Jim is making all kinds of noise about this time. Like turn them blankety blank lights back on before the blankety blank porky pine blankety blank bites me. So, being the good friends that we are we waited while he bitched and moaned some more then turned the lights on.

Jim finished with the porcupine and got back in the truck. I carried that 4x4 around for a couple of month's with a dozen or so quills sticking out of it. Every time I looked at it I got a chuckle over the good laughs and good time we had that evening.

We went back there the next day to look for that deer but it was not there. This was after we all took turns shooting Bob's .357 and each hitting the target with it. ??? Must have had blanks in the gun but Bob never did say.

Came to camp one year for winter weekend. Lots of snow but it was starting to melt. It was about 18 inches deep on the road. Came in by Weaver's camp got stuck about ¼ mile past their camp. Dug myself out. Dug myself a place to turn around and came down Penrose. Got to camp around 2 or 3 on a Thursday afternoon. Built a fire, got something to eat. No one around yet. Jim and Dale were supposed to to be coming in. Decide to take a ride back up Penrose to look for them. Got stuck again somewhere around Buck Harbor. Dug myself out, again, went to the top of the hill. No Jim or Dale. Took hard road toward Forester's house, turned around and came back down Penrose to camp to find Jim McKinley had made it in a @*^#% Buick wagon without getting stuck!

I watched Jim walking in the laurel one year while we were putting on a drive. Spent at least 5 minutes moving his feet but not going anywhere. When he looked up at me he said #*&@ laurel is hard to get through sometimes. I had to agree. I was doing the same thing . That was down on window shutters.

Jim over on Coon Run – a whole gang of us hunting together. Jim, way down over the hill says over the radio, come on down. Why? Don't ask just come down. So, Paul and I truck down there to which Jim says, ok, go back up there and we'll finish the drive. I think he was getting back at me for turning the lights out on him. Ha, Ha. No not really. We found deer that Stevie had shot earlier in the day. Come on down, now go back up. ????

One time I slid the jeep through the crossroads (coon run/penrose) just above camp one day. There was no snow, just ice on the road where water runs out and freezes. Slid down a good hundred yards till it finally stopped. So, I'm out gathering sticks and dirt and leaves and whatever to throw under the truck to try and get some traction. I want to back up the hill. Suddenly, I hear a truck coming out Penrose from buck harbor direction.

Oh, good. It's Jim in the green Chevy. Now I know how observant he is, he's sure to see me down here and come and help. Well, he gets to the corner and turns right headed towards Weaver camp. I'm jumping up and down waving my arms and yelling hey Jim. Of course he can't hear me there's no exhaust on his truck and it's purring along real nice out of sight. He never looked.

He's paying me back for turning the lights out on him. No, not really.

I've known Jim McKinley for a good many years now. Lots of good times riding around together, work weekends, hunting and just hanging out at camp. Jim likes to pull pranks and all that but he would never leave anyone stuck. Jim's the kind of guy that would go without to help someone else.

We were putting on a drive one time up on David's rock. Working our way towards Coon run where spotters were set up. I can still hear Jim's voice, "oh, oh. Hear deer," and all that. Up between us jumps a buck. We were about fifty yards apart and the only shot I had was when the deer first got up and Jim was directly on the other side of the deer. Couldn't shoot. The deer ran back through from the way we had come. So, we finished the drive coming out onto coon run road at about the same time. I look up the road toward Jim and he's looking through his rifle scope at the back of a Toyota pickup, taking aim at one of those "o's" on the tailgate. They were pot hunting off our drive. Jim was a little upset but I knew he wouldn't shoot. He's not like that.

Like I said, we've had our share of good times over the years. I've always enjoyed Jim's stories at camp. He's quite a story teller and he's got a few to tell. A fine and good man he is. Always done right for his children, they are all good people. It's a shame that Jim has this cross to bear when he should be enjoying the stories you young guys have to tell. Maybe, with God's help this will all pass and things will get back to normal for Jim. If anyone deserves it, Jim does.

"My achin' tillies."

Always a friend.

Jim Keenan

## Jim's Sister

Mr. Funk;

I am Jim's sister Sue. He is truly a miracle in that no matter how down you feel when you go to visit him, he always makes you feel so much better when you go home. He has been an inspiration to all of us. We all, our whole family has been blessed in the fact that he has never given up hope that he will get better. He truly believes that God has a plan for him and I for one know that God lives with us each day. He has touched many lives throughout his illness. In all the places he has been located, there is always someone who he has befriended and helped along the way.

The man who was up in Ebensburg in his room that was in the automobile accident and could not move or anything, Jim always talked to him and made sure that he knew someone was with him. He has prayed for anyone who is in need of prayer.

He enjoys having lots of company and it is a joy that he is able to get around by himself, as he likes doing things for himself. He has told me many times that before he got sick, he never wanted to take anything from people but wanted to give to them; but now he has to take things from people and be thankful for what they do for him.

When we go into visit him, you had better take something good to eat that would taste good to him. He likes tomato cheese pie, venison bologna, Ham potpie, cheese of all kinds, stuffed peppers, macaroni with milk and butter, Reese's peanut butter cups, 5th Avenues and candy bars of all kinds and Peanut butter milkshakes from Dairy Queen.

If you have any questions that I can answer; please Email me.

Sincerely,
Sue Porter

# *The Illness*

In the following medically based material, I hope to provide you with some insight into the illness Jim has endured and will likely contend with for some time to come. Guillian Barre Syndrome is the name of the disorder Jim contracted. It's effects on the human body are devastating.

I will provide a URL address (www...) for each piece of information, page or pages I provide. I think you will find great insight into the matter by reviewing this material, but hope you will not consider it the final authority. These sites I referenced simply Googling the name Gullian Barre Syndrome. Ask your doctor about it. Read a book or magazine article on the subject. Such off the beaten path subject matter is in need of our attention.

www.ninds.nih.gov/disorders/gbs/gbs.htm?css=print

# NINDS Guillain-Barré Syndrome Information Page

Condensed from **Guillain-Barré Syndrome Fact Sheet**

## What is Guillain-Barré Syndrome?

Guillain-Barré syndrome is a disorder in which the body's immune system attacks part of the peripheral nervous system. The first symptoms of this disorder include varying degrees of weakness or tingling sensations in the legs. In many instances, the weakness and abnormal sensations spread to the arms and upper body. These symptoms can increase in intensity until the muscles cannot be used at all and the patient is almost totally paralyzed. In these cases, the disorder is life-threatening and is considered a medical emergency. The patient is often put on a respirator to assist with breathing. Most patients, however, recover from even the most severe cases of Guillain-Barré syndrome, although some continue to have some degree of weakness. Guillain-Barré syndrome is rare. Usually Guillain-Barré occurs a few days or weeks after the patient has had symptoms of a respiratory or gastrointestinal viral infection. Occasionally, surgery or vaccinations will trigger the syndrome. The disorder can develop over the course of hours or days, or it may take up to 3 to 4 weeks. No one yet knows why Guillain-Barré strikes some people and not others or what sets the disease in motion. What scientists do know is that the body's immune system begins to attack the body itself, causing what is known as an autoimmune disease. Guillain-Barré is called a syndrome rather than a disease because it is not clear that a specific disease-causing agent is involved. Reflexes such as knee jerks are usually lost. Because the signals traveling along the nerve are slower, a nerve conduction velocity (NCV) test can give a doctor clues to aid the diagnosis. The cerebrospinal fluid that bathes the spinal cord and brain contains more protein than usual, so a physician may decide to perform a spinal tap.

## Is there any treatment?

There is no known cure for Guillain-Barré syndrome, but therapies can lessen the severity of the illness and accelerate the recovery in most patients. There are also a number of ways to treat the complications of the disease. Currently, plasmapheresis and high-dose immunoglobulin therapy are used. Plasmapheresis seems to reduce the severity and duration of the Guillain-Barré episode. In high-dose immunoglobulin therapy, doctors give intravenous injections of the proteins that in small quantities, the immune system uses naturally to attack invading organism. Investigators have found that giving high doses of these immunoglobulins, derived from a pool of thousands of normal donors, to Guillain-Barré patients can lessen the immune attack on the nervous system. The most critical part of the treatment for this syndrome consists of keeping the patient's body functioning during recovery of the nervous system. This can sometimes require placing the patient on a respirator, a heart monitor, or other machines that assist body function.

## What is the prognosis?

Guillain-Barré syndrome can be a devastating disorder because of its sudden and unexpected onset. Most people reach the stage of greatest weakness within the first 2 weeks after symptoms appear, and by the third week of the illness 90 percent of all patients are at their weakest. The recovery period may be as little as a few weeks or as long as a few years. About 30 percent of those with Guillain-Barré still have a residual weakness after 3 years. About 3 percent may suffer a relapse of muscle weakness and tingling sensations many years after the initial attack.

## What research is being done?

Scientists are concentrating on finding new treatments and refining existing ones. Scientists are also looking at the workings of the immune system to find which cells are responsible for beginning and carrying out the attack on the nervous system. The fact that so many cases of Guillain-Barré begin after a viral or bacterial infection suggests that certain characteristics of some viruses and bacteria may activate the immune system inappropriately. Investigators are searching for those characteristics. Neurological scientists, immunologists, virologists, and pharmacologists are all working collaboratively to learn how to prevent this disorder and to make better therapies available when it strikes.


### NIH Patient Recruitment for Guillain-Barré Syndrome Clinical Trials

- **At NIH Clinical Center**
- **Throughout the U.S. and Worldwide**
- **NINDS Clinical Research Collaboration Trials**

# Organizations

## Related NINDS Publications and Information

- **Guillain-Barré Syndrome Fact Sheet**
- Guillain-Barré Syndrome (GBS) fact sheet produced by the National Institute of Neurological Disorders and Stroke (NINDS).
- **NINDS Miller Fisher Syndrome Information Page**
- Miller Fisher syndrome information sheet compiled by the National Institute of Neurological Disorders and Stroke (NINDS).
- **Neurological Diagnostic Tests and Procedures**
- Fact sheet on neurological diagnosis and testing, prepared by the National Institute of Neurological Disorders and Stroke (NINDS).

Prepared by:
Office of Communications and Public Liaison
National Institute of Neurological Disorders and Stroke
National Institutes of Health
Bethesda, MD 20892

NINDS health-related material is provided for information purposes only and does not necessarily represent endorsement by or an official position of the National

Institute of Neurological Disorders and Stroke or any other Federal agency. Advice on the treatment or care of an individual patient should be obtained through consultation with a physician who has examined that patient or is familiar with that patient's medical history.

All NINDS-prepared information is in the public domain and may be freely copied. Credit to the NINDS or the NIH is appreciated.

Last updated May 06, 2010
www.guillianbarresyndrome.net

**Guillian Barre Syndrome** – "Gradually patient loses all his reflexes and goes through a complete body paralysis. Guillain Barre Syndrome is a life threatening disorder and needs timely treatment and supportive care with intravenous immunoglobulins or plasmapheresis."

Go to the website to read more about the symptoms and signs.

## Further reading offered at the site:

http://www.ninds.nih.gov/disorders/gbs/gbs.htm
http://en.wikipedia.org/wiki/Guillain-Barré_syndrome
http://www.mayoclinic.com/health/guillain-barre-syndrome/DS00413

## A History of Gullian Barre Syndrome was also presented at this site.

**"The first and precise incident of Guillain Barre Syndrome was reported on 1859 by Jean Baptiste Octave Landry de Thezillat." Potential causes of the illness are also discussed at this site.**

The authors also offered "**Famous People who suffered Guillian Barre Syndrome;**

- Andy Griffith, actor
- Franklin D. Roosevelt, U.S. president. In 2003 doctors concluded that Roosevelt"s paralysis, long attributed to poliomyelitis, was actually Guillain-Barré syndrome.
- William "The Refrigerator" Perry, former professional American football player with the Chicago Bears was diagnosed with GBS in 2008."

For more from this site, go to <u>www.guillianbarresyndrome.net</u> and click any listing from the "navigation" heading.

<u>www.telegraph.co.uk/health/healthnews/8069426/swine-flu-jab</u>

## Swine flu jab linked to rare nerve disease

Health watchdogs have admitted for the first time that there may be a possible link between the swine flu jab and an increased risk of developing a rare nerve disease.

By <u>Richard Alleyne</u>, Science Correspondent
Published: 12:01AM BST 18 Oct 2010

Experts are carrying out studies to examine a possible association between the vaccine and Guillain-Barre Syndrome, a condition which attacks the nervous system and can cause paralysis and even death.

The authorities have always denied any link although it had been suggested a previous swine flu vaccine had caused cases of the disease in America in the 1970s.

For the complete article see the url listed above, i.e. www. telegraph...

**For other titles on Guillian Barre Syndrome go to google and click on the books link. Below is a page from that search;**

1.)     **Guillain**-Barré **syndrome**: from diagnosis to recovery
by Gareth J. Parry, Joel S. Steinburg – 2007. 264 pages.

1.)     **Guillain-Barre syndrome**: pathological, clinical, and therapeutical ...

---

1.)     Silvia Iannello - 2004 - 234 pages - Preview
2.)     The aim of this book is to describe and discuss this disease that is not exactly rare but is almost the only inflammatory polyneuropathy and the most frequent cause of acute flaccid paralysis in general medical practice.
3.)     books.google.com

---

1.)     **Guillain-Barre' Syndrome**: My Worst Nightmare

---

1.)     Byron Comp - 2004 - 208 pages - No preview
2.)     books.google.com - More editions

---

1.)     **Guillain-barre Syndrome**: A Medical Dictionary, Bibliography, And ...

1.)     Icon Health Publications - 2004 - 184 pages - No preview
2.)     If your time is valuable, this book is for you. First, you will not waste time searching the Internet while missing a lot of relevant information. Second, the book also saves you time indexing and defining entries.
3.)     books.google.com - More editions

## 1.)     The **Guillain Barre syndrome**

1.)     C. P. Petch - 1947 - No preview
2.)     books.google.com

## 1.)     **Guillain**-Barré **syndrome**

1.)     Allan H. Ropper, Eelco F. M. Wijdicks, Bradley T. Truax - 1991 - 369 pages - Snippet view
2.)     The details in this book are based on years of observation and care delivered personally to over more than 250 patients with Guillain-Barre syndrome from 1979 to 1988.
3.)     books.google.com

www.google.books.com

# Works Cited

Alleyne, Richard. "Swine flu jab linked to rare nerve disease." *The Telegraph.* Oct. 18, 2010.

<www.telegraph.co.uk/health/healthnews/8069426/swine-flu-jab>

An Exposition with Practical Observations, St. Luke. *Commentary on the Holy Bible.*

Matthew Henry; volume 5. New York: Funk and Wagnalls Co., date unknown.

Ecclesiastes. *The Preacher's Homiletic Commentary.* Hamilton, Dr. J. Funk and Wagnalls Co., New York: No Date, 18?? (as reported at Wikipedia.orgwiki/Funk_%26_Wagnalls).

Guillian Barre Syndrome; Facts, News an General Information about Guillian Barre

Syndrome. Home Page, *History of Gullian Barre Syndrome, Causes of Guillian Barre Syndrome , and Famous People who suffered Guillian Barre Syndrome.* 2009.

Guillian Barre Syndrome. Home Page. Google. <www.google.books.com>

Leale, Rev. T.H._*Preacher's Homiletic Commentary - Ecclesiastes*; Funk and Wagnalls Co., New York and London. No Date.

NINDS Guillian-Barre' Syndrome Information Page. May 2006. National Institute of Neurological Disorders and Stroke. May 2006. <<u>www.ninds.nih.gov/disorders/gbs/</u>>

Stedman, Ray C. *Is that all there is to life: Answers from Ecclesiastes.* ; Discovery House Publishers, 1999. Page 70.

The Book of Job. *Preacher's Homiletic Commentary.* Robinson, D.D., Thomas. New York: Funk and Wagnalls Co., No Date.

Weaver, Joanna. *Having a Mary Heart in a Martha World.* Colorado Springs, Colorado: Waterbrook, Multnomah, 2002.

*Young's Compact Bible Dictionary*; G. Douglas Young Ph.D. & Co. Tyndale House Publishers, Illinois. 1989.